Glam Italia!
101 Fabulous Things to Do in Florence

Insider Secrets to the Renaissance City

ISBN: 978-1-7323799-4-7 (paperback)
ISBN: 978-1-7323799-5-4 (eBook)

DISCLAIMER
The author is not a travel agent. All opinions and views expressed are those of the author based on personal travel experiences. Businesses, websites and apps recommended by this author may change ownership, rebrand or close through no fault of the author. The author has not received any compensation or sponsorship from any recommended businesses.

Cover art and all images by Marta Halama © Corinna Cooke
www.martahalama.com
Maps by Steve Doubles © Corinna Cooke
Photography by Tracy Battaglia Fully Alive Photography
Formatting by Polgarus Studio
Cover Design by EBookLaunch.com

Contents

And the voices in the waves are always whispering to Florence, in their ceaseless murmuring, of love – of love, eternal and illimitable, not bounded by the confines of this world, or by the end of time, but ranging still, beyond the sea, beyond the sky, to the invisible country far away!

– Charles Dickens

1.
Introduction

Everything about Florence seems to be colored with a mild violet, like diluted wine.

– Henry James, from a letter dated 1869

I fell in love with Florence 30 years ago. In a lifetime of travel I've found there are some places you visit, enjoy for a few days, but feel no great need to return to. Others are like a love affair you can't quite let go of, they just keep pulling you back over and over again.

That's how I feel about Florence. I truly love this city.

My first trip to Florence was with a six-week Contiki tour. A bus load of 18 to 35-year-olds from around the world, itching to experience something new and exciting but lacking the know-how and the confidence to go it alone. It was perfect and it was fun. In fact, for years I looked back at this trip as the best six weeks of my life. I had an absolute blast and made friendships that are still going strong to this day, even though I live clear across the world from everyone else.

My Contiki tour bus departed from Russell Square in London, unloading us at a North Sea ferry journey to the Netherlands, which felt like a cross between *The Perfect Storm* and *Deadliest Catch,* without the fish. (This was to be the first of many North Sea crossings

I would make over the following years, any of which were violent enough to sink the Titanic.) Eight hours later we disembarked in Europe, decidedly green around the gills.

We traveled through France and Spain and then after a quick romp back through Provence, Nice and Monaco we rolled into Florence. From the first breath I drew as we arrived in this beautiful city, I swear I have never been the same. I didn't just *see* Florence, I *felt* it, all the way into the depths of my soul. This would have been entirely remarkable were it not for the fact that every second person who comes to Florence *feels* it. Throughout time writers, musicians, poets and artists have been moved to their very core by Florence. Travelers from far and wide speak of enjoying other places but *loving* Florence. When people tell me about their European travels it is always Florence that calls them back.

Before we head out on this journey together I want to tell you that I am not an art historian – or any kind of historian actually. I'm not an archaeologist or a linguist or a travel agent. I have no degree in Italian or Florentine Studies. I'm a make-up artist who has spent my lifetime traveling the world and who, through a fabulous twist of fate, wound up hosting private tours of Italy for several months each year. I've lived on islands and continents across several countries, but it's Italy that keeps pulling me back.

I've spent years exploring Florence, and the more time I spend here the more new (old) things I discover. One of my friends has lived here for more than 25 years. Every day he walks to and from work, and he often goes out walking at night after dinner. He's *still* finding new things in Florence. Perhaps this is part of the magic of this renaissance city, it always has something new to show you, another secret to let you in on.

2

Unfortunately Florence is also an excessively touristed city. Each year I am more horrified than the year before by the volume of tourists descending on the city's hot spots every day of the tourist season. They seem to stick to the same places, obscuring the view and wasting hours in queues, oblivious to the treasures they could find if they ventured just around the corner.

The purpose of this book is to direct you towards these treasures; to tell you about some of the other places and things to be seen in this beautiful city. Almost everything is 20 minutes' walk (or less) from the Duomo, or the heart of the historic center, so will be within a block or two of where you are likely to be anyway. You'll be amazed at how fantastic these places are and at how few travelers visit them. They will feel like insider secrets that only you know.

I will also include some of the super crowded tourist spots like the Piazza del Duomo and the Piazza della Signoria, simply because these can't be missed, but I'll give you some inside information on accessing them, as well as specific things to look for. For example, the façade of the Duomo is spectacular but some visitors find it overwhelming as there is so much to take in. I've found in my years of private tour-guiding that when you look for a handful of specific features you'll enjoy a better level of appreciation and excitement. I have walked past and studied the Duomo more times than I can count in the many years I've been coming here, and I *still* notice new things every time.

As you visit some of the cool things in this book, you'll be amazed at the thousands of tourists standing nearby, completely unaware of what's here! From Michelangelo's graffiti to Cellini's hidden self-portrait, Baccio d'Agnolo's balustrade to Dante's stone, *Glam Italia! 101 Fabulous Things To Do in Florence* will lead you to wonderful discoveries of treasures hiding in plain sight.

My advice to you is, unless you are in Florence for several days, I don't recommend wasting time standing in long lines waiting to get in anywhere. Instead go and see these extraordinary places nearby, with no crowds, no lines, and which will blow your mind.

If you have already been to Florence – even if you've been many times – you will still discover new things in this book. You may learn about a secluded rooftop bar perfect for a sunset Prosecco, or a hidden workshop where you can order bespoke shoes. There may be a vintage store or a museum you have never heard of. Believe me, there is always more to discover!

Most travelers don't want an enormous amount of information about each building or work of art, so what I have tried to do is to give you just enough information to spark your interest and get you through the door. Entire books have been written about most of these places so if you want more details a quick Google search will provide as much as you could ever hope to learn about whatever has tweaked your interest.

This book is my love letter to Florence. I hope I can help you to love it too.

Andiamo!

Travel After Covid-19

Introduction Addendum

I wrote this book in 2019. It was originally scheduled for publication in early spring 2020, but then Coronavirus struck.

However, I think this book is even more relevant post-pandemic. My focus has always been on getting travelers away from the tourist crowds and taking you to places in Florence that are less frequently visited, yet completely fantastic. I aim to give you strategies to avoid crowded spots and also methods for escaping them should you find yourself in the middle of a tourist mob.

I believe mass tourism is untenable. It is my sincere hope that one day it will be replaced with sustainable travel: small group tours specific to the individual's interests, rather than big bus tours that overcrowd the bucket list sites. I want to encourage individuals, families or groups of friends to plan their own individualised trips, rather than arrive on cruise ships for mass-produced tours. I would like to see travelers supporting local businesses, artisans and craftsmen, rather than tourist money being spent at chain restaurants and high street shops. I want to see visitors hiring licensed local guides and professional drivers, and supporting local industry.

I would love mass tourism to stop, but I know that, while there is demand for that type of travel, cruise lines and big bus tours will continue to squash as many people as possible into every venue. So in the meantime, I'm going to use my *Glam Italia* series of books to encourage as many visitors as I can to be *travelers* rather than tourists, to interact with and support the local people of this amazing country, and to make an effort to discover the hidden treasures of Italy.

What will travel look like after the Covid-19 pandemic? Maybe we will all wear masks, or maybe we won't need them. I'm sure we will all use more hand sanitizer. Of course there will be changes to the way we travel, and at first they will seem strange as they did after 9/11. But after a while we simply won't notice them anymore, just as most of us no longer think about the changes and increased security for air travel since 2001.

I hope this and all of my *Glam Italia* books will inspire you when planning your Italian adventure, and will give you the confidence to get off the beaten path (even in the big cities) and choose sustainable travel over mass tourism.

2.
How To Use This Book

Don't expect to do all 101+ things in this book. Instead, read through the chapters, look for places and foods and experiences that sound interesting to you, and hopefully you'll find things you've never heard of before. Most people won't want to spend their visit to Florence going to every church on the list, but they will get a thrill out of seeing inside a couple of them. (The churches really are remarkable.)

Not everyone wants to go shopping, but finding a cool vintage store or knowing where to buy a fabulous Italian leather jacket can be a fun addition to your trip. After a lifetime of travel I can tell you that walking into a big church, palace or museum without any knowledge in advance can leave you feeling overwhelmed and frazzled, the churches can start to look alike, and this can lead to you overlooking something really incredible.

So I will tell you about a place, give you enough history to put it into context, then direct you to a handful of specific things to look at while you're there.

While tour-guiding, I find the things that get travelers the most excited tend to be those things they haven't heard about before. Everyone knows the Duomo and yes, it's fantastic, but it's the visit to SS Annunizata or Ognissanti that you'll be talking about for years to come. That's what this book is about – introducing you to places that fly below the radar of the average tourist, yet have an incredible wow-factor.

Florence is small. You'll notice how close everything is, and therefore how much you can fit into a single day, with no rush and no effort at all. I put a **What's Nearby** section after each place in the book to help you plan what can be grouped together within a couple of minutes' walk.

This book not only introduces you to some really cool places, but it will also plant the idea in your memory. You may find yourself walking from point A to point B on your planned Florence itinerary and recognise a vintage shop you've read about here, and score a vintage Chanel handbag or Gucci blouse. Or you might spot a church with a non-descript exterior but remember there are genius frescoes inside, and pop in for a quick look. You may walk past one of my favorite wine bars and know that *this* is where to get the best aperitivo, or crostini to die for, rather than the over-touristed one down the street.

I show you amazing things to see and do in Florence, places *not* swamped with tourists, and I give you escape routes for when you do find yourself swallowed up by a crowd. Together we will avoid the long lines and maximize your time in this beautiful city. Do at least skim the sections that you don't think will interest you. You're bound to find bits and pieces within them that you'll be curious to see.

A few places show up more than once in this book. This is because the rest of that chapter would lose context without them, or because a story would be incomplete without that piece added to it. One example is Michelangelo's Graffiti, which is in the **Unusual & Interesting Things** chapter, but also in **A Walk with Michelangelo**.

I love creating walks tracing the story or life of someone interesting, so in this book have included a walk through Michelangelo's life and work in Florence and another that leads you through the Florence of Dante. Fans of Dan Brown's *Inferno* will also enjoy a guided walk through the places that appear in the book and film.

Florence is the city of the Medici, a dynasty you encounter at every turn, in the buildings, statues and art they left behind. The Medici were fascinating, fantastic, sometimes ruthless, and seldom boring. They also can be a little tricky to follow in the beginning because they kept recycling the same names over and over throughout the centuries. Chapter 3 introduces you to the Medici and a handful of other families who show up in stories in this book. If you are interested in history read that chapter when you come to it. If you just want to find some fun things to do in Florence, jump ahead and come back to the Medici chapter when you want to know who someone was or why they were important.

If you want more after reading this book, you can follow me on social media: Instagram **@CorinnaTravels** and Facebook **Corinna Cooke Author**. I also have loads of travel information on Pinterest **@Corinnamakeup**

Visit my blog **CorinnaBsWorld.com** where you can sign up for my Private Member's Newsletter. The newsletter is packed with great, practical information for travelers to Italy.

Now let's explore Florence…

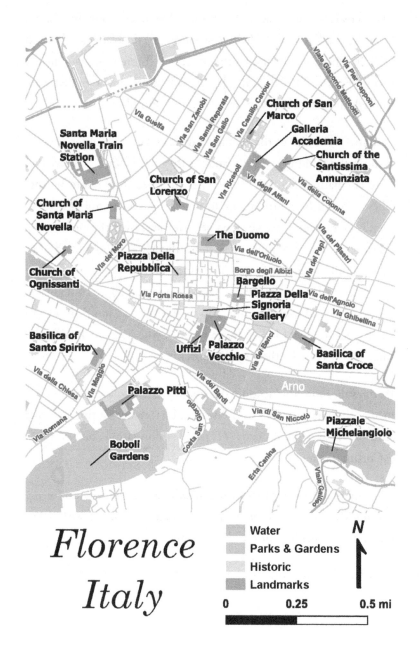

Florence
Italy

Water
Parks & Gardens
Historic
Landmarks

N

0   0.25   0.5 mi

The Medici

MEDICI GENEALOGICAL TREE

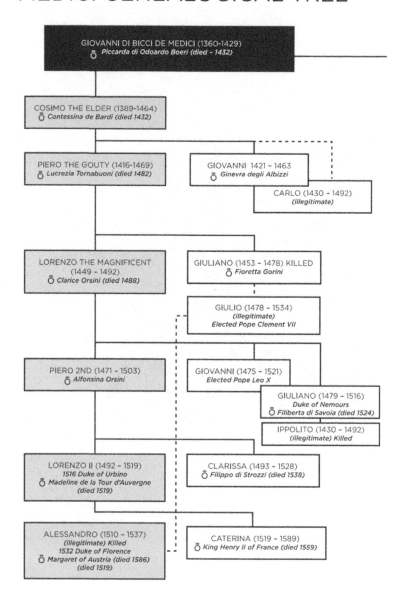

GIOVANNI DI BICCI DE MEDICI (1360-1429)
💍 *Piccarda di Odoardo Boeri (died - 1432)*

COSIMO THE ELDER (1389-1464)
💍 *Contessina de Bardi (died 1432)*

PIERO THE GOUTY (1416-1469)
💍 *Lucrezia Tornabuoni (died 1482)*

GIOVANNI 1421 ~ 1463
💍 *Ginevra degli Albizzi*

CARLO (1430 - 1492)
(illegitimate)

LORENZO THE MAGNIFICENT (1449 - 1492)
💍 *Clarice Orsini (died 1488)*

GIULIANO (1453 ~ 1478) KILLED
💍 *Fioretta Gorini*

GIULIO (1478 - 1534)
(illegitimate)
Elected Pope Clement VII

PIERO 2ND (1471 - 1503)
💍 *Alfonsina Orsini*

GIOVANNI (1475 ~ 1521)
Elected Pope Leo X

GIULIANO (1479 ~ 1516)
Duke of Nemours
💍 *Filiberta di Savoia (died 1524)*

IPPOLITO (1430 - 1492)
(illegitimate) Killed

LORENZO II (1492 ~ 1519)
1516 Duke of Urbino
💍 *Madeline de la Tour d'Auvergne (died 1519)*

CLARISSA (1493 ~ 1528)
💍 *Filippo di Strozzi (died 1538)*

ALESSANDRO (1510 - 1537)
(illegitimate) Killed
1532 Duke of Florence
💍 *Margaret of Austria (died 1586) (died 1519)*

CATERINA (1519 - 1589)
💍 *King Henry II of France (died 1559)*

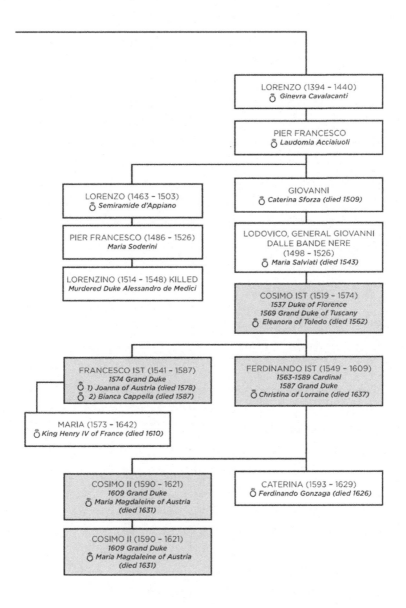

LORENZO (1394 - 1440)
💍 Ginevra Cavalacanti

PIER FRANCESCO
💍 Laudomia Acciaiuoli

LORENZO (1463 - 1503)
💍 Semiramide d'Appiano

GIOVANNI
💍 Caterina Sforza (died 1509)

PIER FRANCESCO (1486 - 1526)
Maria Soderini

LODOVICO, GENERAL GIOVANNI
DALLE BANDE NERE
(1498 - 1526)
💍 Maria Salviati (died 1543)

LORENZINO (1514 - 1548) KILLED
Murdered Duke Alessandro de Medici

COSIMO IST (1519 - 1574)
1537 Duke of Florence
1569 Grand Duke of Tuscany
💍 Eleanora of Toledo (died 1562)

FRANCESCO IST (1541 - 1587)
1574 Grand Duke
💍 1) Joanna of Austria (died 1578)
💍 2) Bianca Cappella (died 1587)

FERDINANDO IST (1549 - 1609)
1563-1589 Cardinal
1587 Grand Duke
💍 Christina of Lorraine (died 1637)

MARIA (1573 - 1642)
💍 King Henry IV of France (died 1610)

COSIMO II (1590 - 1621)
1609 Grand Duke
💍 Maria Magdaleine of Austria
(died 1631)

CATERINA (1593 - 1629)
💍 Ferdinando Gonzaga (died 1626)

COSIMO II (1590 - 1621)
1609 Grand Duke
💍 Maria Magdaleine of Austria
(died 1631)

3.

The Medici

It was a dynasty with more wealth, passion and power than the houses of Windsor, Kennedy and Rockefeller combined. It shaped all of Europe and controlled politics, scientists, artists and even popes, for 300 years. It was the house of Medici, patrons of Botticelli, Michelangelo and Galileo, benefactors who turned Florence into a global power center, and then lost it all.

– Christopher Hibbert, *The House of Medici, Its Rise and Fall*

What do you get when you mix brilliant bankers with ruthless politicians, patrons of the arts, humanists, three *really* controversial popes, and a couple of assassins? You get a dynasty called the Medici.

Love them or hate them, Florence is undeniably the city of the Medici. They ruled Florence for centuries. You'll see the family crest everywhere in the city and all over Tuscany in every town they ruled.

Their story is one of banking genius. They created one of the wealthiest banks in all of Europe from essentially nothing. The family was deeply embroiled in political intrigue. They evolved from no noble status at the beginning, to becoming the self-appointed Grand Dukes of Tuscany. They are responsible for an entire art movement that changed the art world forever, at the same time changing the face of Florence with their massive influence on and participation in its architecture.

I've studied the Medici for years. I've read numerous books about them (There's a list of recommendations at the end of this chapter should you want to learn more). I have watched documentaries and TV shows about them, and even have a friend who is one of them.

While reading this book you'll notice that the Medici recycled the same names over and over through the centuries, especially *Cosimo*, *Lorenzo* and *Giovanni* (you almost wish they could have thrown in a Mike or a Bob somewhere just to make things a little easier to follow). To help you to keep track of who's who, this chapter introduces you to the main players, the ones we meet in Florence. I'm going to take some license, skip some generations and leave some out altogether, but every time that I refer to a Medici as we explore Florence together, you can check back here to see who he was.

So let's meet the family.

Giovanni de Bicci de' Medici (1360–1429)

There were Medici before him, even some sitting as *gonfaloniere* (a highly prestigious office in local government) but our story really begins with a wily and brilliant character named Giovanni di Bicci de' Medici.

Giovanni worked for his uncle Vieri's bank, became a junior partner, then three years later in 1385 became the manager of the Rome branch. Under Giovanni's management the Rome branch made most of Vieri's total profits, so when Vieri retired in the early 1390s Giovanni took the opportunity to turn the Rome branch into his own firm. One of his formidable strengths was the ability to see the big picture and play a very long game; lose money up front but make it back tenfold down the line.

On October 1, 1397 he set up his head office in Florence, the banking capital of Europe. With an initial investment of 10,000 florin (5500 his own money and the balance paid by two non-family partners), Giovanni's Medici Bank ran at around 10% profit the first few years.

Big banking families, like the Bardi and Peruzzi, had gone bankrupt in the not too distant past, so Giovanni changed his business model. He diversified, buying farmland and cloth-producing workshops. Florence's two big industries at the time were banking and wool, with wealthy families often invested in both.

In 1402 he opened a Venice branch of his bank to go with the Rome, Naples and Gaeta branches. Always cautious, other than opening another wool workshop in 1408, this was the full extent of his expansion. In a stroke of brilliance he set each branch up as its own separate business, so if one failed it couldn't bring the others down with it. Giovanni pioneered the double-entry accounting system, tracking debits and credits, and was an early proponent of extending lines of credit.

As the Medici Bank profits increased, Giovanni kept buying property in Florence, laying a solid foundation for what would become a massive family fortune. At all times he avoided the obvious trappings of wealth, and showy, ostentatious behavior, instilling in his sons the importance of appearing to be regular folk. They didn't dress to reflect their financial status and didn't show off the way the other wealthy families did.

THE PIRATE POPE

In a stroke of absolute genius, Giovanni di Bicci de' Medici bet on a Neopolitan pirate named Baldassare Cossa. (You'll find more on Baldassare Cossa at the end of this chapter.) Cossa wanted to become pope but this meant first becoming a cardinal. He asked Giovanni for a loan of 12,000 florins to buy his cardinalship. This was a staggering amount at the time. Despite the risk and knowing he likely wouldn't be repaid, Giovanni backed the pirate – which totally paid off. In 1410 Baldassare Cossa, the pirate from Naples, became Pope John XXIII and made his friend and backer the new papal banker, propelling the Medici further into extreme power and wealth.

Although there were much bigger names in banking, and at various points over the years the papal account was taken from the Medici and given to others, they all lacked the infrastructure of the Medici Bank, so it always came back to them. The foundation that Giovanni di Bicci de' Medici set up for his banking operation was genius. He passed his brilliance and strategic thinking on to his son Cosimo (and to his other son, Lorenzo).

To get a really good understanding of how the Medici Bank made its money and how innovative it was, I recommend reading the Tim Parks' book listed at the end of this chapter.

Cosimo the Elder (1389–1464)

Cosimo de' Medici, also known as Cosimo the Elder, the 'Father of Florence', is my favorite Medici. Partly because of his patronage of the arts and the enduring impact on art as we know it today; partly because of his patronage of the architects Brunelleschi and Michelozzo and the visual impact that that still has on the face of

Florence six centuries later; partly because he was a strategic thinker and skilled diplomat; also because underneath his polished surface he was a shrewd political operator and a ruthless powerbroker. Mix it all together and you have one of the most interesting characters in history, who left a visual legacy like no other.

Born a twin on April 10, 1389, named for the saints Cosmas and Damian, his twin Damiano died in the first year of their life. He later had a younger brother, Lorenzo.

Cosimo had a passion for the arts. Beginning with Cosimo, the Medici family were, in my opinion, history's greatest patrons of the arts. They took art out of the exclusivity of the church and its ecclesiastical themes, and brought it into the humanistic realm.

If you were an artist at that time you couldn't just paint/sculpt something and sell it, you had to be commissioned to create it. Commissions were generally made for churches (with few exceptions), so the subject matter revolved around bible stories. Cosimo commissioned artists not only to do religious work but also to create beauty outside of those confines – sometimes crossing the two. Donatello's *David* is a good example: the story is biblical but the work itself crosses boundaries, being flamboyant and innovative, erotic and quite sensational.

Cosimo and the next few generations of Medici were prolific but strategic patrons. They elevated the family's position to dominate the city of Florence by being everywhere. The art and architecture they commissioned was not just for the wealthy – their Renaissance utopian ideals meant this beauty had to be accessible to all.

Cosimo told his biographer Vespasiano de Bisticci, 'Before 50 years are up we will be expelled, but my buildings will remain.' Most of his buildings were church-related, so not only would they get him a place in Heaven but also huge fame on Earth. Could he have imagined that nearly 600 years later we would still be enjoying them?

THE PALAZZO MEDICI

Cosimo didn't just impact art, he also changed domestic architecture. Deciding he needed a palace to reflect his status, he built the glorious Palazzo Medici. Rather than build on top of existing buildings, which was the norm at the time, he razed them to the ground and started afresh. His palazzo, although fortress-like from the ground floor exterior, was a beautiful new concept in architecture that was then copied all over Florence.

COSIMO'S WIFE

At age 25, Cosimo married Contessina Bardi. She came from the noble and influential Bardi family, who had lost their banking fortune but retained their prestige. The Medici were nouveau riche so needed some of that prestige via noble marriages to raise their image in Florence.

They had two sons, Piero and Giovanni. Marriages weren't love matches back then, they were alliances, but it is said that there was great warmth between these two.

COSIMO'S MISTRESS

While exiled in Venice, Cosimo bought a Circassian slave named Maddelena. The plagues had wiped out much of the servant population, so it was commonplace for families to buy slaves. In most cases slaves were well-treated and would even eat at the table with the family.

Cosimo and Maddelena shared a love of art, and he was thought to have been in love with her. They had a son, Carlo, who was raised by Contessina alongside her own sons. It was not unusual for illegitimate children to be raised in the home of their father, and they were frequently destined for a life in the church, which is what befell poor Carlo. He had no say in the matter. Two generations later, Cosimo's grandson Giuliano would have a son out of wedlock who also was given over to the church. Carlo was different from the legitimate sons in another way too. If you look at the Medici family tree you will see there was only one Carlo. He was given a name that separated him from all the others with their revolving door of Cosimos, Lorenzos, Giulianos and Giovannis.

THE LIBRARIES

During his exile in Venice in 1433, Cosimo had Michelozzo design a library for the Venetians as a symbol of his gratitude. This was calculated politicking – creating something to bring him huge accolades and to last long after he was gone.

In 1444 Cosimo founded the first public library in Florence. Situated in San Marco and again designed by Michelozzo, Cosimo financed construction of the library itself and all the books, which people of his choosing were then able to use at no charge. By selecting who had access, he was able to shape the politics of the Republic.

Only the very wealthy had books at this time, so creating a public library was a big deal. Put into perspective, growing up Cosimo had had only three books. By the time he was 30 he had more than 70. He sourced manuscripts from all over Europe, Syria, Egypt and Greece. A team of 45 scribes translated and copied them, including the works of Livy and Plutarch and Plato. Although it doesn't get as much acclaim as his patronage of the arts, this preservation, translation and copying of ancient manuscripts has been of enormous benefit not only to Renaissance Florentines, but to all of us even today.

Michelozzo also designed a small library for Cosimo's much adored grandson, Lorenzo (the Magnificent).

POLITICS

Cosimo de' Medici was a shrewd politician, which makes him all the more fascinating. His father taught him to play a really long game and he became masterful at it. Paul Strathern's book (at the end of this chapter) goes to great lengths explaining Cosimo's brilliant political maneuvers, but I want to give you just a couple of examples:

Suspecting that Rinaldo degli Albizzi was going to stage a major attack on him, Cosimo quietly moved massive amounts of Medici money out of Florence over the course of several months. This way neither his nor his bank's money could be confiscated were he exiled or assassinated. Each branch of the Medici Bank was a separate business, so if Albizzi got his hands on the Florence branch he couldn't access the money in the others.

For years Cosimo had built solid and strategic relationships in other parts of Italy, so when he was imprisoned and then exiled to Venice, he was well prepared. Not only did he go, his money went with him. Within one year, the effect of the loss of capital (his money) in Florence was so extreme they had to lift his exile and bring him back! Once back he instigated constitutional changes giving him much more power behind the scenes. A few years later Pope Pius II said Cosimo was 'a King in everything but name'. By this time Cosimo was the richest man in Europe.

Another example was during a time of non-stop war amongst the various factions that made up Italy. Wars were prohibitively expensive and a waste of money. Each side would hire mercenaries to fight on their behalf and, even if they won, were left with nothing much to show for it beyond a huge bill.

When the ruling Visconti died, Cosimo funded the mercenary Francesco Sforza's takeover of the Duchy of Milan, thus preventing a military attack on Milan from Venice, which would have further empowered Venice's ability to attack Florence. The long game that Cosimo envisaged and achieved was a balance of power, with allies Milan and Florence on one side and Venice and the Kingdom of Naples on the other. This created 50 years of peace that in turn enabled the Renaissance to take hold in Italy, and of course, the Medici Bank to become even more prosperous.

SHREWD CHARITY

In around 1442 Cosimo formed a charity, the Good Men of San Martino, a religious confraternity helping those who had fallen on hard times but were too proud to ask for assistance. The Good Men would solicit donations then quietly provide help to those in need, preserving the recipients' anonymity. Fifty percent of the contributions came from the Medici Bank. Cosimo entered these funds into the books as donations under 'God's Account'.

This was another example of his political wiliness. Rather than make a grand gesture of publicly giving his own money, his massive contribution was hidden behind a religious organization and in the name of a commercial entity (the bank). Offset by the donations of other good men, this enterprise made Cosimo's largess appear even more dramatic. While squashing some of the economic unrest, he was able to help the poor, which he genuinely wanted to do. And to top it all off, the act of shunning recognition by doing it all behind the scenes actually garnered him more recognition and adoration.

The amount of food and wine handed out to the poor by the Good Men of San Martino at Christmas and Easter, courtesy of Cosimo de Medici, valued at more than 500 florins, was more than 3 bank managers' annual salaries! (You can find more about this in Tim Park's book.)

Cosimo was the most brilliant of all the Medici, creating the colossal family fortune.

Now let's skip a generation and meet his magnificent grandson.

Lorenzo the Magnificent (1449–1492)

Lorenzo the Magnificent was the most influential patron of the arts in the history of the world. His benevolence impacted the careers of Michelangelo, Leonardo da Vinci, Botticelli, Domenico Ghirlandaio, and Andrea del Verrocchio, just for starters.

The son of Piero de' Medici and Lucrezia Tornabuoni, and much adored grandson of Cosimo de' Medici, he was a politician, a diplomat, and a patron of scholars, poets, and the arts. He ruled Florence with his brother Giuliano from 1453–1478 (when Giuliano was murdered) and then alone until his own death in 1492.

His father Piero was the first Medici to combine running the Medici Bank with running the Republic of Florence. Piero was also a patron of the arts and his mother Lucrezia loved the poets and philosophers of the Medici Academy, and also wrote sonnets herself. When her husband died she became advisor to Lorenzo.

From childhood, Lorenzo showed great wit, incredible intelligence, a spectacular memory and great curiosity, all of which would serve him well.

THE POLITICIAN AND THE DIPLOMAT

Lorenzo entered politics at 16, traveling on diplomatic missions for his father, even meeting with the pope on his behalf. Piero (known as Piero-the-Gouty) was frequently too ill to travel. This early entry into and experience with the world of diplomacy proved beneficial as the years unfolded. When Piero died, 20 year old Lorenzo took over running Florence. He was not only responsible for reforming state institutions but also for using his influence and friendships to maintain peace among the various Italian powers.

Rather than officially accepting power, Lorenzo wanted to be thought of as just another citizen so, like his grandfather and father before him, he ruled Florence from behind the scenes through a series of surrogates in the councils, strategic marriages, payoffs and threats. Technically he was a despot, albeit an altruistic one. Florence flourished under his rule.

However, the other noble families resented the Medici dominance, so Lorenzo had many highly placed enemies, the most virulent being the Pazzi, who tried to murder him in 1478. The **Pazzi Conspiracy** is detailed at the end of this chapter, but the short version is Pope Sixtus IV, some priests, an archbishop and the Pazzi family cooked up a scheme to murder Lorenzo and his brother Giuliano inside the Duomo during Easter service. (In case you missed the gravity of that last sentence, *the Pope was part of a murder conspiracy scheduled to happen at Easter, inside the cathedral!*) It gets even crazier as, in the aftermath of the murder and attempted murder, the Pope excommunicated Lorenzo (the victim!) and the Florentine government, and seized all the Medici assets that he could get his hands on. When Florence stayed loyal to Lorenzo, the Pope made an alliance with King Ferdinand I of Naples, and orchestrated an invasion of the Florentine Republic. With allies Bologna and Milan unable to help, it was Lorenzo's spectacular diplomatic skills that saved the day (and the Republic). While the war raged, Lorenzo traveled to Naples and resolved the crisis using only his diplomacy. He beat the Pope at his own game and emerged even more celebrated and powerful than before!

From this point forward he worked on maintaining the peace. He kept the power balanced amongst the northern Italian states, and kept invaders such as France and the Habsburgs out of Italy. Lorenzo maintained good relations with the Ottoman Empire's Sultan Mehmed II, trade with whom was a major source of Medici wealth.

A PASSION FOR THE ARTS

What I love most about Lorenzo the Magnificent is his passion for the arts. He understood artists weren't like regular folk and couldn't thrive when shackled by the confines of normal rules. As such he worked *with* them, indulging their crazy behaviors. He created environments where they could thrive, and provided income and opportunity never seen before.

As an avid collector of classic sculptures, Lorenzo created a sculpture garden school in San Marco where up and coming artists could study and copy the brilliance of the sculptors from ancient Greece and ancient Rome, honing and refining skills lost for more than 1000 years. Imagine being a poor child in fifteenth century Florence with no access to blocks of marble to practice on, being swooped up by

Lorenzo the Magnificent, given a place to learn and practice, and the opportunity to become a master sculptor!

One such fortunate artist was Michelangelo. Observing him working in the sculpture garden, Lorenzo was so taken with the boy and his talent, he moved him into the Medici Palace and for several years raised him as his own son. Some of Michelangelo's most formative years were spent with the greatest humanists, philosophers, artists, musicians and poets of the time. Not only was he exposed to this incredible mental stimulation, but Lorenzo created an environment where the young Michelangelo could achieve his full potential. When you look at the sculptures he created for the tombs of Lorenzo and Giuliano you can see Michelangelo's devoted love for Lorenzo. Lorenzo was not a handsome man, but in Michelangelo's hands Lorenzo became beautiful.

LORENZO'S LIBRARY

Lorenzo inherited the Medici Library, created by his grandfather Cosimo. The library was a source of great pride – only the most cultured and wealthy could own collections of books, let alone have their own library. During his lifetime he amassed a collection of more than 600 manuscripts, all of which he had translated into Latin.

More than just acquisitions, he understood the importance of making books available to scholars in order to further new developments and discoveries. From the writings of Plato, Livy and Plutarch, to more recent works, Lorenzo shared his collection, promoting humanism and greater education. So much had been lost during the Dark Ages, enlightened thought had given way to barbarianism and religious fundamentalism. But Lorenzo, the ultimate Renaissance Man, used his generous patronage to open a new world where art, beauty, music and writing emphasized the goodness, the potential, and the value of human beings, while finding a way to reconcile Christianity with ancient and modern philosophies. Part of why I love Lorenzo is that beyond his colossal impact on the art world lay a concern for finding ways to solve human need.

LORENZO THE LOVER

What Lorenzo lacked in beauty he made up for a thousand times over in charisma. Paintings of Lorenzo don't depict a handsome fellow but if you look at his death mask at the Palazzo Pitti you can see signs of something alluring.

Lorenzo is said to have been quite the ladies' man. Historian Guicciardini described him as 'licentious and very amorous'.

In 1469 Lorenzo married Clarice Orsini. This was an advantageous match, she was from a noble Roman family and a descendent of England's King John. The marriage was a political alliance, not a love match. He was an extrovert and a humanist and she was deeply religious and an introvert. However, their letters do suggest they respected and held great affection for each other, and after her death Lorenzo wrote to Pope Innocent VIII that he missed her dearly. When she traveled she did so as a representative of her husband, which was quite unusual at the time, but it implies the level of trust, care and value he placed on her. They had 10 children together, three of whom died in infancy.

However, the love of Lorenzo's life was the very beautiful Lucrezia Donati. Some say it was a platonic love, others say she was his mistress. Either way, he wrote her many love poems.

DEATH

Lorenzo suffered from the family ailment of gout. At the end of his life his gout was so bad that he couldn't walk and had to be carried around on a litter. He spent the last months of his life at his villa in Careggi, surrounded by his friends. As he lay dying in his final hours on April 8, 1492, several omens are said to have happened in Florence: ghosts roamed the city, Florence's lions killed each other, and Verrochio's golden ball on top of the cathedral was struck by lightning.

Lorenzo the Magnificent was only 43 when he died. The people of Florence were devastated by his death. He is buried in the New Sacristy at the Basilica San Lorenzo.

Giuliano de' Medici (1454–1478)

Giuliano was Lorenzo the Magnificent's younger brother. The Medici were generally an unattractive bunch but Giuliano was the one handsome member of the family. Athletic, elegant, kind and passionate, he was denied reaching his full potential when he was brutally murdered inside the Duomo at the age of 25 (see **Pazzi Conspiracy** below).

Giuliano was well-liked and judging by Michelangelo's sonnet written to him, well loved (learn more about this in the Medici Chapel at Basilica San Lorenzo in **Chapter 14: Churches**). Michelangelo's sculpture of Giuliano is arguably his most beautiful.

Giuliano never married but had a lover named Fioretta Gorini, who was eight months pregnant at the time of his assassination. She gave birth to a boy, Giulio di Giuliano, who Lorenzo the Magnificent raised as his own. Giulio became the second Medici pope.

Giovanni de' Medici, Pope Leo X (1475–1521)

Giovanni was the second son of Lorenzo the Magnificent. He was raised in the Medici Palace with his siblings, his orphaned cousin Giulio and, for a while, Michelangelo. Living in the court of Lorenzo the Magnificent, these children received the finest education in all of Europe and, in addition to traditional academics, they were exposed to and learned from some of the greatest minds in Italy; from philosophers to humanists, artists to scientists, poets to musicians. This education would account for the huge accomplishments in their lives (and in some cases where things went a little sideways).

From childhood, Giovanni was destined for the church. He received the tonsure (a religious shaving of the head or part of the head) at the age of seven, and in 1488 when he was 13 his father Lorenzo the Magnificent had Pope Innocent VIII make him cardinal, although he couldn't wear the robes or get involved in deliberations for three more years.

Giovanni de' Medici was 37 when he became Pope Leo X. At the time, having a pope in the family was the ultimate tool for expansion of power and influence. The papacy was already corrupt and Leo X was not the first to buy his way into the top job.

On the bright side Giovanni was a huge supporter of the arts. The world is better off for his magnificent patronage of the artist Raphael. He worked with leading literary figures, reorganized the University of Rome, and set up a Greek College and publishing house. Leo X loved music, in fact the second highest salaries paid from the papal accounts were to musicians, with the goldsmith taking first place.

The previous pope, Julius II, spearheaded the building of St Peter's Basilica, but Leo X accelerated the effort, also massively increasing the holdings of the Vatican library. The Medici family library in Florence had more books and manuscripts than the Vatican library, so Leo X had a huge appreciation of the value of a substantial library.

Under Leo, Rome became a major European cultural center and political power.

As pope, he was head of the church and head of the papal states, but he was also head of Florence, so wielded enormous power and influence.

Leo X made substantial charitable donations each year to the crippled, the sick and the unfortunate, poor students, discharged soldiers and pilgrims, convents, retirement homes and hospitals. He was well thought of, intelligent, engaging and witty and promoted the pursuit of knowledge and learning.

It is said that, after the debauchery of the Borgia popes, he restored some of the piety to the papacy. Clearly the Borgias must have been much, much worse than I realized, because Leo X was known as the hedonistic pope.

When he was elected he had a six-year-old boy painted top to toe in gold and paraded through the streets of Florence with the celebratory procession. It was total propaganda, implying that the golden era had returned to Florence via the Medici. Unfortunately the boy died from paint poisoning, but the party carried on.

Leo X was accused of debauchery, atheism and murder. Like plenty of the popes that preceded him he was charged with throwing orgies, leading a wild and lewd lifestyle, and there were rumors that he was gay. This would be of no consequence whatsoever other than the

Catholic Church taking such a strident position on homosexuality, pre-marital and extra-marital sex. At parties he would have naked young boys jump out of cakes and there was talk that he was having relationships with the handsome young sons of noblemen (although these may have been stories made up by his enemies).

Pope Leo X was also an excessive spender, running the papacy into borderline bankruptcy. It took him only two years to blow through the entire treasure amassed by the previous pope, who was known for his frugality. Leo X's massive patronage of the arts cost a small fortune, as did his personal expenses and wild lifestyle. He is reputed to have justified his hedonism by saying, 'Let us enjoy the papacy since God has given it to us,' but now that is thought to be up there with Marie Antoinette's 'Let them eat cake' propaganda – not necessarily historically accurate.

Constantly running out of money, Leo created extra church revenue by selling off relics and valuables belonging to the church, even selling papal furniture when the going got rough. He is also famous for the 'selling of indulgences', even though it had been going on for decades, but Leo X took the practice to a whole new level. 'Indulgence selling' shortened the buyer's time in purgatory by forgiving the sins of those willing to pay. If you spread the practice out across all of Christendom, there was a great deal of cash to be made.

Another way of fattening up the coffers was the practice of selling cardinalships. Again, Leo X was not the first to do it, but he was prolific. After an assassination attempt on him in 1517, Leo X named 31 new cardinals. (The cardinals implicated in his attempted murder were imprisoned and executed.)

One of Leo X's greatest mistakes was failing to recognize the danger of Lutheranism and the rise of Protestantism. When he died suddenly in 1521, Pope Leo X left Italy in political turmoil, and the Catholic Church across Europe (especially northern Europe) in religious turmoil.

Giulio de Giuliano de' Medici, Pope Clement VII (1478–1534)

Giulio di Giuliano de' Medici was the illegitimate son of Lorenzo the Magnificent's murdered brother Giuliano, born a month after Giuliano's murder. His godfather Antonio da Sangallo the Elder raised him for his first seven years until Lorenzo took over, moving him into the Medici Palace and raising him as his own son.

Giulio was shy, handsome, and a good musician. He wanted a life in the clergy but his illegitimacy prevented him from achieving a high position in the church, so Uncle Lorenzo helped him build a military career instead.

When Lorenzo died in 1492 and Giovanni became a cardinal, Giulio became more involved with church affairs. He studied canon law at the University of Pisa and went with Giovanni to the conclave of Rome for the election of the Spaniard Roderigo Borgia to Pope Alexander VI. From 1494 to 1500, Giovanni and Giulio roamed Europe together, even getting arrested twice (which is hilarious considering they both became popes!).

In 1510 while living in Rome with his cousin Lorenzo II de' Medici, Guilio had an illegitimate child with Simonetta de Collavechio, a black slave working in the home. Because Giulio still wanted a career in the church, Lorenzo was named the child's father. However,

Giulio always showed clear favoritism to the child, Alessandro, including bypassing Ippolito de' Medici to make Alessandro the first Duke of Florence in 1530.

Meanwhile, in 1513 Giovanni de' Medici became Pope Leo X and made Giulio Archbishop of Florence. He then gave a papal dispensation making Giulio legitimate, before making him a cardinal, all within one short year. Giulio was by all accounts clever, respectable, and a hard worker. Leo X gave him great power and authority. More than just a trusted papal advisor, Giulio lived with Pope Leo X; they were brothers to the end. In 1517 Leo X made Giulio his vice-chancellor, the pope's second in command. Giulio was chief advisor both to Leo X and his successor Pope Adrian IV. By the time he was elected Pope Clement VII, Giulio was considered an excellent statesman.

Unfortunately Giulio's papacy was marked with all kinds of problems, earning him the moniker 'The Most Unfortunate of Popes'. He became pope at a time of crisis, with foreign armies invading Italy, the Protestant Reformation spreading across Europe, and the church near bankruptcy.

While he was pope, England broke away from the church (Henry VIII got divorced) and Emperor Charles V led the violent Sack of Rome which resulted in Giulio (now Pope Clement VII) being imprisoned for a time.

Interestingly, in 1533 he approved Copernicus theory that the earth orbited the sun, 99 years before Galileo would be labeled a heretic for the same theory! He was also credited with issuing orders affording protection to Jews.

Although his papacy was troubled, Clement VII/Giulio was considered to be devout, of dignified character, clever both in theology and the sciences, and with a profound understanding of European politics. Were he pope during a different set of years chances are he would have helmed a successful and prosperous papacy. Giulio de' Medici was pope from 1523 until 1534.

Lorenzo II de' Medici (1492–1519)

Lorenzo II, or Lorenzo di Piero de' Medici was born in 1492. He ruled Florence from 1516 until he died in 1519. Titled the Duke of Urbino, he was the father of Catherine de' Medici who married Henry II de Valois, the future King of France.

Alessandro de' Medici (1510–1537)

Alessandro, the illegitimate son of Pope Clement VII and a slave in the Medici house, was known as '*Il Moro*' (the Moor), due to his dark skin and African features.

In 1527 Emperor Charles V sacked Rome and most of the Medici fled, including Alessandro (interestingly eight-year-old Catherine de' Medici was left behind).

In 1530 Pope Clement VII made peace with Charles V and the Medici went back to ruling Florence. The pope put his 19-year-old 'nephew' (son) Alessandro in charge, and a few months later made him the first Duke of Florence, one of the most powerful men in Europe. Technically this honor should have gone to Ippolito de' Medici. By surpassing Ippolito and giving it all to Alessandro, Clement VII furthered the theory that *Il Moro* was his son.

The Medici rule of Florence had become succession. The republic was over. This makes Alessandro the first black head of state in the modern western world.

Unfortunately Alessandro is said to have been somewhat of a maniac. His rule was not only incompetent, but harsh and depraved. Supposedly he organized orgies, raided convents and would bust into private homes searching for new women. It is hard to know how much of this actually happened or if he was written about this way because he was the first black ruler in Europe.

In 1535 the Florentine opposition sent cousin Ippolito to appeal to Emperor Charles V against Alessandro, but Ippolito died on the way, rumored to have been poisoned by Alessandro. Instead of taking up their cause, Charles V married his illegitimate 14-year-old daughter Margaret of Austria to Alessandro. Margaret had been promised to Alessandro when she was five, was moved to Florence when she was 11 and was married in 1536 when she was 14. (Luckily for her, Alessandro died the year after they were married. Unluckily for her, Charles V then married her off again to the grandson of Pope Paul III.)

Alessandro was murdered in 1537. His cousin Lorenzino lured him without a bodyguard to a promised sexual rendezvous with a beautiful woman *Il Moro* had been coveting. While waiting for the meeting that would never happen, Alessandro got drunk and passed out on the bed, at which point Lorenzino and an assassin slipped into the room and stabbed him to death.

Margaret and Alessandro had no children. Alessandro had two children by his mistress Taddea Malaspina: a boy named Giulio and a girl named Giulia.

Catherine de' Medici (1519–1589)

Catherine only appears in this book in the context of the perfume shop and the fragrance created for her by the monks at Santa Maria Novella, but she is a really fascinating character. Catherine was the great granddaughter of Lorenzo the Magnificent

At 14, her uncle Pope Clement VII arranged for her to marry Henry de Valois, the second son of King Henry I of France. Catherine became Queen Consort of France from 1547–1559 while her husband was King Henry II. Then from 1559–1589 she was Queen Mother to three French kings: Francis II, Charles IX and Henry III. The years during which her sons reigned are known as 'the age of Catherine de' Medici'. Her political influence in France was massive.

Catherine was ruthless, doing everything possible to keep her sons on the throne and to keep the Valois monarchy running. In all likelihood, they would have lost the throne without her. Due to all the civil wars raging during her sons' rules and the persecution of the Hugenots, she is often considered quite villainous (which I think just makes her more interesting).

Biographer Mark Strage describes her as the most powerful woman in sixteenth century Europe.

Cosimo I de' Medici/ Grand Duke Cosimo (1519–1574)

Cosimo I is another really likeable character from the Medici dynasty.

After the fiasco with Alessandro, a new Medici was needed to take over the line of succession. There was a problem though – Alessandro died leaving no legitimate heirs. He was the end of Cosimo the Elder's line. So they rustled up the great, great grandson of Cosimo the Elder's brother Lorenzo. Cosimo I was a 17 year old living in the countryside in Mugello. (Just for fun have a look at that side of the family tree – everyone is called Lorenzo or Pier Francesco or Giovanni until this new Cosimo comes along!)

Cosimo I was at a disadvantage, having not been educated at the Medici court. When he arrived in Florence the power brokers thought they could take advantage of the 17-year-old duke, but he proved to be clever, astute, ambitious and wily like his namesake. Not trusting the important families, he stripped them of their charges and replaced them with officials from regular life.

AN AUSPICIOUS LEADER

Although an authoritarian, Cosimo I was a good leader. He reformed the administration of justice with a new criminal code that created a police force and a decent judicial system. He promoted economic growth, strengthened the army, and commissioned the construction of roads, ports and drainage systems.

Cosimo I built the Tuscan Navy. He protected Florence and Tuscany from constant foreign invasions by building fortresses and walls, creating strongholds throughout Tuscany. In 1555 he successfully conquered Siena, then divided the region into *Old State* (Florence and its territories) and *New State* (Siena with its territories), running the two administrations separately.

In 1569 Pope Pius V made him Grand Duke of Tuscany. His effective leadership restored the Medici power, enabling the family to rule Florence and Tuscany until their dynasty ended in 1737.

A MAN OF THE ARTS

Cosimo I is best remembered for his contribution to the arts. In 1563 with Giorgio Vasari he founded the Academy of Art and Design, with dual purposes of creating a guild for all working artists and an academy for the most eminent artists in his court (including Vasari, Giambologna, Cellini, Ammannati, Bronzino and Francesco da Sangallo). The Academy protected and supervised all art in Medici-controlled Tuscany. Throughout this book and all over Florence you will find loads of art credited to the patronage of Cosimo I.

He moved his family from the Medici Palace into the Palazzo della Signoria, and then across the river to the Palazzo Pitti. He created the Uffizi, consolidating government offices that had been spread out over the city into one centralized location, which at the time was a brilliant move. He had Vasari create a secret passageway, the Vasari Corridor, allowing Cosimo I to walk unimpeded and unattacked from his home at the Palazzo Pitti, to work at the (now renamed) Palazzo Vecchio. The Uffizi has since become one of the most famous art museums in the world.

Cosimo I expanded the Pitti Palace and Boboli Gardens, turning it into the Palace of the Grand Dukes, of which he was the first. He commissioned the incredible artwork in the Palazzo Vecchio's Salone dei Cinquecento. He had a passion for archaeology and natural sciences, and was responsible for research into Etruscan ruins and artifacts. From his grandmother Caterina Sforza of Forli' he inherited an interest in alchemy. Everywhere you look in Florence, you see him.

MARRIAGE

At 19 Cosimo I married Eleanora of Toledo, a beautiful Spanish girl related to Emperor Charles V. They had seven sons and four daughters. He was a family man who enjoyed eating his meals at home with his wife and children. By all accounts they were happily married for 23 years, until her unexpected death. Eleanora died of malaria along with two of their sons while en route to Pisa. Devastated, Cosimo I largely stepped down from government life two years later, handing the reins over to his son Francesco.

Three years after the death of his wife, Cosimo I took a mistress, Eleanora degli Albizzi. In 1566 she bore him a daughter (who died as a baby) and then a son, Giovanni. Cosimo I wanted to make the child legitimate and marry Eleanora. He told his trusted chamberlain who in turn told Cosimo's eldest son Francesco. Francesco wanted neither a step-mother nor a new heir to the title, so confronted his father about it. Apparently Cosimo was so furious that his chamberlain had betrayed his confidence that he stabbed the man to death.

The affair between Cosimo I and the mistress cooled off quite quickly and he set her up with a dishonored nobleman facing execution, Carlo Panchiati. Not only was Carlo pardoned, Cosimo also gave him a 10 thousand scudi reward to marry her and take her off his hands. They had three children before Carlo accused her of adultery and had her locked away in a monastery where she lived the rest of her long life. Meanwhile Cosimo I moved on to another mistress, Camilla Martelli. She was 26 years his junior, and bore him one child, Virginia. His other children hated Camilla, finding her vulgar and ostentatious compared to their own beloved mother. Cosimo married her anyway, on the pope's orders.

He eventually abdicated due to poor health, handing everything over to Francesco, and lived the final 10 years of his life in borderline seclusion at the villa di Castello, with Camilla at his side. He had at least one stroke and was unable to speak, eventually dying in 1574. Camilla was forced into a convent, only allowed out to witness the marriage of her daughter Virginia to Cesare d'Este in 1586. With Francesco dead, she asked Ferdinando for permission to leave the convent, but he sent her back and she died there in 1590.

Eleanora of Toledo (1522–1562)

It was important that Cosimo I marry someone of noble/royal blood, for the political alliance and, as a newly minted duke, he needed to *trade up*. He had wanted to marry Margaret of Austria, daughter of Charles V and widow of Duke Alessandro de Medici, but she wouldn't have him, so the Emperor placated Cosimo by getting him this 17-year-old Spanish hottie with blue-blooded lineage, Eleanora of Toledo. Eleanora was renowned for her beauty and her charm. At a time when it was normal for a man of Cosimo's wealth and standing to have girlfriends and mistresses galore, he was happily faithful to the lovely Eleanora until her death.

She is considered the first modern First Lady, serving as regent of Florence when Cosimo was away. Although during her life Cosimo I was only a duke, he became a grand duke after her death, a title that would be taken on by their sons: Francesco and then Ferdinando.

Eleanora was more than just a pretty arm-piece for Cosimo I. She was a patron of the arts, founded several churches in Florence, and was a decent business woman. She owned considerable amounts of land in Tuscany, which she ran well, shipping goods as far away as Spain, while building the Medici holdings.

Behind the scenes she loved traveling and gambling. She didn't much care for living in Florence's city center, so in 1550 bought the Pitti Palace, which she considered far more suitable for the family of a duke. She turned it into a palace of similar standing to the other great European palaces, but she died of malaria before all the renovations and her fabulous Boboli Gardens were completed.

Francesco I (1541–1587)

Francesco was the first son of Cosimo I de' Medici. He became the second Grand Duke of Tuscany, from 1574–1587. Francesco was a despot and wasn't well-liked, although he did helm some good ideas, which were brought to fruition by his brother Ferdinando after his death.

Francesco had a huge interest in chemistry and the sciences and would lock himself away in his Studiolo in the Palazzo Vecchio, his private lab where he would work on his chemistry experiments.

Francesco married Joanna of Austria. It is said they couldn't stand each other and he was never faithful to her. They had seven children: the first six were girls, then finally with number seven he got his son, Filippo. Having at last produced an heir, Francesco's wife Joanna mysteriously fell down the stairs (while pregnant again) and died, leaving poor Filippo motherless. For all of five minutes.

Francesco had a Venetian mistress, Bianca Cappello. (Mysteriously/conveniently her husband was murdered in the street in Florence in 1572.) When Cosimo I died in 1574, Francesco bought her the beautiful Palazzo de Bianca Cappello in the Oltrarno (via Maggio, 26), flaunting the relationship in front of his wife Joanna. At that time Francesco had had no heir, and in 1576 he had an illegitimate son with Bianca, named Antonio.

Within months of Joanna's death in 1578, Francesco secretly married Bianca, making it public and acknowledging Antonio as his son the following year. Bianca was crowned Grand Duchess of Florence, but her position wasn't secure. Francesco's brother Ferdinand loathed her, and Francesco's legitimate son Filippo was the heir, so if Francesco were to die she would have had a problem. But then Filippo died of hydrocephalus at age four, so Francesco had Antonio legitimized and declared his new heir. Bianca must have been relieved.

But neither she nor Francesco had factored in his brother Ferdinando…

Ferdinando I (1548–1609)

Ferdinando I was the fourth son of Cosimo I de' Medici. His future was somewhat uncertain until his mother and two of his three older brothers died of malaria. The elder of these two brothers, Giovanni, had been a cardinal, and upon his death Cosimo I had Pope Pius IV transfer the cardinalship and all its benefits over to Ferdinando.

Ferdinando moved to Rome and for 10 years worked at making strategic alliances and influential contacts. He was happy to be in Rome as he couldn't stand his brother Francesco. In 1576 he bought Cardinal Ricci's villa in Rome (to this day still known as the Villa Medici) and began amassing his incredible art collection.

Ferdinando was handsome, with a great personality, so he was popular in both Rome and in Florence. His fellow cardinals could see substance beneath his outwardly fun appearance, and they liked him too. However, beneath it all he was ruthless.

In 1587 Francesco and Bianca died under fantastically suspicious circumstances: Ferdinando was staying with them at Poggio a Caiano, just outside Florence when the couple suddenly got sick. Cardinal Ferdinando stepped in, controlling the environment, keeping them isolated, not allowing their confidants near them. He sent dispatches to the Holy See saying Francesco was sick due to his poor eating habits and that Bianca was sick with grief over her husband's health. Within 11 days of his arrival both were dead. Cardinal Ferdinando ordered immediate autopsies to document it being a 'non-toxic' death and to protect himself from any accusations. He gave a solemn funeral for his brother but supposedly had Bianca buried in a common grave in San Lorenzo.

I found some fascinating information in a 2006 National Center for Biomedical Information report via the US National Library of Medicine, National Institute of Health. (You can Google the report.) Apparently, when the bodies were autopsied, four terracotta jars containing the viscera were buried in the crypt at the nearby church of Santa Maria a Bonistallo, close to the villa at Poggio a Caiano. The 1587 Book of Births, Deaths and Marriages recorded the day and time of death of the Grand Duke of Tuscany and his wife, and documented the four terracotta jars containing their viscera being brought to the crypt. In 1857 Grand Duke Leopold III ordered that the Medici tomb be opened so that Francesco could be identified and have his final burial in the Medici Chapel. They discovered his body in surprisingly good condition, which indicated arsenic poisoning. Arsenic causes massive fluid loss pre-death, and the chemical preserves bodies, so when exhumed after a long time they appear mummified. The doctor's reports from Francesco's final days also reflect the symptoms of arsenic poisoning, not malaria, which was the official cause of death. More recently the Medici Project accessed

Francesco's remains (there was actually skin, beard hair and quality matter from a leg bone) as well as the remains from the terracotta jars, and they confirmed that they had indeed been poisoned with arsenic!

And so now, with his brother and sister-in-law dead, the only thing between Ferdinando and the Grand Duchy was Antonio, Francesco's son. He had witnesses swear the boy wasn't Francesco's son, then sent him off to join the celibate Order of the Knights of San Stefano. Then he had Pope Sixtus V confer his cardinalship to Francesco Maria del Monte, and stepped into his role as the Grand Duke of Tuscany.

MARRIAGE

Ferdinando married Christina of Lorraine in 1589. Christina was Catherine de' Medici's favorite granddaughter, and Catherine had worked hard to make this marriage happen. In addition to her *huge* dowry, Christina brought the rights to Catherine's Duchy of Urbino into the marriage, which would become Medici property on the death of Queen Catherine of France.

Beyond the financial gain, the marriage brought Ferdinando into an alliance with France. Catherine de' Medici had wanted this for years, and for Ferdinando it was a chance to get out from under Spain's influence. Ferdinando and Christina had nine children, of which one died as a child and three died unmarried.

GRAND DUKE FERDINANDO

If you ignore the whole family murder thing, it would appear that Ferdinando was a pretty good guy. His brother Francesco had been an awful ruler and was hated, but Ferdinando was loved. He cared about the welfare of his subjects, was generous and approachable, and ruled compassionately.

He regained Tuscany's independence, forfeited during Francesco's rule, and re-established the justice system. He also seemed to have a decent world view, making Livorno a safe haven for foreigners and Spanish Jews, and decreeing tolerance for Jews and heretics. Interestingly Ferdinando created the Medici Oriental Press (*Typographia Medicea*), publishing some of the earliest books ever printed in Arabic.

He built up commerce (fattening the Medici Bank's accounts), and supported an irrigation project in the Val di Chiana, enabling the areas around Pisa and Val di Nievole to be farmed. Ferdinando strengthened the Tuscan Navy, winning battles against pirates on the Barbary Coast in 1607 and the Turks in 1608. Also in 1608, he organized an expedition to Brazil to set up a colony base for trading.

Ferdinando was responsible for introducing opera to Europe. In 1600 when his niece Marie de' Medici married France's King Henry IV, his court put on a sumptuous performance of *Euridice*, one of the first important operas.

Ferdinando was a pretty interesting character. Of course he did more than I have talked about here, but you'll find his statue on the horse in Piazza della SS Annunziata much more interesting now that you know these details!

Baldassare Cossa, the Pirate Pope (1365–1419)

This is one of those fantastically outrageous stories that would be considered too bizarre to be true, except for the fact that it *is* true.

This event was instrumental in the Medici family bank catapulting from moderate wealth to super wealth.

Baldassare Cossa was born to an impoverished noble family on the island of Procida, in the kingdom of Naples. He and his brothers maintained the family's standard of living and dignity by becoming pirates. After a brief spell in the military, Cossa studied law at the University of Bologna, obtaining a doctorate. He was no dummy. He then sidestepped into his third career when he began working in the office of Simony, selling church offices and positions, for Pope Boniface IX.

In 1402 he borrowed 12,000 florins from Giovanni di Bicci de' Medici and bought himself a cardinalship (mentioned in the profile on Giovanni). During his eight years as a cardinal, the pirate's house was notorious for housing large numbers of women: 200 maids, wives and widows, and many nuns.

Cossa needed more money to finance a run on the papacy, and Giovanni saw this as a fantastic risk – success would mean the Medici became the papal bankers. He put up the money and in 1410 the gamble paid off. Baldassare Cossa became Pope John XXIII.

Known as Antipope John XXIII, his papacy didn't last long. He was charged with and found guilty of piracy, sodomy, simony, heresy, incest, tyranny and immorality. (Apparently the even more scandalous charges were suppressed in public record!) When asked to abdicate he ran away disguised as a mailman, was caught and imprisoned, ransomed (the Medici paid his ransom) and then the new Pope, Martin V made him Cardinal of Frascati (which may be the craziest twist of all).

Baldassare Cossa, the Pirate Pope, died in 1419 and is buried in the Baptistery of San Giovanni in Florence.

Medici Enemies

Rinaldo degli Albizzi (1370–1442)

The Albizzi family were the leaders of a group of wealthy oligarchs who ran Florence during the second half of the fourteenth century. As Giovanni di Bicci de' Medici and his son Cosimo began building wealth, influence and power in Florence, the Albizzi felt threatened, seeing the nouveau-riche Medici family as a challenge to their own supremacy. Rinaldo degli Albizzi became the Medici's fiercest enemy, coaxing other important families to side with him.

Rinaldo was belligerent, impulsive and haughty. Cosimo thought him dangerous (which is an understatement). On September 7, 1433, Cosimo was summoned to the Palazzo della Signoria where Rinaldo convinced the members to imprison Cosimo in the tower. (He'd wanted Cosimo beheaded but had to settle for him being exiled.) With Cosimo gone, Rinaldo ruled Florence. He was a war monger and a villain and lacked Cosimo's intellect and understanding. Under his guidance, Florence quickly ran out of money. The suffering people were desperate to have Cosimo back. Even the pope, Eugene IV, wanted Cosimo back – the Medici were still the papal bankers. A little over a year after being exiled, Cosimo returned triumphant to Florence and Rinaldo was exiled. He never made it back to Florence, dying in Ancona in 1442.

The Pazzi

The Pazzi were an old, wealthy banking family in Florence who loathed the new money Medici.

In 1099, Pazzo di Ranieri was one of the first men over the wall in the Siege of Jerusalem, bringing back to Florence the flints of the Holy Sepulchre, supposedly used to light the lamps when Jesus was buried. The flints are now held in the church of SS Apostoli. (See **Chapter 14: Churches** for more details.)

Andrea di Pazzi was the patron of the Franciscan chapter house at Santa Croce, and commissioned the fabulous Pazzi Chapel at Basilica Santa Croce (also in my **Churches** chapter). His son Jacopo became head of the family in 1464, and then things started getting interesting.

THE PAZZI CONSPIRACY

This was a particularly heinous crime, as it happened *inside* the cathedral of Florence and involved a pope (Sixtus IV), an archbishop, and some priests.

The conspiracy began in 1477 when Francesco de' Pazzi, son of Jacopo and manager of the Pazzi Bank's Rome branch, cooked up a plan to assassinate two of the Medici. He wasn't alone – Girolamo Riario (the pope's adored nephew) and Francesco Salviati (made Archbishop of Pisa by Pope Sixtus IV) were also involved, *supported by the pope* who is supposed to be God's voice on Earth. Their plan was to kill Lorenzo the Magnificent and his brother Giuliano, and thus be rid of the Medici forever. (At this time the Medici Bank had lost the papal account to the Pazzi, but still remained the wealthiest financial institution in Europe.)

At Easter on April 26, 1478, Ascension Day, Lorenzo and his entourage arrived at the Duomo, securing seats at the front of the church. Giuliano trailed behind with his friends Francesco de' Pazzi and Bernardo Bandini. When they arrived at the Duomo he saw his brother at the front of the church surrounded by friends and two priests, one of whom was a Pazzi tutor. The church was full, so Giuliano chose to stand at the back by the doors, with his friends.

The ringing of the sacristy bell and the priest raising the host was the signal, prompting two events. The two priests behind Lorenzo pulled out daggers. One held Lorenzo's shoulder, but he whipped around just in time to stop being stabbed in the neck, the dagger merely cutting him instead. Lorenzo wielded his cape as a shield, pulled out his sword and jumped over the altar rail, running to the safety of the sacristy.

Meanwhile poor Giuliano hadn't fared so well. At the signal, Bandini had pulled out his own dagger and stabbed it into Giuliano's skull with enough ferocity to split his head right open. Francesco had stabbed Giuliano's body with such a frenzy and fury he ended up stabbing himself in the thigh. After his assault on Giuliano, Bandini raced through the crowded cathedral, his sword drawn, trying to reach Lorenzo before he could escape. Lorenzo's friend Francesco Nori tried to block him, but Bandini ran him straight through with his sword, killing him instantly. In the pandemonium and panic inside the cathedral, the bad priests, Bandini and Pazzi, were able to escape.

Simultaneously, over at the Palazzo della Signoria, Salviati (Archbishop of Pisa) said he had a message from the pope for the *gonfaloniere*. He was led in with his entourage and a disguised team of mercenaries. The gonfaloniere (perhaps sensing something was awry) had the mercenaries wait in the chancellery while he spoke to Salviati. The chancellery doors didn't open from the inside, leaving the mercenaries trapped – for a while anyway. A fight broke out between Salviati's entourage and those of the gonfaloniere, who managed to lock themselves in the tower, run up the stairs and start ringing the *vacca* (the giant bell that warns the city of emergencies and calls everyone to the piazza below).

Much more happens in this conspiracy story, with Jacopo de Pazzi escaping the city, the mob hauling Francesco de' Pazzi from his bed where he was nursing his stabbed thigh, and dragging him naked through the streets to the Palazzo della Signoria, where the gonfaloniere personally put a noose around his neck and threw him out of the window. Salviati was hung out of another window for all to see, wearing his purple archbishop's vestments. The bad priests were found hiding at the Badia Fiorentina and met a hasty demise too. The pope was so enraged at the failure of the plot and at the archbishop being hung wearing his ecclesiastical robes that he excommunicated Lorenzo, then, along with the Kingdom of Naples, he declared war against Florence. (You seriously could not make this stuff up!) The Pazzi were exiled from Florence, but they returned when Piero de Medici was overthrown in 1494.

The most compelling version I have ever read of this story is in Paul Strathern's fantastic book, *The Medici: Power, Money and Ambition in the Italian Renaissance.* I highly recommend reading it (or listening to the audiobook) to get the full scope of what happened. The story is quite incredible and Strathern is a master at telling it.

Recommended Reading

This chapter has offered a quick dip into the lives of only the members of the Medici family mentioned later in this book. Their full stories are fascinating and if you are interested in learning more about this incredible dynasty and everything they achieved, I recommend the following books/audiobooks:

- *The House of Medici: Its Rise and Fall,* by Christopher Hibbert (William Morrow Paperbacks, 1999).
- *The Medici: Power, Money and Ambition in the Italian Renaissance,* by Paul Strathern (Pegasus Books, 2016).
- *Medici Money: Banking, Metaphysics and Art in Fifteenth-Century Florence,* by Tim Parks (W. W. Norton & Company, 2006).

Another fantastic way to experience the Medici and learn enough about them to inform your trip is to watch *The Medici: Masters of Florence* series on Netflix (there are three seasons). Although not entirely historically accurate, it serves the greater purpose of connecting you to the characters of Giovanni, Cosimo, and Lorenzo the Magnificent. I promise your experience in Florence will be much more exciting for watching it! I try to get my Glam Italia tour groups to watch it prior to our visiting Florence.

Those who watch it get so much more out of their time in Florence and I enjoy seeing them half lose their minds at some of the places we go. The show gets you invested in the characters, and I have found that if you know and care about the characters of Cosimo and Lorenzo the Magnificent you will get more pleasure out of seeing something they created in real life.

Alternatively, *The Medici: Godfathers of the Renaissance* is a PBS docudrama about the dynasty. This is a good one to watch if you want something a little more serious.

Piazza del Duomo, the Duomo, Campanile & Baptistery

4.

Piazza del Duomo, the Duomo, Campanile & Baptistery

Santa Maria del Fiore, the Duomo (cathedral) of Florence, is one of the most beautiful buildings in the world. No matter how much time I spend here, even if I was just here the week before, every time I lay eyes on her she completely takes my breath away. In all the years I have been coming to Florence, Santa Maria del Fiore has never looked more beautiful than she does today.

I was 21 years old the first time I came to Florence. Back then traffic could drive around the cathedral (the now pedestrian-only area of the piazza). Not only did this make visiting the Duomo a cat and mouse game of dodging cars, it also meant the walls of the Duomo, Campanile and Baptistery were blackened with pollution. It wasn't until Matteo Renzi became mayor that the nearly 10,000 vehicles per day were rerouted away from the area. Though the cathedral was still mesmerizing on my first time in Florence, it didn't gleam in the light the way it does now.

Recently the Duomo complex has undergone a $30 million+ cleaning project. While writing this book (2019) there are sections at the back of the basilica and the northeast side that are still being cleaned. Walking the circumference of the cathedral, you can see how remarkable the project has been, as you compare the dirty sections at the back with the sparkling clean front and sides.

It doesn't matter how many times you come to Florence, you will always notice new things on the façade of this cathedral. When I'm in Florence, I walk past the Duomo at every opportunity, multiple times, day and night, because I just can't believe I get the opportunity to look at something so spectacular. The way the light plays on the walls keeps changing, so it always looks a little different. If you just look at one tiny section each time you pass, you are guaranteed to spot some detail you haven't noticed before. Unfortunately, for much of the day the piazza is overloaded with tourists obscuring your view. I recommend coming early in the morning when you'll have it (almost) to yourself, before the cruise and bus tour groups hit town.

The Duomo complex is made up of the Campanile, the Baptistery and the Duomo itself. In this chapter I want to highlight a handful of details about each building, giving you some specific features to look for. I find my Glam Italia tour groups get more pleasure having a few specific things to look for, rather than trying to see the complex in its entirety.

The Cathedral Before the Cathedral

Dig anywhere in Italy and you'll find ruins from a previous age, and so it is with the Duomo of Florence. During the Roman era there were villas here; the remains of one was found beneath the Baptistery. Roman coins and various other bits and pieces have also been discovered below Santa Maria del Fiore.

The Church of Santa Reparata

Prior to Santa Maria del Fiore, a smaller cathedral stood on this site – the Church of Santa Reparata. Built between the fourth and sixth centuries, it served Florence until a population explosion in the thirteenth century required a bigger cathedral to be built. Santa Reparata remained the cathedral of Florence until the current one was up and running.

Inside Santa Maria del Fiore, you can go downstairs and visit the ruins of Santa Reparata. There is an entrance fee, but for history buffs it's well worth it. You can see pillars and parts of the walls of the old cathedral, fantastic mosaics, marble carvings, ceramics, glass and a bas-relief plaque that dates back to the middle ages.

Some notable Florentines are said to be buried here. In 1972 archaeologists found a plaque matching Vasari's description of Giotto's final resting place. They also found a tomb with the inscription, 'Here Lies a Body of the Great Talent Filippo Brunelleschi of Florence'.

There are three places I usually take my travelers to show them underground Florence. One is here, the second is below Palazzo Vecchio and the third is the wine cellar in my favorite Florentine restaurant, built into the remains of a Roman amphitheater. A visit down here, to Santa Reparata, not only connects you with the region's Roman history, but also lets you appreciate an old church that operated for nearly 1000 years.

A statue of Santa Reparata stands above the central portal on the façade of the cathedral.

Building a New Cathedral

On September 8, 1296, the first stone was laid for the new cathedral designed by Arnolfo di Cambio. It would take 140 years to complete and would become the third largest church in the world after Saint

Peter's in Rome and Saint Paul's in London. At the time of its completion it was the largest church in Europe. (Saint Peter's was built 1506–1626 and St Paul's 1675–1697.)

Di Cambio's original design had three wide naves ending under an octagonal dome. The central nave would have covered Santa Reparata. However, when di Cambio died in 1302, work on the cathedral stopped for 30 years. In 1330 the relics of Saint Zenobius were discovered in Santa Reparata, reigniting the excitement. The Wool Guild (*Arte della Lana*) assumed patronage of the project, hiring Giotto in 1334 to oversee everything. Working with Andrea Pisano, Giotto continued di Cambio's plans until he died on January 8, 1337. Giotto's greatest accomplishment was building the Campanile (bell tower). Pisano continued until the Black Plague halted work again in 1348.

Di Cambio's design was smaller than the church we see now. After Pisano, another architect, Francesco Talenti, took over and increased the size of the cathedral. Five more architects were involved after Talenti. By the time work was completed in the fifteenth century, the cathedral had grown to 153 meters in length, 90 meters in width at the crossing, and 90 meters in height in the dome.

Santa Reparata was pulled down in 1375. In 1412 the cathedral was dedicated to the Virgin of the Flower, *Santa Maria del Fiore*, the flower (the lily) being the symbol of Florence. In 1418 the only part of the new cathedral that remained unfinished was the dome.

The Competition

For 100 years this magnificent cathedral stood with no dome – the Wool Guild had a problem. Technology had not yet been developed that would allow a dome of such height and width to be built. How could a dome that size not fall in on itself or have its weight collapse the walls of the cathedral?

On August 19, 1418, the Wool Guild announced a competition for a plan to build the dome. Various architects submitted proposals, but their plans were flawed. To the annoyance of all, a goldsmith and artist named Filippo Brunelleschi found a solution. Writing his notes in code and keeping them hidden so no one could steal his ideas, he was able to convince Cosimo de' Medici and the Wool Guild of their merit and won the commission – with a caveat. No one trusted this crazy goldsmith/sculptor/artist to be able to pull off architecture independently, let alone something this huge, so Brunelleschi was made to work with his arch rival, Lorenzo Ghiberti. (Fortunately, Ghiberti, busy with other projects at the time, soon realized the dome project was beyond his abilities, so he quit and the job was left to Brunelleschi alone.)

Prior to beginning work on the dome, Brunelleschi was assigned his first architecture commission and in 1419 he completed the beautiful loggia for the Oespedale degli Innocenti, 500 meters away in Piazza SS Annunziata.

Work began on the cathedral dome in 1420 and the completed cathedral was consecrated by Pope Eugene IV on March 26, 1436.

The Dome

It is hard to comprehend just how extraordinary a feat of engineering the creation of this dome really was. I didn't really get it until I watched a segment about the construction of Brunelleschi's dome on British architect Kevin McCloud's *Grand Tour of Europe* in 2010. (Highly recommended viewing if you can access it.)

In 1420, this was the largest dome ever raised and remained the largest for the next hundred years until it was copied for Saint Peter's. And it was all innovation – Brunelleschi didn't have any examples to look to as he figured out this incredibly complex equation.

The big issue when building a dome is the exerted pressure. It can fall inward as it inclines, or it can push out and down, collapsing the walls below it. The only existing dome of similar width was the Pantheon in Rome, which was nowhere near as tall. Brunelleschi studied the Pantheon but there were fundamental differences: the Pantheon relied on solid 10-foot-thick walls to support the dome's outward thrust, also, the concentric circles of squares making up the Pantheon dome grew smaller and used lighter stone in each ring upward, and had an oculus at the apex pushing the weight back out. None of this was an option for Brunelleschi's dome. He also couldn't construct wooden arches to break up the internal weight of the dome as (among other reasons) there wasn't enough lumber available to make arches that enormous. Basically any existing technology was ruled out.

How He Solved It

Brunelleschi made his dome as light as possible. He built two domes, one inside the other, with a stone staircase jammed between them, creating a hollow space. The outer dome supported the roof and protected the inner dome from the elements. His outer dome had eight arching ribs supporting the weight and between each of these were two more internal vertical ribs, further dispersing weight. Then, just as a wooden barrel has iron rings around it to help hold the wood together, he chained the internal ribs horizontally, like an architectural girdle, holding the belly in.

Next he had to figure out how to stop the brickwork from collapsing and crashing downward. He couldn't lay bricks in concentric circles, as with the circular walls of a tower or a well, because the dome was not only vertical, it also inclined. So Brunelleschi came up with another ingenious concept. He created a herringbone pattern for the bricks making them push back on themselves. They were set one circular layer at a time, each brick locking into place, dispersing pressure perfectly and becoming self-sustaining.

His solution came with a new series of problems. As the technology to execute it didn't yet exist, Brunelleschi had to create it. He invented an ox-driven hoist with pulleys and counterweights to lift the heavy stone 80 meters high. Oxen walked in circles turning a wooden tiller that powered the hoists and pulleys. But there was another issue – what went up had to come back down, and you can't make a team of oxen walk in reverse, nor could they be turned around, so Brunelleschi invented gears. The oxen kept walking in one direction and when the pulleys needed to come back down the gear was shifted into reverse. The entire enterprise was completely astounding. Brunelleschi's Dome is 376 feet tall. Michelozzo's lantern, installed on top in 1461 adds another 66 feet in height. When Verrochio's ball was put on top of the lantern they had to use Brunelleschi's technology and machines to lift it all the way up there.

During construction they found that if the workers came all the way down to ground level for lunch (which was usually accompanied by wine), there would be no getting them back up again, especially if they were drunk. To resolve this, packed lunches were invented, enabling the workers to stay up high all day.

There is much, much more to the story of the dome and I really hope you will take the time to watch some videos online about its construction prior to coming to Florence. It will completely change how you see the dome and your appreciation of what an amazing achievement it really is!

Climbing the Dome

There are many places in Florence where you might turn a corner and run into me, but this is not one of them! I am so claustrophobic that unless it was just me and a CPR-trained guide, I would rather die than climb up to the dome of Santa Maria del Fiore. Just watching videos of people climbing the dome makes me nervous.

The ticket to the dome is part of the OPA ticket letting you into Santa Reparata below the cathedral, the Baptistery, the Campanile and the Museo dell'Opera. You need to book a time slot to climb the dome and I sincerely recommend getting the earliest possible time. It is cramped inside the stairwells and you will be squished in with 100 other hot and sweaty tourists, so the earlier you go the better. Every 15 minutes 100 more go up. There are 436 steps and some stretches are very steep. The ceiling is low and in many places the walls are narrower than your wingspan. There are several stretches where although the space is not two-people wide you will encounter downward traffic as you head up. You can get stuck, squashed in with everyone as traffic thins out above you (just the thought horrifies me). There is no elevator, so if you have an emergency or need a bathroom the only way back down is the way you came up.

> ### An Alternate View
>
> If you are claustrophobic (like me) but still want to see the view, I suggest you try the tower of the **Palazzo Vecchio** instead. It is only 233 steps to the top, nowhere near as cramped as the passage up the Duomo, and sees a fraction of the tourist traffic. Plus you get a sensational view of the entire Duomo and Campanile.

The Façade

The original front façade of Santa Maria del Fiore was designed by Arnolfo di Cambio but is often attributed to Giotto. In the Museo dell'Opera del Duomo you can see drawings of *Giotto's Façade*. It was in fact a collaborative project featuring the work of several artists, begun after Giotto's death. Only the lower part was completed, standing unfinished until 1587 when Grand Duke Francesco I de' Medici had it removed as after 200 years it no longer fit the city's Renaissance style.

Bernardo Buontalenti made a model for a new design (which can be seen in the Museo dell'Opera del Duomo). A huge corruption scandal erupted as multiple entries for the design competition had been submitted but not accepted, and the front of the cathedral remained bare until the nineteenth century. Work on the new front of the cathedral began in 1871 and was completed in 1887, designed to blend with Giotto's bell tower and the existing side walls of the cathedral.

Examine the detail on any exterior surface of the cathedral — they're all astounding.

Random Fact

Michelangelo's *David* was supposed to be one of 12 statues of Old Testament prophets to stand along the northeast roofline of the cathedral, where the wall meets the dome. That plan for these statues was shelved, in part, because there was no way to get the enormous statues up that high.

When *David* was completed he was instantly recognized as a masterpiece. So even if there had been a way to hoist this 17-foot statue up to the roof without breaking it, how would the people possibly be able to appreciate it from 80 meters below?

There were several other location choices for *David* but in the end it was decided he should stand outside Palazzo Vecchio where everyone could enjoy him. *David* remained there for 370 years until 1873 when he was moved to the Accademia, where he currently resides. (Learn more about the statue of *David* in **Chapter 5: Piazza della Signoria**.)

The Main Portal

The front of the cathedral has three huge bronze doors dating from 1899 to 1903. (In **Chapter 13: Unusual & Interesting Things**, I'll tell you a cool detail to look for in the doors on the right.) Above the doors are lunettes with mosaics designed by Niccolo Barabino. It would be worth coming if these were the only things to see. They are tremendous. From left to right they are *Charity Among the Founders of Florentine Philanthropy, Christ Enthroned With Mary and John the Baptist,* and *Florentine Artisans, Merchants and Humanists.*

To the right of the main door a niche contains a statue of Saint Zenobius, who in the 400s was the first bishop of Florence.

Above the central door is a half-relief by Sarrochi of *Mary Enthroned Holding a Flowered Scepter*. Look higher and see niches holding statues of the 12 apostles, six each on either side of the *Madonna and Child*. Above the rose window there are 12 more niches, each holding the bust of a famous Florentine artist.

On the north side of the cathedral (where the ever-present line of tourists waits to enter the cathedral), is the Porta della Mandorla (Door of the Almond), the entrance to the dome named for the almond shape above the door from which the virgin ascends to heaven. Be sure to look at the mosaic of *The Annunciation* above the door by Ghirlandaio, created 1489–1490.

Around the exterior and inside the cathedral you will see signs saying OPA. This is not a Greek cheer or a German granddad, but instead is the sign for the Opera del Duomo (not a musical opera, it's the organization that oversees the cathedral complex and museum).

The Interior

As much as I think that the exterior of Santa Maria del Fiore is one of the most beautiful buildings in the world and I absolutely love it, I seldom go inside. At the risk of offending everyone, I find it to be one of the least interesting church interiors in Florence. This could be due to it having had to survive without a hat for a century. If comparing the interior to that of the nearby Basilica Santa Croce, which is astounding, Santa Maria del Fiore is quite spare. During the century that the Duomo had no roof there was prolific painting happening inside Florence's other churches.

While I have devoted multiple pages to the interiors of several churches whose interiors I prefer, such as Santa Croce, SS Annunziata and Ognissanti, here I will just point out a few things to look at. (If you do go inside Santa Maria del Fiore definitely visit the crypt and the ruins of Santa Reparata.)

The Clock

As you come through the doors, turn back and look above the entrance. You'll see a very unusual clock. This nearly 600-year-old clock, decorated by Paolo Uccello in 1443, is still functioning but can seem quite confusing. It is a 24-hour clock that works in accordance with the *ora italica*, which makes sunset the 24th hour, not midnight.

Lorenzo Ghiberti's Stained Glass Windows

The Duomo has 44 stained glass windows, 36 of them designed by Lorenzo Ghiberti, who famously created two of the three sets of bronze doors at the Baptistery. The windows were created between 1394 and 1444. One of the benefits of the interior of the cathedral being so bare is that it draws your eye immediately to the stained glass windows, many of which have been being painstakingly restored. Their colors are vivid and bold, helping you focus on how striking the artwork is. Other artists who worked on the stained glass windows include Donatello, Paolo Uccello, Andrea del Castagno and Agnolo Gaddi.

Dante, Before the City of Florence

This fresco painted by Domenico Michelino in 1465 is on the left nave of the cathedral. I find it particularly interesting because it shows us a snap shot of Florence in 1465, built into scenes from *The*

Divine Comedy. Dante was exiled from Florence in 1302 and never laid eyes on the city again. As such he never saw the cathedral completed, nor its majestic dome, so this painting makes him somewhat of a time traveler. With his love of the *Battistero di San Giovanni* and the hours Dante spent sitting on his stone in the piazza watching the cathedral being built, it's nice to see him depicted here with the final product, 144 years after his death.

The Last Judgement

By far the largest artwork inside the cathedral is Giorgio Vasari's *Last Judgment*, in the interior of the dome, which was started 136 years after the dome's completion.

Due to the limited amount of light that could get in, Brunelleschi had wanted the interior of the dome to be covered in gold mosaic, but his death in 1446 ended that idea and instead the interior was whitewashed.

In 1572, Grand Duke Cosimo I de' Medici hired his favorite artist, Giorgio Vasari, to fresco the interior. Using the Baptistery next door for inspiration, Vasari designed a series of concentric rows inside which he had groups of figures separated from each other along the lines of the dome's eight vertical sections. He matched the subjects along the dividing lines so the pattern could be followed both horizontally and vertically. Each segment features four themes, a chorus of angels, a series of saints, three figures representing the gift of the Holy Ghost, and Hell. In the east section opposite the nave, he condensed it to three themes to make way for *Christ in Glory* between the Madonna and Saint John, which sits above the three Virtues of Faith, Hope and Charity, who in turn are above the figures of Time and the triumphant Church.

When looking up into the dome you'll notice two distinct painting styles. Vasari died after completing the upper portion, Grand Duke Cosimo I died two months prior, and his son Francesco I hired an artist from Urbino, Federico Zuccari, to complete the job.

Zuccari didn't like Vasari's style, so he ceased painting in *fresco* (wet), instead painting in *secco* (dry), which was easier but more perishable. Then he changed everything – the body types, the colors, the costumes and the very language of the painting. Using a technique he learned painting theater backdrops, he abandoned the delicacy of Vasari's style, from the subtle color transitions to the beautiful ornamentation. He felt that would all be lost anyway from such a distance. What Zuccari lacked in quality he made up for in pizzazz. He inserted a gallery of contemporary personalities into the faces, painting his Medici patrons, the Emperor, the King of France, Vasari, Giambologna, himself (of course), other artists and his friends and family.

Zuccari's *Hell* was inspired by Luca Signorelli's work in the cathedral at Orvieto. Look closer and see how violent it is. His color palette for *Hell* changes drastically into dark colors offset by blood red. I think this section brings the whole thing to life, and is, at least in terms of color, by far the most interesting part of the dome's interior. The painting of the dome was completed in 1579. The paintings of Hell are considered Zuccari's life's work or masterpiece.

A couple of items to look for if you are able to get close enough under the dome to see:

- At the top layer where the lantern starts, the figures are climbing down over the railings and you can see arms and legs and feet going over the edges.

- Look for concentric rows of eight black holes in rows two and four. These are the windows from inside the dome that look down over the church!

The Campanile

Designed in 1334, this bell tower on the south side of the cathedral is also known as Giotto's Campanile. At the time he was the master builder of Florence, but when Giotto died in 1337 the work was taken over by Pisano and later was completed by Talenti in 1359. However, the design was kept exactly to Giotto's original plan with the exception of the spire he had wanted on top, which would have elevated the tower to a height of 400 feet. Giotto completed the first of five levels of the tower before his death in 1337.

The exterior is geometric patterns of white marble from Carrara, green marble from Prato and pink/red marble from Siena. Look for seven hexagonal panels with bas-reliefs on each side. The west side panels tell the history of mankind based on Genesis. Find the creation of Adam and Eve, the beginnings of mechanical arts and creative arts, Jabal (animal husbandry), Jubal (music, harp and organ), Tubalcain (the first blacksmith), and Noah (the first farmer). The panels on the south side depict astronomy, building, medicine, hunting, wool-working, legislation, and flight. The east side only has five panels (due to the position of the door) and they are navigation, social justice, agriculture, art of festivals, and architecture (Euclid). The lunette has *Madonna and Child* and then *Two Prophets and the Redeemer* above the gable, both by Andrea Pisano. The north side has sculpture, painting, teaching grammar, logic, music and poetry, arithmetic and geometry, and Tubalcain. The bas-reliefs are tremendous and are low enough that you can examine them and identify what's going on. I find everything else too high up to see well.

Pisano completed the next layer of the exterior of the bottom level, adhering strictly to Giotto's original design with seven diamond shaped panels, each of which have more bas-reliefs inside. Then Pisano added the second level of the bell tower. The exterior of this section features two layers of rectangular shaped panels with four niches on each side, and each layer with statues in the niches of the bottom layer. The upper layer niches stand empty. The statues themselves are interesting and were created in different periods between 1343 and 1435. (All of the statues and bas-reliefs on the Campanile are duplicates. You can see the originals up close in the Opera del Duomo museum. They are tremendous.)

Pisano's work on the Campanile stopped in 1348 when he died of the black death. Talenti built the top three levels. A random, cool fact about these is that each level is larger than the one below it. This is a trick that counters perspective, so from below they all look the same height and equal in size.

Instead of the spire Giotto had planned for the top, Talenti built a large projecting terrace. The Campanile is 277.9 feet tall. You can visit the terrace if your knees and hips (and whatever other parts) are up for tackling 414 steps. If I were to choose between going up the Campanile or to the top of the dome I would do the Campanile. The views are spectacular and you have the added benefit of being able to look at the dome, which is, after all, the most iconic monument in Florence. I don't recommend going up there if you have heart problems, health issues or are even remotely claustrophobic. There's no elevator so your only access in or out is by the stairs.

The tower has seven bells, the largest of which is named *Santa Reparata*. Each have names tied to the Madonna – *Misericordia, Apostolica, Assunta, Mater Dei, Annunziata* and *Immacolata*. During construction of the dome, if mixed mortar was left to sit while the workers ate lunch it would become too hard to work with, so Brunelleschi had an 11:30am bell rung to warn them to stop mixing any more mortar. The bells still ring at 11:30am every day.

OPA PASS

An OPA pass costs €18 giving you 72 hours to access the Baptistery, Campanile, Santa Reparata, Brunelleschi's dome and the Museo dell'Opera del Duomo. You can only access each place on this ticket one time. You will need reservations for the Duomo and they are recommended for the bell tower, although fewer people go up there.

The Baptistery of Saint John (*Battistero di San Giovanni*)

Immediately in front of the Duomo stands an octagonal building with a matching geometrical marble façade – the Baptistery of Saint John. It bifurcates the Piazza del Duomo and the Piazza San Giovanni, but I'll call this entirety the Piazza del Duomo just to make things easier.

The Baptistery recently underwent a $2 million cleaning project. For a couple of years it was hidden behind screens, but is now is back out in the open, its white marble sparkling in the sunshine, looking more beautiful than ever.

WHAT IS A BAPTISTERY?

All over Italy you will see free-standing baptisteries outside major churches and cathedrals, because for centuries you couldn't go inside a church without first being baptized. Ideally your new baby would be baptized soon after birth. Infant and child mortality rates were high and if your baby died before baptism, their access to Heaven would be denied.

There is record of baptisteries dating back to the fourth century. Initially baptism was a full immersion affair so there would be a pool of sorts inside. Over time the pool was replaced with the baptismal font and eventually the font made its way inside the church.

WHY ARE THEY OCTAGONAL?

Baptisteries are typically octagonal instead of square or rectangular. According to Saint Ambrose this is because on the eighth day Christ rose and loosened the bondage of death, receiving the dead from their graves. Saint Augustine said the eighth day is everlasting and hallowed by the resurrection. I also read that the original man-made baptismal pools were cross-shaped and became octagonal by connecting the edges around the cross.

The History of the Baptistery

There is seldom a simple story behind any older building in Italy and this one is suitably long and interesting. It was thought the Baptistery was originally a Roman temple dedicated to Mars. Mars was the guardian god of ancient Florence, and looking at the shape of the Baptistery it makes sense. My obsession with ancient Rome and its deities would love this to be true, however 20th century excavations discovered a 1st century Roman wall running through here, so the Baptistery may have been built on the remains of a guard tower or some other building.

We do know an octagonal baptistery was built on this site at some point around the late 4th century or early 5th century, making it one of the oldest Christian buildings in Florence. That baptistery was either replaced or renovated in the 6th century by Theodolinda, Queen of the Lombards. In 897 it was described as a minor basilica, second to San Lorenzo and predating Santa Reparata. (On March 4, 897, the envoy of the Holy Roman Emperor sat here administering justice. I imagine *that* was terrifying!)

Back then the Baptistery was surrounded by a Roman cemetery with ancient sarcophagi that became the tombs of important Florentines. The pilasters of the Baptistery were taken from the Roman Forum, located up the street in what is now Piazza della Repubblica. The Romanesque style building was re-consecrated on November 6, 1059, by Florentine Pope Nicholas II with the current building's construction completed in 1128.

The Baptistery of Saint John is considered the oldest religious monument in Florence. Until the end of the 19th century all Catholics in Florence were baptized here. That means every historical figure mentioned in this book (from Dante to the Medici, the Pazzi, Pucci, Albizi and Strozzi, the artists and architects, the gonfaloniere and the guild members...) all came through these doors. As far as buildings go, this one is pretty auspicious.

The Baptistery Exterior

The eight sides of the Baptistery were originally sandstone but during the 1059–1128 renovation the exterior walls were given their geometrical pattern in white Carrara marble with a green Prato marble inlay. In 1293 (or thereabouts) Arnolfo di Cambio changed the original grey stone pilasters to a dark green and white horizontal stripe. In 1150 an octagonal lantern was added to the roof. If you look under the roof, in the corners you will see huge lion head with a human head in its claws. This is Marzocco, the Florentine lion and symbol of Mars, the Roman god of war, Florence's tutelary god, and protector of the city.

The bronze doors usually get all the glory, but first let's look at some other things on the exterior:

THREE SCULPTURES

Above the doors directly opposite the Duomo (*The Gates of Paradise*) look for a sculpture of Christ with John the Baptist and an angel looking on. The Baptistery is named for Florence's patron saint, John the Baptist. This is a copy of the original created by Andrea Sansovino in 1502. The original is in the Opera del Duomo Museum.

Above the north door of the Baptistery is *The Preaching of Saint John the Baptist* by Giovanni Rustici. Brilliant in its own right, this also comes with a story linked to the Medici. Rustici came from a well-to-do family in Florence but also benefitted from Lorenzo the Magnificent. Lorenzo had Rustici study in his sculpture school in San Marco at around the same time Michelangelo was there. (Rustici and Michelangelo were both born in 1475.) From San Marco, Lorenzo then installed Rustici in Verrochio's workshop, and when Verrochio moved to Venice he placed him with Verocchio's former student, Leonardo da Vinci. Rustici shared lodgings with Leonardo while working on the Baptistery.

There is a third sculpture on the exterior, which appears in another part of this book. Above the south doors of the Baptistery is a replica of *The Beheading of Saint John the Baptist* by Vincenzo Danti. The original is in the Opera del Duomo Museum. (Again, this sculpture is fantastic in its own right and is worth seeking even without a story.) Vincenzo Danti came from a family of brilliant mathematicians, astronomers, writers and architects. At a time when most were illiterate, the members of this family were prolific writers on many subjects. Vincenzo himself was a published author and a very interesting character (you might want to Google him, as his life intersects with a few different places in this book. If I were writing a book about the artists working in Florence during the Renaissance he definitely would get his own section.) In **Chapter 13: Unusual & Interesting Things**, I talk about Vincenzo's brother Ignazio, who invented the Gregorian calendar with astrological tools he left hiding in broad daylight on the front of the Basilica Santa Maria Novella. It's fun to see the genius work of these two brothers, just down the street from one another.

THE SARCOPHAGUS

To the left of Pisano's door look for a Roman sarcophagus built into the wall. It seems odd to see a pagan sarcophagus on a Christian wall, don't you think? Remember at one time this was a Roman cemetery and wealthy Florentines co-opted sarcophagi to bury themselves in. The images on this sarcophagus illustrate picking grapes and transporting wine on boats. I read that perhaps the sarcophagus carried the remains of a wine merchant, tied to the church's use of wine symbolizing the blood of Christ. Who knows? Maybe it was just slipped in there to link the Roman origins of the site to its (then new) construction. Either way, I think it's cool to see it.

The Doors of the Baptistery

The Baptistery of San Giovanni is famous for its three sets of bronze doors. These were commissioned by the Cloth Guild of Florence (*Arte della Calimala*) who oversaw the Baptistery. The doors were created between 1330 and 1452, each door being made up of square panels telling stories of the bible. At this time the general public couldn't read, so they learned the stories of the Bible, and to fear the fate of non-believers and sinners, from the artwork in and around churches.

PISANO'S DOORS

The first set of doors were made by Pisano, and tell the story of the life of St John the Baptist. The 28 panels were executed between 1330 and 1336. Each scene is made up of relief images sculpted in bronze. The 20 panels from the top down tell stories from the life of John the Baptist and the bottom eight represent the virtues of hope, faith, charity, humility, fortitude, temperance, justice, and prudence. At the top of the doors look a little closer and see two cherubs surrounded by foliage and fruit, symbolizing the baptism of little children and the health and wealth of the life ahead of them.

Initially these doors faced the Duomo, but they were later moved to the south side and the primo spot was taken by Ghiberti's doors. However it is fitting that Giotto's beautiful Campanile stands diagonally opposite his friend Pisano's doors.

GHIBERTI'S DOORS

After the huge success of Pisano's doors the Cloth Guild decided to commission another set and in 1401 held a competition to see which local artist could win the job. Each artist competing had to submit a bronze panel depicting the Sacrifice of Isaac.

Interestingly Giovanni de Bicci de' Medici was one of the judges. Until then he had strictly been a man of business, but perhaps this experience gave him an appreciation of something bigger than money. Maybe it gave him an inkling that there was a way to look powerful and important and leave your mark eternally on this earth via a medium that all could appreciate?

Of all the major artists who entered the competition, including Donatello, it came down to two finalists – Lorenzo Ghiberti and Filippo Brunelleschi. Each submitted a panel that was spectacular but ultimately the commission was awarded to Ghiberti. Some say this was because his was lighter-weight, used less bronze and therefore cost less to produce. Of course we will never know for certain, but when you look at them side by side in the Bargello Museum it is impossible to say one is better than the other. We know the judges found Brunelleschi's to be exemplary too because all the other panels submitted were melted back down so the metal could be reused. Brunelleschi's was returned to him intact, too outstanding to be destroyed.

Brunelleschi was so devastated by his failure to win the competition he turned his back on the art form, never returning to it. Luckily for us he channeled his energy into architecture.

Ghiberti's doors followed the same system as Pisano's. Twenty-eight quatrefoil panels portraying stories from the bible. This time 20 New

Testament scenes from the life of Christ followed by eight scenes of Matthew, Mark, Luke and John, Augustine, Ambrose, Jerome and Gregory the Great. The job was supposed to take 10 years but ended up taking 21 years to complete. Once again, originally the doors were placed on the east side of the Baptistery, facing the Duomo, but they were moved to the north side, and are now the entrance you pass through.

THE GATES OF PARADISE

The Cloth Guild was so thrilled with this second set of doors that they decided to commission a third set, this time with no competition, instead awarding the job directly to Ghiberti.

The project took 27 years to complete, from 1425 to 1452, and is considered to be the first major work of Florence's Renaissance.

Telling the story of the Old Testament this time, Ghiberti changed things up, creating only 10 panels in the space that took up 28 panels in the previous two sets of doors. He also used a new technique. Instead of using quatrefoils he placed his sculptures inside open spaces, using greater perspective to create foreground, middle ground and background. He put more than one story inside each panel, using depth and three dimensions to separate them, making them easily distinguishable from one another.

The doors are so staggeringly brilliant that Michelangelo deemed them worthy of Paradise. He is frequently credited with naming them the *Gates of Paradise*, but the name comes from an annual procession during the Middle Ages on the day of St John the Baptist. Converts to Christianity were anointed in the Baptistery and through these doors would enter and earn the right to Paradise (remember, only the baptized can go to Heaven).

Look at the frames around the doors. They are filled with figures and small busts of prophets, biblical characters and sybils. At eye-level you can see a self-portrait of Ghiberti. He is easy to spot – a small bust of a peaceful, serene-looking bald fellow.

Ghiberti died a few years after his *Gates of Paradise* were installed. From the beginning his doors were considered a masterpiece (*capolavoro*) and have always been well cared for. During World War II they were removed and hidden for safe keeping, and when the great flood of 1966 damaged the lower panels they were again removed and this time replaced with replicas. Restorations took 27 years. The original doors are now on display inside the Opera del Duomo Museum.

The *Gates of Paradise* are a huge tourist draw, and during the day this can make them hard to get close to. If you're staying overnight, I sincerely recommend visiting them early in the morning. In the early morning, you seem to be the only person around other than the locals going to work, so you'll have a perfectly unfettered view of the doors. As with most things in this beautiful city, you can look at them 100 times and still notice something new on visit 101.

The Baptistery Interior

The interior of the Baptistery is sensational: Byzantine mosaics, Roman sarcophagi, dramatic Romanesque arched windows, funerary monuments to a Medici family member and the Pirate Pope, and above it all an astounding dome with a Byzantine mosaic ceiling. There is so much to see inside the Baptistery, every inch of surface is embellished, so I'll just direct you to my favorite things.

THE CEILING

Florence never lets us down when it comes to wow-factor, and this is yet another example of the city's artistic genius.

Beginning in the 1200s this stupendous ceiling with its complex and incredibly detailed account of the Universal Judgement took more than 100 years to complete. It can seem totally overwhelming at first as so much is happening. I recommend studying the ceiling online prior to coming, so that you A) have an idea what's going on and B) can identify the parts that interest you.

The easiest place to start is the huge circular mosaic of Christ. He is massive, you can't miss him. Everything is either to his left or to his right. In the concentric circles making up the dome, you'll see stories of the Apostles, St John the Baptist, stories from Genesis, and stories from the life of Joseph. But the most intriguing cycle to look at here is the Last Judgement. On Christ's right hand is Salvation, those who were saved are released by gorgeous angels and emerge from their tomb in joy. Meanwhile on Christ's left hand is Damnation. (Interesting side note: in Italian the word for left is *sinistra*, from which we get the word *sinister*. The left is always associated with bad things.)

Imagine living in pre-19th century Florence. You couldn't read or write, and even if you could there were no newspapers or free press. All your information came from the church. There wasn't room for free thought or expression. Not only was there a tithe to be paid but there was also mental extortion. The church told you what to think and how to behave. They told you what would happen if you followed their rules – whatever suffering they caused you on earth was irrelevant because by obeying them you would make it into their perfect heaven. And what happened to non-believers or anyone who disobeyed? Look to Christ's left hand. Here you see the horrors of damnation in a series of mosaics that must have been terrifying to the devout – black winged devils release the sinners from their tombs to a scary, horned Satan who sits eating a man while snakes come out of his ears, gorging themselves on two more humans; people panic, trampled on as ugly demons push more sinners into their midst; the damned are thrown into fires, burned on spits, hanged, and beaten; monsters, snakes and demons bite them, tear them to pieces and in some cases come at their naked behinds like sodomites. The story is so vivid, gruesome and frightening it influenced Dante's description of Hell (*Inferno*) in his *Divine Comedy*.

What's hilarious here is the clergy (*especially* the popes) didn't follow the rules they laid out for the congregation. In the most ironic juxtaposition, one of the most nefarious popes, the Pirate Pope Baldassare Cossa (Pope John XXIII) is laid to rest here. With no means to learn about him you can be sure that the people of Florence had no idea they were baptizing their babies beside the tomb of a pope found guilty of heresy, simony, sodomy, tyranny, incest, piracy, and immorality!

THE TOMB OF THE ANTIPOPE JOHN XXIII

As bad as he was, Antipope John XXIII (aka Baldassare Cossa) was a friend to Florence and to the Medici, who financed his ascent to the papacy. He gave the city of Florence the pilfered relic of John the Baptist's finger – supposedly the right index finger John pointed at Jesus when he said, 'Behold, the lamb of God.' This had huge religious significance to the city.

The Pirate Pope made four men executors of his will. Two died, one wasn't interested and the 4th was Giovanni de' Bicci de' Medici.

Giovanni handed the job to his son Cosimo who, following Baldassare's wishes, organized the creation of the Pope's tomb inside the Baptistery. To the left of the mosaic of Christ (his sinister side) you will find the tomb of Pope John XXIII, the Antipope.

Cosimo hired his favorite architect, Michelozzo, and his favorite artist, Donatello, to create the tomb. Notice how the tomb is very vertical – they weren't allowed to build outward into the body of the Baptistery. The tomb fits between two columns to the right of the altar and is the first example of a coffin being carved on top of a tomb.

At the bottom three niches hold bas-reliefs of the virtues Faith, Hope and Charity. Above this is the tomb with a child sitting on either side of the inscription: *John the former pope XXIII. Died in Florence AD 1419 on the 11th day before Calends of January.* Pope Martin V, who took over after the pirate was de-poped, didn't like the implication that the pirate was still pope when he died, but instead of ex-communicating him, Martin had made him a cardinal (which was *crazy*) and wanted his tomb to reflect that lesser status.

Above the tomb is a bronze statue by Donatello, depicting the pirate pope lying on a bed. Rather than traditionally looking up to the heavens, Donatello has positioned his face looking out at us. Above the bed a canopy with an apex, drawing the eye heavenward, and inside the canopy is Madonna and child. It is all quite incongruous, yet brilliant.

ALSO BURIED HERE...

Not many are buried here but once again the Medici show up. Guccio de Medici, who made an appearance in the city's government in the early 1300s, somehow managed to get himself buried in one of Florence's holiest sites. Guccio's tomb is a Roman sarcophagus depicting scenes of boar hunting, a famously popular Tuscan pastime. On the upper left hand corner of the sarcophagus, look for the Medici crest.

THE MARBLE FLOOR

Construction of the marble floor of the Baptistery probably begun in 1209. It features intarso marble designs in geometric patterns and in the signs of the zodiac. You can see them in the floor on your left as you enter. There once was a hole in the dome that let light flood down and hit the signs of the zodiac, and on the summer solstice, June 24 – the feast day of John the Baptist, the light would hit this inscription of a mysterious and untranslatable palindrome:

en giro torte sol ciclos et rotor igne

In the middle of the floor look for the base of the octagonal font, placed there in 1128. It once stood in Santa Reparata. Supposedly Dante broke one of the basins while rescuing a drowning child. In 1571 Grand Duke Ferdinando ordered the font removed. The current font was installed in 1658 but is much older, its reliefs attributed to Andrea Pisano.

Museo dell'Opera del Duomo

From the outside you don't realize how huge and modern this space is. Rather than a dusty old cathedral museum, it is light and bright and cleverly laid out.

The OPA (Opera del Duomo) has cared for the cathedral of Florence for 700 years. It oversaw construction of the complex, then became the conservation arm, taking care of its monuments.

The museum holds the original works of art, statues, reliefs et. al from the exterior of the Duomo, the Campanile and the Baptistery, protecting them from vandalism and pollution. Spread across 25 rooms on three floors , there are more than 750 works of art, and a sensational sense of space and light. It's not at all what you would expect.

Some noteworthy things (my favorites) to find here are:

- **The Corridorio dell' Opera.** This really cool wall displays the names of some of the thousands of people who worked on the Duomo complex, from architects, artists and musicians, to workmen, artisans and humanists. To a degree it gives you a sense of how enormous the project was from its inception in 1296 to now.

- **Galleria delle Sculture/The Sculpture Gallery.** These sculptures were created for the Baptistery and the sides of the cathedral, plus here you'll find a rare view of the back of Ghiberti's Baptistery doors.

- **Salone del Paradiso/Hall of Paradise.** This is astounding! A monumental, life-sized re-creation of the original cathedral façade and Baptistery. The statues that covered the original façade, torn down in 1587, have been repositioned in what would have been their original spaces. Ghiberti's original *Gates of Paradise* are also here.

- **La Salla della Maddelena/Room of the Magdalene.** Adjacent to the area with all the relics, the main work of art here is Donatello's haunting wooden statue of the *Penitent*

Saint Mary Magdalene. Kept safely behind glass, this is not to be missed.

- **Tribune di Michelangelo.** This will suck the breath right out of you, even when you're expecting to see it. The room holds Michelangelo's second-to-last sculpture, intended to be placed at the altar of the church he expected to be buried in. It was begun around 1546 and abandoned around 1555 when he smashed it, frustrated at flaws in the marble. After it was put back together, Cosimo III de' Medici acquired it in 1671 for the crypt at the Basilica of San Lorenzo. In 1721 it was moved to the Duomo and stationed opposite the Holy Sacrament altar. The *Pietà* is the deposition of Christ from the cross into Mary's arms, with a self-portrait of Michelangelo as Nicodemus. The lighting in this room will bring you to your knees – it is quite dramatic.

- **The Galleria del Campanile/Gallery of the Bell Tower.** This gallery holds the artwork from the exterior of the Campanile: the 54 reliefs from the hexagons and the lozenges, and the 16 statues from the niches above them. It is hard to appreciate them fully on the Campanile as they are so much higher than eye line, but here they are at eye level.

- **The Galleria del Cupola/Gallery of the Dome.** This is perhaps the most fascinating room in the museum as it focuses on Brunelleschi's masterpiece – the dome (or cupola) of the cathedral. There is a short film about the construction, you can see the tools Brunelleschi invented, the design of the windows, the friezes, the lantern… all of it is here. You'll get a greater appreciation of the creation of the dome and what makes it so special. Brunelleschi's death mask is also here.

- **Galleria dei Modelli**. This gallery contains the models for the statues submitted for the new façade. This time the originals are still at the Duomo (and can be seen on the rooftop tour). They were thought to be too big to be brought down without damaging the Duomo itself.

- **Belvedere della Cupola/The Terrace**. Here you get the chance to see the dome up close, allowing you to see some of the smaller details. From the inside there is a big, modern skylight which gives you yet another viewing experience. This room has an incredible wow-factor.

Address: Piazza del Duomo, 9 (at the back of the Duomo).

Things to Look for in the Piazza

DANTE'S STONE

There are more details in **Chapter 23: A Walk with Dante**, but while we are here in the piazza I want to point this out:

Dante Alighieri is Italy's most celebrated poet. During the early construction of the cathedral he would sit on a stone in the Piazza Duomo, catching the cool breeze on summer evenings, thinking his big thoughts. In 1291, in his work *La Vita Nuova,* he wrote about sitting and thinking of his beloved Beatrice who had died the year before. The actual stone he sat on is long gone, and in its place is a commemorative plaque. On the southeast side of the piazza next to via dello Studio, look for a pink and grey marble plaque, low on the wall, with the inscription, *Sasso di Dante.*

THE BALUSTRADE ON THE CUPOLA

I had been to Florence more times than I could count before learning about this detail on the cupola of the Duomo. At the time I was walking with a friend who is one of the city archivists, and who kept up a running stream of stories about fascinating things as we passed them. As he is an Italian, this story was delivered at great verbal velocity, with much hand gesturing, a fabulous outfit, a scarf artfully wrapped around his neck, walking at a snappy pace, and a sense of drama. I thought it was fantastic! So here it is:

Baccio d'Agnolo (1462–1543) was an architect and sculptor. He collaborated with Antonio da Sangallo on the church of SS Annunziata and the restoration at Palazzo Vecchio. Between 1508 and 1515 he worked on the Duomo and was nominated master builder, but was fired after Michelangelo criticized his work.

One of the things d'Agnolo worked on was the decorative walkway around the drum of the dome. He'd designed and built the first section, but when asked for his opinion, Michelangelo denounced the balustrade, saying, 'it looks like a cricket cage to me.' With Michelangelo's condemnation, the job was abandoned, leaving just the one section.

Walk along the south side of the cathedral, you'll find the statue of Brunelleschi. Follow his gaze up to the dome and you will spot the 'cricket cage' – d'Agnolo's aborted balustrade. Then observe how many people walk past it, oblivious.

Another fantastic position to see the balustrade is from the terrace restaurant and bar at the Biblioteca delle Oblate, which gives you an unimpeded view.

WHERE THE BALL DROPPED

As you walk to the back of the cathedral from the south side, past Brunelleschi's statue and Dante's Stone, look for a white marble circle on the ground. In 1468 Verrochio designed a 2000 kilo gilded bronze ball measuring 2.3 meters in diameter. (At that time Leonardo da Vinci was an apprentice in Verrochio's workshop so he probably worked on the project in some way.) The golden ball was given a cross on top and in 1471 it was positioned on the lantern, on top of the dome of the cathedral, as its crowning glory, a golden beacon that could be seen from afar, and a proud symbol of Florence.

The sphere was struck by lightning on April 8, 1492, when Lorenzo the Magnificent died, and several more times over the next hundred years. It remained steadfast until, on January 27, 1601, a massive thunderstorm raged over Florence. A lightning bolt hit the highest point of the cathedral, the gilded bronze ball with the cross on top that had been in place for 118 years. The lightning was so powerful it knocked the ball off its perch. The ball rolled down the cupola causing massive damage, before it crashed to the ground below, making a terrifying noise on impact. The sphere took a year to repair and in 1602 it was put back on top of the lantern on the dome. The exact spot the golden ball landed is marked with a circle of white marble. When you've found it, it's fun to stand back and watch how many tourists walk right past it without noticing it's there!

THE LOGGIA DEL BIGALLO

With the cathedral, Campanile and Baptistery creating such an astounding visual, it is easy to miss another spectacular structure here in the piazza, the Loggia del Bigallo.

This incredibly beautiful building would get more attention if it was in its own separate piazza. Frescoed and sculpted, with statues in niches above the entrance, I am always stunned to watch the hordes of tourists descending on the Piazza del Duomo, passing right in front of it, unaware it's even here!

Dating to 1352–58, the Loggia was a shelter for abandoned and orphaned children and babies, left here in the care of the Campagnia della Misericordia (the monks of the Company of Mercy). Not only did they care for the little ones, they also gave shelter to others in need, including those afflicted with the plague. In 1425 the Compagnia del Bigallo, who from 1244 had been housed by Orsanmichele, moved in too. They cared for pilgrims and travelers, so it seems fitting that the piazza that held Europe's biggest cathedral and its beautiful Baptistery also held the refuge for those most in need of God's help.

The Loggia is now the entrance to the Museo del Bigallo, with artwork telling the history of the fraternity over the centuries. There is a lot to see here including a remarkable fresco with the oldest known view of the city of Florence, *Madonna of the Misericordia*, painted by Bernardo Daddi in 1342.

Address: The Loggia is on the corner of Piazza San Giovanni and via Calzaioli.

UNUSUAL & INTERESTING THINGS IN PIAZZA DE' DUOMO

In **Chapter 13: Unusual & Interesting Things,** I'll tell you about three more things to look for here in the Piazza Duomo. Be sure to check it out and look for *The Bull of Santa Maria del Fiore, The Devil's Wind* and *The Strangled Artist of the Duomo.*

Piazza della SS Annunziata

Florence

5.

Piazza della SS Annunziata

This is one of the loveliest piazzas (*piazze*) in all of Florence and I'm going to let you in on a secret. When the crowds around the Duomo get too overwhelming (and believe me, they get *very* overwhelming), one of my favorite escapes is just a stone's throw away – to the peace and tranquility of this gorgeous city square. It takes all of three minutes to walk here yet it feels like a world away.

This square (it is actually a square shaped piazza) is a testament to Renaissance elegance. From the harmony of the color palette to the classically inspired archways of the loggia, to the pleasing geometry within this space, the Piazza della SS Annunziata is the ideal place to let your mind rest for a minute, to escape the crowds, and to discover some fabulous and fascinating things.

With Piazza della SS Annunziata, I think the approach is important. Rather than taking a side entrance, start in the Piazza Duomo. Walk along the north flank of the cathedral, past the long line of hot, sweaty tourists waiting to get inside, loop around the back and you'll see a little street only two blocks long, the via dei Servi. With your back to the Duomo walk down via dei Servi, past the little shops and eateries towards the huge statue of Ferdinando I de' Medici welcoming you to the piazza from his horse.

Piazza della SS Annunziata is an open, airy space, built according to the Renaissance utopian ideals in architecture – the concept of beauty and order being accessible to all. Before we look around, I want you to get your bearings. With the Duomo at your back, the church of SS Annunziata is directly in front of you, beyond the huge statue of Ferdinando. (We met him in the Medici chapter.) On your right is the Hospital of the Innocents or *Ospedale degli Innocenti* also known as the Foundling Hospital . The Servi monastery is on your left, and the Palazzo Grifoni is at your left shoulder.

The Church of SS Annunziata

This is one of my favorite churches in Florence for several reasons. The building itself is spectacular, the artwork is breathtaking, and the piazza this church resides in is full of cool things to see.

Before you go inside the church, take a moment and look around the piazza. It is so peaceful and pretty and feels light years away from the crowds at the cathedral, yet it's only *500 meters away*!

THE STORY BEHIND THE CHURCH

In 1081 a small oratory was built on this site just outside the city walls, to thank the Virgin Mary for protecting the city from the siege of Enrico IV. At some point it was abandoned and fell into disrepair. Fast forward to the mid 1200s, a group of seven men got together, calling themselves the Order of the Servite (Order of the Servants of Mary), dedicated to honoring and serving the Virgin. As the Order grew they needed somewhere to hang out, so requested use of the abandoned oratory. They built this church on the site in 1250 and in 1252 commissioned Fra Bartolomeo to paint *The Annunciation*. All was going swimmingly until he got to the bit where he had to paint the Virgin's face. Despairing he wouldn't be able to paint a face beautiful enough, he fell asleep, exhausted from his attempts and worrying about getting it right. When he woke a miracle had occurred. While he slept, an angel had completed the painting with an exquisitely beautiful face.

You know how well pilgrims and miracles go together. Word got out about the miraculous *Annunciation* and pilgrims arrived from all over. They would leave votives in the church, sculptures made of wax, plaster and wood, even a life-sized sculpture of a nobleman and his horse.

The church grew in importance and consequently grew in size. The magnificent church that we see today is the product of centuries of reconstruction and additions, all adding to its beauty.

The Puccis

I love finding odd things you wouldn't otherwise notice. On the corners of the church and underneath the portico look up into the vaulted ceilings and you will see the symbol of the Pucci family, a black head offset by a white background. The Pucci family funded this section of the church in the late 1400s.

You also see the Pucci crest inside the church on the floor. Here you can get close enough to look at the headband the figure is wearing. It originally bore three hammers, the symbol of their ancestral profession, but was later amended to three Ts, representing the family motto: *Tempore tempora tempera* (Time is a great healer).

THE CLOISTER OF THE VOTI

If this is the only thing you see it would be worth taking time out of your day!

The entrance to the basilica is through the magnificent Cloister of the Voti. Remember the endless stream of pilgrims coming here with their wax sculptures? Well, they had to be put somewhere, so Michelozzo was commissioned to design this cloister/entryway to house them.

The cloister is decorated with marble reliefs and twelve frescoes by major Florentine artists. The first lunette, Baldovinetti's *Nativity*, was begun in 1460 but the second, Cosimo Rosselli's *Dressing of S Filippo,* didn't start for another 16 years. In 1509 Andrea del Sarto began the first of his five frescoes detailing stories from the life of the Virgin Mary, but in 1516 he handed off the final two works to his best pupils, Pontormo and Rosso Fiorentino.

The cloister recently underwent massive restoration. Over the centuries, weather, humidity and more recently pollution, had damaged the fresccos. A glass ceiling was constructed over the atrium and an organization named Friends of Florence took on the four year project which was completed in November 2017. The restored beauty we are able to enjoy now and hopefully for centuries to come is thanks to their work.

THE CHURCH

As you enter the church be prepared to be completely wowed by the ceiling. To this day, every time I walk inside the basilica my eyes are instantly drawn upward.

The church may seem a little off-kilter, due to the chapel of SS Annunziata which is on the left as you enter. In 1447 Piero de' Medici funded the friars' decision to create a 'temple' for the painting of the miraculous *Annunciation*. Designed by Michelozzo, it is rich with bronze, Carrara marble, ceramics and artwork, signifying how important this painting was.

Before exploring the enormity of the artwork housed in the chapels along the sides, take a moment to step back and soak in the entirety of this church. It is dazzlingly beautiful. I know I am repeating myself, but it is *magnificent*.

Moving through the church, follow the signs from the left transcept to the Sacristy, from where you can observe the dome and the altar up close.

There is also a free bathroom behind the Sacristy.

THE CLOISTER GRANDE

Opposite the entrance to the Sacristy look for a rich red curtain behind which you'll find the doorway to the peaceful and harmonious Cloister Grande, also known as the *Cloister dei Morti*.

Here you will see 25 more lunettes, painted by an assortment of artists. Also look for the sarcophagus with the Falconieri family logo on it – two falcons and a ladder. This is the family that gave the church Saint Giuliana, preserved in glass up by the altar, and her uncle Alessio Falconieri, one of the founding seven Servites who was also sainted.

The Cloister Grande leads to the Capella di San Luca, where many artists including Pontormo and Cellini are buried.

The Architects of the Piazza

The first construction in the piazza was the original church, built for the Servite Order in 1298. As the church grew in importance due to the miraculous painting inside, the piazza needed to reflect its new celebrated status. The beauty of the design seen today stems from the genius of Brunelleschi.

In the early fourteenth century, Florence was one of the wealthiest cities in Europe. Its robust economy was based on two things – a very effective banking system and a strong textile industry. The textile industry's merchants and artisans belonged to a variety of powerful guilds. In 1419 one of these, the Silk Guild, commissioned Brunelleschi to design an orphanage or foundlings hospital here in Piazza SS Annunziata. The *Ospedale degli Innocenti* (Hospital of the Innocents) may actually have been Europe's first foundlings hospital.

OSPEDALE DEGLI INNOCENTI (HOSPITAL OF THE INNOCENTS)

This was an orphanage for babies and children. Initially babies were left in a large basin in front of the building. In 1660 the basin was replaced with a horizontal wheel and a special door. The baby would be put on the wheel and rotated through the door, allowing the parents some anonymity.

The hospital provided wet nurses, and once the baby was weaned and old enough the boys learned to read and write before being taught a skill to match their individual aptitude. Girls learned sewing, cooking and other jobs thought suitable for females, then had the choice of being provided a dowry so they could marry or becoming nuns.

The building was constructed in several phases. Brunelleschi was part of Phase I, from 1419–1427. He laid the foundations, built the walls, basement and cloisters and perhaps most famously, designed the beautiful loggia along the front façade.

The loggia were designed using Classical Roman and Italian Romanesque architectural styles. Brunelleschi had spent time studying the beauty of ancient architecture in Rome with his buddy Donatello. His loggia, with their rounded columns and classic capitals, circular arches, and segmented domes inside, were considered novel and incredibly beautiful. He offset the white walls with what would become his signature grey stone, *pietra serena*.

The loggia and eventually the entire piazza, look so harmonious because of Brunelleschi's use of geometry. It would become a defining characteristic of his architecture, but this loggia was the beginning of his use of the logic of proportion. If you draw an imaginary line along the top of the columns you will see perfect squares created out of the height of the columns and the distance between them. This became an important feature of Renaissance architecture, and it started right here. It wasn't until after this commission that Brunelleschi created the dome for the cathedral.

Brunelleschi intended the circles between the rounded arches on the façade of the loggia to remain empty, but 44 years after his death in 1446, Andrea della Robbia was hired in 1490 to decorate them. The 10 *tondi* have light blue backgrounds and white *putti*, dressed in swaddling cloths to represent the abandoned children.

A Work in Progress

It was a century before another architect, Antonio da Sangallo the Elder (godfather to Giulio de Medici), transformed the piazza into one of the most beautiful in Italy by building a portico onto the monastery, the *Confraternita dei Servi*. He created arches identical to Brunelleschi's loggia, directly opposite. Instead of blue and white *tondi* with *putti*, the circles between Sangallo's arches simply feature the letter S for Servi.

When you enter the Piazza della SS Annunziata it looks like the buildings are all part of the one entity, but they're not. Stop for a moment and look at della Robbia's *tondi* on the hospital on your right and the Servi S on your left. You would never know 100 years separate them!

Sangallo's work here in the piazza influenced Michelangelo's design for the Piazza del Campidoglio in Rome in 1536. He used the same pattern of two identical buildings with long porticos flanking a center building – in that case, the Palazzo Senatorio.

It was almost another hundred years before the third portico was created. The church had a plain façade until 1601 when architect Giovanni Battista Caccini imitated Brunelleschi's façade, albeit using a little stretching to get the height of the portico consistent with the *Ospedale degli Innocenti*. So it took almost 200 years to get these three sides of the piazza matching!

Another famous architect seen in the Piazza della SS Annunziata is Bartolommeo Ammannati. In 1563 he designed the Palazzo Grifoni, starting a new trend by mixing color with stone. The Palazzo delle Due Fontane, which is on your immediate right as you enter the piazza, wasn't given a façade to match the Palazzo Grifoni until the late nineteenth century.

The Ospedale degli Innocenti Museum

I think this one is pretty fantastic. You can experience 600 years of history and art by the likes of Botticelli and Ghirlandaio without crowds of tourists. No one seems to know this gem is here!

The museum reopened its doors in 2016 after a three year renovation. It spreads out over almost the entire complex, divided into three sections: History, Architecture and Art. There is a multimedia presentation at the beginning, which I highly recommend as it puts everything you are about to see in context.

The History section depicts stories of the day-to-day care of the children. Most were left here due to extreme financial hardship. Parents often left their child with the broken half of a charm known as a *mark*, so in time they might be reunited, with their own half of the charm proving the child was theirs. The hospital kept archives on all the children, and there is a heartbreaking section with the marks of children never claimed by their families.

The Art Gallery starts on the second floor, once home to the children and wet nurses. The renovations here are tremendous with the art work well lit and well displayed. See work by artists including Botticelli, Ghirlandaio and Lucca della Robbia. There is a really beautiful *Madonna and Child with Angel* by Botticelli which is probably the most important piece in the collection, along with Ghirlandaio's *Adoration of the Magi*. At the big staircase there is a statue of St John the Baptist by Simone Talenti, created for the Silk Guild's tabernacle at Orsanmichele. (See **Chapter 14: Churches** for more details.)

On the top floor a terrace called *the Verone* was a place to hang the washed clothes to dry, and for workers and children to socialize. **The**

Verone is now a café where you can take a break with a fabulous view of the Duomo.

The Statue of Ferdinando I

Back in Rome in 1538, Michelangelo moved the monument of Marcus Aurelius, a 13.9 foot tall bronze of the emperor on his horse, to the center of the Piazza del Campidoglio. In 1608 sculptor Giambologna, famed for his life-sized sculptures of horses, placed his bronze statue of Grand Duke Ferdinando I de' Medici in the Piazza della SS Annunziata, creating yet another similarity between these two piazzas.

Giambologna's statue was created with bronze from melted down cannons from captured Turkish galleys. The inscription on the horse's girth says '*De' metalli rapiti al fero Trace,*' which means 'Metal taken from the savage Thracians' (a traditional enemy of the ancient Romans from the area that now makes up Turkey, Greece and Bulgaria).

Other Fascinating Things to Look for in the Piazza

I love a good story, so anything quirky, secret or offbeat is fascinating to me. While you are here in Piazza della SS Annunziata I have some additional cool things for you to look for, each with its own story.

THE FOUNTAIN

In the midst of this peace and tranquility there is a fountain that doesn't quite match the rest of the piazza. Have a closer look and you will see creatures looking like they belong in the movie, *The Creature from the Black Lagoon.*

The fountain was created by Pietro Tacca', a student-of and successor-to Giambologna, the sculptor who created the giant Ferdinando on the horse. Tacca' created the fountain for the Port of Livorno, hence the sea-beast theme, but Ferdinando II, grandson of he on the horse, insisted that it live here. There is a copy of this statue in the Port of Livorno near the statue of the Quattro Mori.

THE OPEN WINDOW AT PALAZZO GRIFONI

Who doesn't enjoy a good ghost story? This one involves Palazzo Grifoni, the reddish palazzo at your left when you enter the piazza. The last window on the top floor on the right hand side has remained open for centuries.

Near the end of the 1500s one of the Grifoni sons was called away to war, leaving his young bride behind. Her last view of him was from this window as he rode away. She waited at the window for decades, sure that one day he would ride back into the piazza. She loved him so much she never gave up hope, waiting each day at the window until she eventually died. Upon her death, once her body had been carried away, the family tried to close the window. Legend says that when they tried to close it all hell broke loose. The furniture started shaking, books flew off the shelves, paintings fell off the walls…

Since then the window has remained open, for more than 400 years, just in case her husband ever rides back into the piazza to come for her.

Ferdinando's Mistress

There is another story that goes with the same window at Palazzo Grifoni. This story says the room with the open window belonged to Grand Duke Ferdinando I's mistress and that he had the statue placed exactly there so that he could keep an eye on her. If you look at him it kind of makes sense – he is acting all macho and his eye line looks directly at that window. Theoretically it could keep other gentleman callers away. The only problem with this story is – why would the window have to remain open? The timing of the statue's placement and the window staying open also doesn't fit. But Ferdinando could have been getting it on with the subsequent occupant of the room. Have a look when you are there and let me know which story you think is most likely!

Ferdinando and the Bees

Ferdinando's statue has another interesting feature. At the back, on the pedestal there is a bronze relief of a swarm of 91 bees circling a queen bee. Supposedly this symbolizes his magnificence and superlative leadership skills, with him being the queen bee and the 91 others being the people of Florence and Tuscany. Except I don't really think that equating yourself with a queen bee is particularly masculine, do you? Apparently his motto was *Maiestate Tantum* which means *Great Majesty*.

It's funny to think of the ghost of Ferdinando's girlfriend looking out the window at the queen bee. The bees weren't put there until 1640, so the poltergeist wasn't throwing books around because her macho man had decided he was a queen – the ghost action happened 50 years prior.

THE SEALED WINDOW

I absolutely *love* random things like this! Unless you know to look for it, you'll walk right past the walled-in window on the northeast corner of via dei Servi and via del Pucci, midway between the Duomo and Piazza della SS Annunziata. This is the Palazzo Pucci, former home of the Pucci family and the site of a Renaissance tale of conspiracy and revenge.

The Pucci have been a prominent family in Florence since the 1200s. They were important politically, were magistrates, 23 of them held priories, eight of them became *gonfaloniere*, three of them even became cardinals. They were wealthy and powerful and were staunch allies of the Medici throughout the Renaissance. In the sixteenth century they were trusted members of the Medici's ducal and grand ducal courts.

Things went sideways in 1559 when Pandolfo Pucci was kicked out of the court of Grand Duke Cosimo I de' Medici, either for accusations of immorality or for wanting to restore the Republic of Florence. (Who knows which it really was?) Regardless Pandolfo fell from grace. So he conspired with some other noble families to kill Cosimo. The plan was to shoot him with an arquebus as he and his entourage walked past on their way to mass at SS Annunziata. The plan was aborted but the Medici got wind of it and had to make an example of him. Pandolfo was hung from a window in the Bargello and the Pucci properties were seized.

Whether it was superstition or just to remind everyone never to plot against the Medici, Grand Duke Cosimo I ordered the window from where the attack was to have occurred be bricked up. To this day it has remained sealed. The sealed window is one block up via dei Servi on your left as you walk to piazza della SS Annunziata. I still get a kick out of it every time I see it.

The Pucci made good with the Medici and three years later they not only got the palace back but they were also awarded the title of Marchese di Barsento, a noble title handed down within the family ever since.

6.

Piazza della Repubblica

Piazza della Repubblica is one of the main squares in Florence, and is the most central point of the city. To me it's the least interesting of Florence's piazzas, but you'll pass it multiple times in any given day so I want to give you a little background on it.

The Colonna dell' Abbondanza/ Colonna Dovizia

During the Roman era this was the heart of the city of Florentia, home to the Roman Forum, the political and commercial center. It was the intersection of two important Roman grid roads, the Cardo and the Decumanus Maximus. There will have been a monument marking the spot, but it's long gone. Now the ancient intersection is celebrated with a column in the piazza. Made of grey granite from the island of Elba, the Colonna dell' Abbondanza was erected in 1431. The top of the column held a *pietra serena* statue by Donatello, telling the allegorical story of *La Dovizia* (Abundance), which was fitting as, by then, this square had become the old market, or *Mercato Vecchio*.

There is a little intrigue here. Over the next three centuries the statue suffered weather damage and eventually the head fell off. In 1721 the statue was replaced, and the original promptly disappeared – vanished without a trace. In fact *La Dovizia* is considered to be Donatello's most important lost work. You have to wonder if it was destroyed or is hiding in a private collection. Maybe like the statues found in Rome, one day someone will be digging in the street or in their garden and this statue will be discovered, having been buried for centuries.

In 1721 Giovanni Battista Foggini's marble replacement statue was installed on top of the column. The current statue is a replica of Foggini's work. The original is in the bank *Cassa di Risparmio* on the via dell'Oriuolo. The column used to have two chains attached. One rang a bell signaling the open and close of the market, the other apparently was used to detain swindlers and debtors. I've read that the second bell also rang to warn market shoppers that pickpockets were about.

The Old Market/ Mercato Vecchio

In the Middle Ages, Piazza della Repubblica was the Old Market/Mercato Vecchio. Bursting with market stalls and churches, it was the site of the city's food market. It also became the location of the Jewish Ghetto after the Papal Bull of July 14, 1555, revoked the rights of the Jewish people. (Having grown up in New Zealand, I think we must have a different Bible over there, because I don't remember any part where Jesus ordered the persecution of the Jews. Or for that matter any other group who have been or currently are being persecuted in the name of Christianity...)

The piazza remained the home of the city market until the nineteenth century.

In 1865 Florence became the capital of the new Kingdom of Italy. It was decided the city needed modernizing, with plans to tear down old buildings and make way for new, wide boulevards and public squares. The historical buildings were seen as a sign of the old, divided Italy. The capital moved to Rome in 1871, but the morons in charge moved forward with their plans anyway and began demolishing the historic center of Florence in 1885. Thankfully this caused an outrage across Europe and petitions and campaigns were created to stop the destruction. In 1895 the city ran out of money and the project ground to a halt, but the old market had already been razed to the ground. The people still needed a market place so its replacement was erected in San Lorenzo – the Mercato Centrale.

The ghetto was cleared out, historic buildings were pulled down and the big new public space, the Piazza della Repubblica was created. The Colonna della Abbondanza was dismantled, the various pieces were stored around town, not to be reassembled until 1956. When it finally was re-erected it had a bronze replica of Foggini's statue and was placed two meters from the original site.

The Piazza Now

You'll notice this piazza doesn't really mesh with the medieval buildings that make up the historic center of Florence. To me it has a very Napoleonic feel to it. The most prominent feature of the Piazza della Repubblica is the *Arcone*, the triumphal arch at its center. Built in 1895 it has an inscription celebrating the destruction of the history that once surrounded it:

> *L'Antico Centro Della Citta' Da Secolare Squallore A Una Vita Nuova Restituito.*

Roughly translated it says, 'The old city center restored from an area of squalor to a new life.'

Piazza della Repubblica is now home to hotels and modern shops like the Apple Store. You have to wonder how long it will be before Starbucks, McDonald's and Old Navy move in and further homogenize this space. I know it's just business and that high streets are full of chain stores now, but personally I want Florence's historic center to remain a place for Florentine businesses.

Piazza della Repubblica is home to one of Florence's oldest and best known cafes, Caffè Gilli. Gilli first opened in 1773 in Piazza Duomo, selling Swiss pastries and sugared donuts. In the 1800s it moved to via degli Speziali, then eventually moved to Piazza della Repubblica, where it has become an institution along with other historic eateries such as Giubbe Rosse and Paszkowski. Sitting outdoors in the piazza at Gilli with a glass of wine or a coffee is a lovely (albeit expensive) experience putting you in the footsteps of a legion of artists, writers and actors who whiled away the hours here over the decades.

Caffe Gilli is the perfect place to enjoy the signature cocktail of Florence, the Negroni. The head barman at Gilli, Luca Picchi, is internationally recognized as the authority on both the drink and Count Camillo Negroni, for who the drink was named. He will happily tell you the story as he mixes you the world's best Negroni!

The piazza is home to a twentieth century carousel, owned for generations by the Picci family. The carousel has 20 brightly painted wooden horses and two gilded carriages, whirling round and round from 10am–8pm, May to November. On summer nights street musicians fill the air with music, adding to the atmosphere.

Nonetheless, to me this piazza always feels somewhat sterile, and in odd juxtaposition to all the medieval piazzas that make up the historic heart of this city.

What's Nearby: This is midway between the Duomo and Ponte Vecchio. Immediately nearby are the Porcellino Market, Orsanmichele, Piazza della Signoria and the Uffizi.

7.

Piazza Santa Croce

Piazza Santa Croce shows up multiple times in this book, mostly because I come here all the time.

In my personal opinion the Basilica Santa Croce contains the greatest church art in all of Tuscany (not that I have been inside every church in Tuscany, but you know what I mean). When my Glam Italia tours are in Florence – even for just one day – we skip going inside the Duomo in favor of coming here. Even if you are not into church art I emphatically recommend visiting Basilica Santa Croce. **If you only visit one church in all of Florence, let it be this one.** I go into depth about this church and suggest many things to look for in **Chapter 14: Churches.** I sincerely hope you will read it and make the time to visit this basilica.

The piazza itself is one of the most important Renaissance piazzas. It is beautiful, historical, and you need to see it.

An Island Outside the City Walls

In the twelfth century this was an island outside the city walls, formed by a fork in the Arno River. The Franciscans arrived in the early 1200s and wanting to be isolated from the town, settled here. By 1294 the current church was under construction and Santa Croce stood inside the newer, expanded city walls.

Events for Centuries

Not only is this piazza home of the largest Franciscan church in the world, but Piazza Santa Croce is a social hub and home to annual events, some dating back centuries:

Every December there is a German Market here, with stalls full of wooden toys and trinkets, Christmas decorations and gifts, steins of German beer, and German street foods.

On summer nights, Piazza Santa Croce fills with local young folk, making it fun to meander and people watch here. If you're lucky, you might stumble upon a concert: Il Volo did a show with Placido Domingo in this piazza. Radiohead, George Michael and Patti Smith have played here too.

CALCIO STORICO

One of the most famous annual events takes place here every June, the Calcio Storico. For this event, the piazza is ringed with metal stadium-style seating, the ground is covered in dirt, and a crazy, violent combination of rugby, soccer and wrestling takes place. Calcio Storico dates back to the 1500s. The four historical neighborhoods, Santa Croce (blue), Santa Maria Novella (red), Santo Spirito (white), and San Giovanni (green) don traditional uniforms and play against each other in a three game series. There are two semi-finals and then the big final on June 24. To make it more authentic (and more rugged) the teams play barefoot, just as they did nearly 500 years ago.

One theory suggests Calcio Storico began in 1530 when the city was under siege by Charles V and his troops. The citizens staged an improvised, violent football game while musicians played from the roof of the basilica. It was designed to show their scorn for Charles V and that, as a people, they were not defeated. I don't know if it's true or not, but it's fun to think of them giving him the giant finger by playing this riotous game.

DANTE

In front of the basilica is a statue of Dante, Italy's most celebrated poet. (Learn more about him in **Chapter 23: A Walk With Dante**.)

Italian actor and Oscar-winner Roberto Benigni (*Life is Beautiful*) once put on a performance here reciting the entire *Divine Comedy* (*Divinia Commedia*) under Dante's gaze.

Palazzo Cocchi-Serristori

Directly opposite the basilica there is a beautiful Renaissance-style palazzo, the Palazzo Cocchi-Serristori. This is a reconstructed palazzo built on a pre-existing medieval building belonging to the Peruzzi family. In the 12th century (pre-basilica), this building stood just *inside* the city walls.

The current structure is attributed to Giuliano da Sangallo, architect, sculptor and military engineer favored by Lorenzo the Magnificent. Sangallo built a villa for Lorenzo as well as a monastery. Popes Julius II and Leo X (the first Medici Pope) commissioned him to design and work on several structures including the beautiful Villa Farnesina and St Peter's Basilica, both in Rome.

Cube-shaped and made from polished stone, it is the perfect Renaissance palazzo. If you step back and look at it you can imagine

Brunelleschi would have appreciated the geometry of the façade. From the three equal arches in the middle layer, framed by pilasters that create perfect squares, to the upper level with its square windows inside more squares made from the pilasters, the palazzo is a study in symmetry.

It is a regional office now, and not open to the public, but it has a beautifully frescoed private chapel and a staircase lined with eighteenth century frescoes.

Palazzo dell' Antella

The south side of the piazza is home to one of the most beautiful palaces in Florence, the Palazzo dell' Antella.

The façade of this palazzo is deliciously frescoed and always stops me in my tracks, because how on earth can something this lovely survive hundreds of years, through wars, floods, discord and difficulties, and annual matches of Calcio Storico?

The palazzo was originally a group of several houses joined together, owned by the Ricoveri family. In the second half of the 1500s it was raised by one floor and a mezzanine, then in the early 1600s it became the property of Niccolo dell' Antella as part of his wife's dowry. In 1619 he hired architect Giulio Parigi to make the façade look more unified (remember this was several buildings joined together). Between 1619 and 1620 Parigi had the entire façade frescoed by a team of 13 artists who completed the work in just 20 days! (This blows me away. Could they have even imagined that 400 years later you and I would be standing in the piazza, looking at their three weeks of work?) The paintings depict allegorical figures, foliage, cherubs/*putti*, flowers and arabesques, centered around a bust of

Cosimo II de' Medici above the central doorway. If you read my Glam Italia guide to Rome you will know that I'm a huge Caravaggio fan. Look at the fourth tile from the left and you will see a copy of Caravaggio's *Sleeping Amorino*. In 1925 the building was purchased by the writer Delfino Cinelli who had the paintings restored.

The frescoes covering the front of the palazzo serve as a distraction to an architectural trick designed to make the building look grander. Standing in the middle of the piazza you will see that from right to left the windows start getting closer together as they head toward the basilica, creating the illusion that the palace is bigger than it actually is.

What's Nearby: The leather school (*Scuola del Cuoio*) is immediately behind the basilica. The piazza is one large city block from Palazzo Vecchio, a five minute walk to the Uffizi, the Badia Fiorentina and the Bargello. It is half a block along Borgo dei Greci from my favorite restaurant, Francesco Vini.

Piazza della Signoria

8.

Piazza della Signoria

Possibly the most well-known piazza in Florence, Piazza della Signoria has been the central hub of the city since the early middle ages. Situated a couple of large city blocks from the Duomo and just meters from the Arno River, the piazza is the home to Palazzo Vecchio and the Uffizi Gallery. It was the original home of the statue of *David* and now holds its replica, with the original residing safely in the Accademia museum. While visiting Florence, you will find yourself in the Piazza della Signoria multiple times, so I want to draw your attention to some fantastic things to look for while you're here.

If you're staying overnight in Florence I sincerely recommend getting up early and coming for a walk through here before the bus and cruise tours arrive. I love early morning walks through Florence. The city is still and quiet, only delivery trucks and early workers are out and about. The piazza is empty in the early morning, I have it all to myself. I can examine the statues, look for hidden secrets and see it all without a thousand tourists getting in the way. (Normally I follow an early morning visit to the piazza with a walk through the Uffizi courtyard to the Arno, and then head over the Ponte Vecchio to have coffee in the Oltrarno.)

You must also visit the piazza at night, it is so beautiful. There will be people around, but in manageable numbers. Musicians fill the night air with song, and you will find yourself completely overwhelmed by the history of this place.

If you're in Florence for a day trip only, especially between May and October, try to get to Piazza della Signoria before 9:30am when the tours descend en masse. If you get here and it's packed, go do some of the other things recommended in this book and come back in the afternoon when the crazy crowd is whittled down a bit.

Who were the Signoria?

From 1115–1532 Florence was a republic, ruled by a council known as the Signoria. There was a nine-member body known as the *Priori*, made up of six men chosen from the major guilds, two from the minor guilds, and a *gonfaloniere* who ran the show. The city hall from which they ran the Republic was alternately called the Palazzo della Signoria and Palazzo della Priori. Later it became known as the Palazzo Ducale (the Duke's Palace) until Cosimo I moved into the Palazzo Pitti, at which point it was renamed the Palazzo Vecchio (Old Palace).

The Palazzo Vecchio was (and still is) the City Hall of Florence. The tower has a huge bell called *La Vacca* (the cow) which tolled to call the people of Florence to the piazza during times of crisis or when they needed to vote on anything (including executions). Since the Palazzo Vecchio's construction in 1299, the square in front of it, Piazza della Signoria, was the most important piazza in Florence.

On our little walk through the piazza, let's start on the far left and work our way back across…

The Statue of Cosimo I de' Medici

This is a Florentine masterpiece. Ferdinando I de' Medici commissioned Giambologna, renowned for his huge equestrian statues, to create this statue of his father Cosimo I de' Medici. It resembles the classical Roman equestrian statues which were traditional monuments to a ruler's power. This one specifically bore a likeness to the statue of Marcus Aurelius in Rome – the trotting horse with its right leg raised, a breeze blowing through its mane. Slightly different from Marcus Aurelius though is Cosimo's use of stirrups and the horse's head being gently restrained by the bridle.

The statue was placed in the piazza in 1594. Positioned next to the Fountain of Neptune, which had been commissioned by Cosimo I to symbolize his power over the sea, the statue celebrated his power over the land of Tuscany.

Much of what we see in the Piazza della Signoria is due either to Cosimo I or his family. From the statues to the frescoes in the palazzo courtyard, to the Salon dei Cinquecento, the Uffizi, to the Vasari corridor, it's all Medici.

The statue of Cosimo was removed for safety during World War II. On its return, Florentines lined the streets welcoming him back. He had left Florence in an oxcart but returned in a US Army truck. Cosimo was separated from the horse for the trip, and instead a soldier rode the horse on the back of the truck, lifting up powerlines as necessary. As they entered the city the convoy was joined by MPs on motorcycles with their sirens blaring, giving this important historical figure a suitable welcome home!

The Fountain Of Neptune

In 1559 Cosimo I de' Medici held a competition to design the first public fountain in Florence. The greatest artists of the time vied for the job – Cellini, Bandinelli, Giambologna. Cosimo chose Bandinelli but when he died before work began, it was handed to Bartolomeo di Ammannati, who worked on the center sculpture of Neptune from 1560–1565. Carved from white marble from Carrara and nicknamed *Il Biancone* (the great white one), his Neptune is exquisite. He looks just like Cosimo. The statue rests on a pedestal decorated with sea monsters from Greek mythology, surrounded by an octagonal basin that took some of the best sculptors in the city more than 10 years to create.

In Greek mythology amphibians were Neptune's sons, or the gods of the rivers. At Neptune's feet there are three of them playing on water flutes. Four horses pull Neptune's wagon and on the edges of the basin there are four Greek sea gods: Thetis, Doris, Oceanus and Nereus.

The Fountain of Neptune is spectacular. In 2019 restoration and cleaning was completed, giving Neptune back his dazzling shade of white.

VANDALS AND THIEVES

Poor Neptune has had more than his fair share of damage to deal with.

- From 1580–1592, the fountain became a basin for laundresses to clean clothes until a fence was built to keep them away.
- In 1830 during a carnival, thieves stole one of the statues, a satyr created by Giambologna. They danced around the fountain, dressed the statue and then slipped away with it. To this day no one knows what happened to it or where it

is. In 1831 a Milanese sculptor named Pozzi created its replacement.

- In 1848 when the Bourbons bombed the city, the fountain was damaged by cannonballs.
- In 2005 the most recent act happened when vandals climbed onto Neptune, breaking off one of his hands and his trident, and damaging the pool beneath him.

Savonarola's Memorial Plaque

In front of the Fountain of Neptune is a round marble plaque set into the ground, commemorating Savonarola.

Girolamo Savonarola was born to a noble family in Ferrara in 1452. The third of seven children, by all accounts he had a good life and got an arts degree, which is ironic considering what was to follow. He began writing apocalyptic poetry, then, according to his brother Maurelio, was spurned by his neighbor Laudomia Strozzi whom he had asked to marry. In 1475 he joined the Dominican Order, studied theology, preached his looney apocalyptic ravings to fellow priests, and was sent on a break from his studies to work with the novices in Ferrara in 1478. In Ferrara his personal brand of crazy ruffled so many feathers that he was sent to the convent of San Marco in Florence. His time in Florence didn't go so well and before long he became an itinerant priest, roving the countryside preaching repentance, piety and austerity. As with any proficient lunatic some parts of his religious diatribe held merit. He hated corruption in the Catholic Church, didn't approve of popes and cardinals cavorting with wives and mistresses and hookers, and fought against the exploitation of the poor. On the other hand he preached of biblical floods and the arrival of a divine scourge.

Florence could have been rid of Savonarola but for a humanist philosopher named Mirandola, who heard him preach in Reggio Emilia and was impressed with his piety. Mirandola's unorthodox ideas had gotten him in trouble with the church so he was living under the protection of Lorenzo the Magnificent, then ruler of Florence. Mirandola persuaded Lorenzo to let Savonarola come to Florence to be his spiritual counsellor. Interestingly Fra Bandelli, a vicar general, tried to stop them bringing Savonarola to Florence, knowing full well the madness he would inflict on the city. Unfortunately they didn't listen and in 1490 crazy Savonarola was back in San Marco. Savonarola's sermons to the poor became so popular and his following grew so big, that he had to move them to the cathedral. Although the clever saw him as a zealot, his followers were so busy weeping and wailing they couldn't see what a fanatic he really was. (Or maybe they were so desperate they would have hung on to anything if it could bring them an easier life?) Regardless, they supported his campaign to rid the city of vice. New laws were passed against homosexuality, adultery, public intoxication and other moral transgressions. His sidekick, Fra Maruffi, had bands of boys patroling the streets monitoring bad behavior and immodest dress, essentially licensing the harassment of women. This evolved into banging on people's doors demanding vanities – artworks, jewels, books, and cosmetics – and on February 7, 1497, Savonarola held his bonfire of the vanities, burning it all. We will never know how many great art works were destroyed by this madman, but even Botticelli is said to have thrown some of his paintings on the fire.

On May 12, 1497, Pope Alexander VI excommunicated Savonarola. He kept preaching, now bragging an ability to perform miracles. A Franciscan monk challenged him, suggesting he walk through fire to prove it. The first trial by fire in 400 years was scheduled for April 7,

1498. Savonarola appointed another priest to be his surrogate. (Right there you might think his followers would get a clue that he was a fraud.) The crowds waited to see on whose side God would intervene, meanwhile the nervous priests used delay tactics, pushing out the start of the proceedings for hours until it began to rain, drenching everyone. The mob finally saw through Savonarola's game and marched on the fresco-adorned convent of San Marco. Savonarola and his lieutenants Fra Domenico and Fra Maruffi were arrested and tortured. Ultimately Savonarola admitted that his visions and prophecies were made up. On the morning of May 23, 1498, the three were led into the Piazza della Signoria where a tribunal of government officials and clergy condemned them as heretics. They were stripped of their Dominican garments, hanged until *nearly* dead and then burned at the stake over giant fires. Their ashes were collected and disposed of in the Arno, preventing any remaining devotees from turning them into relics.

The day after his death by fire, Savonarola's remaining followers covered the spot where he died with flowers, palm leaves and rose petals. The anniversary of his death is still commemorated each year by Florentines bringing flowers to his memorial plaque in the Piazza della Signoria, and they throw leaves and petals into the Arno where Savonarola's ashes were scattered.

The Palazzo Vecchio

The Old Palace was built in 1299 by Arnolfo di Cambio, the architect of the Duomo. It was designed to be secure and defendable while also reflecting the importance of the city of Florence. It was built on the ruins of two other palazzi, owned by the ousted Uberti family in order to make sure the family of Ghibelline rebels would never rebuild on that land. The former Uberti palaces had in turn been built over Roman ruins.

When looking at the Palazzo Vecchio you will notice the tower is not centered, but sits slightly to the right. Counting the crenellations along the rooftop, there are seven of them, then the tower, then four more, because when di Cambio designed the palazzo he incorporated the existing Foraboschi Tower, rather than pulling it down and rebuilding a new one. The tower stands 94 meters tall and houses two prison cells, which in 1435 held Cosimo de' Medici (the Elder) and in 1498 Girolamo Savaronola.

The palazzo was designed to house the chief members of the guilds (the *Priori*) during their time in office. You can visit these apartment rooms and see the fabulous artwork on the ceilings and walls.

When Cosimo I de' Medici became Duke of Florence he left the Palazzo Medici and moved into the Palazzo Vecchio (at that time called the Palazzo della Signoria). Extra rooms were constructed to house the family. You can walk through this entire section of the palazzo at the end of the *Secret Passages* tour.

AN ARCHEOLOGICAL SITE

The Palazzo Vecchio is built on top of a first century Roman theater. This site can be visited either as part of a combined ticket with the Palazzo Vecchio museum or by itself for €4. The ruins are well signposted and there is also a short movie explaining what you are seeing. It is very cool.

THE ENTRANCE TO THE PALAZZO

The stairway entering the palazzo from the Piazza della Signoria is flanked by two sculptures. On the left is the replica of Michelangelo's *David*. Until 1873 the original *David* stood here in the people's square, outside the city hall. He was a symbol of Florence rising up and beating its own Goliath, becoming a republic. On the right is a statue of *Hercules and Cacus* by Baccio Bandinelli. This was created as the partner piece to the *David*, although oddly, they are not positioned equidistances from the doorway.

THE FIRST COURTYARD

This is one of my favorite public spaces in Florence. I always make a point of stepping inside even if only for a few minutes, because it is so beautiful and because I can't quite wrap my head around the fact that Florentines get to see this all the time.

I talked about this to my friend Elisabetta once when I was in town and she told me that if her husband is having a bad day at work he takes a stroll to Palazzo Vecchio and walks around the first courtyard a few times. As he says, 'How can you be stressed out or have a bad day when you can come here and see such beauty?' I think of this every time I step through the entrance into the Palazzo Vecchio.

The first courtyard was designed by Michelozzo in 1453. The lunettes around the tops of the arches hold the crests of the church and the city guilds. The center of the courtyard has a porphyry fountain by Battista del Tadda, on top of which is the *Putto with Dolphin* by Verrochio. (This one is a copy, the original is on display in the museum on the second floor of the palace.) The water flowing through the nose of the dolphin is piped in from the Boboli Gardens.

Inside the arched colonnade there are frescoes of Austrian cities belonging to the Habsburg monarchy, painted by Vasari in 1565 for the wedding of Cosimo I's son Francesco to the Archduchess Johanna of Austria. Until that time the columns had been smooth, but then they too were decorated, with the gilt stuccos we still see today.

THE SALON DEI CINQUECENTO

The largest and most important room in the palace is the *Salon dei Cinquecento* (Hall of 500).

Savonarola built this huge room in 1494 to house his newly created Council of 500. He wanted a more democratic rule and thought a group of 500 men could make all the decisions. No doubt it looked good on paper, but I'm sure in reality it was a circus. The hall is 54 meters long, 23 meters wide and 18 meters high. Savanarola liked austerity, so it was left bare.

After Savaronola was burned at the stake, *gonfaloniere* Piero Soderini took over management. Wanting to spruce up the big room he hired the two greatest Florentine artists of the time, Leonardo da Vinci and Michelangelo, to paint giant murals on the walls. Leonardo was assigned the *Battle of Anghiari* and Michelangelo the *Battle of Cascina*. Neither work was completed. Leonardo tried out a new technique, mixing wax with the paint, which proved disastrous. The paint didn't dry quickly enough, so when heat was added, the wax melted, and the painting slid off the wall. Meanwhile Pope Julius II called Michelangelo to Rome to work on the ceiling of the Sistine Chapel, so the *Battle of Cascina* was put on hold.

In 1540 Cosimo I, Duke of Florence, moved from the Palazzo Medici into the Palazzo della Signoria. He hired Giorgio Vasari to transform the palace into a work of art. Now the paintings would have to glorify the Medici family. To make the Salon of 500 even more majestic, Vasari raised the ceiling by seven meters, covering it with a 42 panel coffered ceiling. Each panel is its own giant painting in an enormous gilded frame. A ceiling as heavy as this couldn't possibly hold itself up, so Vasari created an ingenious two-part double-truss system to support it. One truss system keeps the roof attached to the palazzo while the second truss system holds up the ceiling. (You can see this in detail both on the *Secret Passages* tour and in the movie *Inferno*). The center ceiling panel is a painting of Cosimo I. Surrounding it are allegorical paintings of scenes depicting Florence and Tuscany in submission to him along with scenes from the War of Pisa (1496–1509) and the War of Siena (1553–1555). Archways in the room contain sculptures of the two Medici Popes (Leo X and Clement VII), and niches around the room hold statues of other important Medici family members.

There is so much to see inside the Palazzo Vecchio, including the Medici apartments, which alone are fantastic. The palazzo is a museum, so you need a ticket to go beyond the first courtyard and the foyer area. The Salon dei Cinquecento should definitely be on your must-see list.

THE *SECRET PASSAGES* TOUR

I recommend taking a walking tour of the palace. The Palazzo Vecchio offers a variety of tours and tour combinations. There is much here to see and so many details that you'd otherwise miss, having a guide is a great idea.

I love doing the *Secret Passages* tour. There are secret rooms inside the walls of the palace where the various Medici kept their art and treasures, and could spy on the political goings on in the rooms below. On this tour you'll walk through secret staircases, see how the palace occupants could escape unseen at night, and visit the area above the ceiling of the Salon of 500. The tour ends in the Medici apartments where you can spend as much time as you like wandering through their rooms and enjoying the views from the Medici balconies.

THE TOWER

The Palazzo Vecchio ticket also allows you (weather permitting) to go up the tower and see the cell where Cosimo was held prisoner. When going anywhere up high in Florence, ultimately you want a view of the Duomo. I don't send my tour groups up the Duomo, instead I bring those who are interested (and enjoy climbing stairs) up here. I haven't ever encountered a line or a crowd here, and once up top (and breathing regularly again) you have a perfect, unfettered view across Florence, encompassing the majestic Duomo. While up here, look out for glass bricks in the floor of the outer part of the tower. They are placed directly over the head of *David*, giving you a different view of the statue!

Fans of Dan Brown can take the *Inferno* Tour of the Palazzo Vecchio. There are multiple tour options, and each one I've tried has been tremendous.

The ticket office is in the back left hand corner of the Palazzo Vecchio. If there's a big crowd in the piazza when you arrive, take the short cut inside by using the entrance immediately behind the Fountain of Neptune. I drop in and buy whatever tickets I need (they sell out quickly), then I take my time exploring the piazza before going in the main entrance.

David

Not everyone reading this book will make it to the Accademia to see the original *David*, so I want to tell you about him here – after all, this was his original home. The *David* you see at the doorway to the Palazzo Vecchio is a replica.

Perhaps the most recognizable sculpture in the world, Michelangelo's *David* was created between 1501 and 1504, starting when the artist was 26 years old.

The 17-foot-tall work was commissioned by the Opera del Duomo to stand on the roofline at the back end of the cathedral. Michelangelo was handed an unfinished work, initially started in 1464 by Agostino de Duccio and re-attempted by Antonio Rossellino in 1475. Both artists walked away from the job, deeming the block of marble to have too many *taroli* (imperfections) for it to safely stand on the roof of the Duomo. This giant block of marble spent 25 years lying neglected in the courtyard of the Opera del Duomo (*opera* means *workshop*, so Opera del Duomo is the workshop of the Duomo).

Michelangelo enthusiastically took on the job, working around the clock for two years, barely sleeping or eating. He worked outdoors in his courtyard, in utmost secrecy. He stood in the pouring rain working on his *David* – which may be how he came up with his method of sculpting. Michelangelo would make a wax model of his design and submerge it in water. As he worked, he would let the level of the water drop slowly, so that he could chisel only that which he could see emerging from the water.

Although they gave him the subject for his statue, the vestry had no idea how revolutionary the final product would be. *David* was traditionally depicted *after* beating Goliath, normally standing over his head. Michelangelo instead chose to show his *David before* the battle. Deep in concentration, *David* looks relaxed but alert, resting in *contrapposto* (a classic pose where the weight is on the back leg while the front leg is forward, creating an S shape to the torso, the hips and shoulders at opposing angles). The slingshot is over his shoulder, nearly invisible, telling us his victory was won not by brute force, but by cleverness. We see concentration and exceptional self-confidence, the Renaissance's ideal of the 'thinking man' personified.

In January 1504, the completed *David* was secretly shown to members of the vestry and to Piero Soderini, the *gonfaloniere*. All agreed that *David* was too perfect to be up high on the cathedral, and that a new location must be found. A council committee convened with 30 members, including Leonardo da Vinci, Sandro Botticelli and other artists. Nine potential sites were discussed but in the end they decided *David* should stand for all to see, outside the Palazzo della Signoria in the political heart of Florence. It took 40 men four days to move the statue half a mile to its new home.

David became the city's symbol of freedom, liberty, and readiness to defend herself. He stayed in the Piazza della Signoria until relocated to the Accademia in 1873, where he now stands under a skylight built especially for him, protected from weather and vandalism.

Wondering why his head and right hand are so unusually large? *David* was designed to be placed 80 meters high on the cathedral roofline, so both needed to be accentuated in order to be seen from below.

One last thing about his right hand: although seemingly relaxed it gives us our only insight into the tension *David* was feeling. Look at the engorged veins on the back of the hand. You can almost imagine the thrumming of his fingers with his next breath.

DAVID'S BROKEN ARM

On April 26, 1527, anti-Medici rioters occupied the Palazzo Vecchio (Palazzo della Signoria) while soldiers tried to battle their way inside. As rioters threw furniture from the parapets at the soldiers down below, a bench struck *David's* left arm, breaking it off in three pieces.

Giorgio Vasari said the broken arm lay on the ground for days as the fighting continued in the piazza. Two young boys (one of them Vasari himself) pushed their way through the melee to rescue the pieces of their beloved *David*, hiding them for years until it was safe to bring them out and have *David* repaired. It is said a new arm was carved and reattached, but according to Vasari the broken pieces he had saved were reattached with copper nails. Who knows which is true?

FINAL DAVID FACT

The original *David* had gold leaf on the slingshot and on the wood behind his leg, but 400 years of exposure to the elements has washed it away.

Hercules and Cacus

Once *David* was in place in the piazza it was decided he needed a partner piece, so in 1508 Piero Soderini ordered a massive block of marble from Carrara, and Michelangelo was commissioned to create a second statue.

Plans went sideways when the giant marble block was transported back to Florence. The marble was to travel up the river to Signa, then by land to Florence, as the river between Signa and Florence was too shallow to transport such a heavy block of marble. When they docked at Signa and tried to move the marble, it fell into the river and was so deeply stuck in the mud it couldn't be recovered. Engineer Piero Rosselli had to divert the river and drain the banks to retrieve the marble. It didn't arrive in Florence until 1525, by which time things between the Medici and Michelangelo were hairy to say the least.

Pope Clement VII (the second Medici pope) withdrew the commission from Michelangelo and awarded it to Baccio Bandinelli. Bandinelli made a wax model for his sculpture, but once the marble arrived he realized it wasn't suitable for his design, so he had to travel to Rome with the measurements of the block to explain the problem to the pope and create a new design. Again, the statue was delayed.

In the 1527 Sack of Rome, Pope Clement VII fled and the Medici lost their authority in Florence. Bandinelli fled to Lucca. Meanwhile Michelangelo took an active role in the new republican regime, including designing the new defenses of the city. In 1528, a new contract returned the commission to Michelangelo. Once he saw the marble block Michelangelo decided to sculpt Samson and the Philistines, but before he could get started the Medici returned to power and gave the job back to Bandinelli.

Is your head spinning yet?

Eventually Bandinelli's statue of *Hercules and Cacus* was completed and became partner to Michelangelo's *David*. It tells the story of Hercules defeating the evil bandit Cacus, a cave dweller who preyed upon travelers to Rome. The statue was completed in 1534 but as it made its way from the Opera del Duomo to the Piazza della Signoria it was pelted with stones by the public showing their hatred for the current Medici ruler, Duke Alessandro, *Il Moro*. The statue had multiple errors and received much criticism. Unlike *David*, it wasn't carved from a single block.

It's an interesting piece but an odd juxtaposition to *David*. Where *David* is lithe, *Hercules* is bulky. Where *David* is the thinker, *Hercules* is brute force. Perhaps they are at odds with one another, or perhaps they represent two opposing sides of strength and power.

One last note on *Hercules and Cacus*, unlike Michelangelo, Bandinelli signed his work. The pink stone on the pedestal has the inscription:

BACCIVS BANDINELL.FLOR.FACIEBAT.MD XXXIIII

Baccio Bandinelli of Florence made this in 1534

The Loggia dei Lanzi

Florence is essentially a huge, beautiful outdoor museum. One place to see its incredible art and beauty is outside Palazzo Vecchio at the Loggia dei Lanzi (the arches with the sculptures on the south side of the piazza). The Loggia was built between 1376 and 1382 to hold public ceremonies. It wasn't until the 1500s when the Medici became the Dukes of Florence that it became an art museum, filled with sculptures for all to see and enjoy. The staircase to the loggia is flanked by two huge lions. The one on the right dates back to ancient Rome while the one on the left was sculpted for the Villa Medici in Rome by Flaminio Vacca in 1598. It was moved to the loggia nearly 200 years later, in 1789.

Everything in the loggia is fantastic, but I want to draw your attention to my two favorite sculptures here.

1. *Perseus*

Cellini sculpted this mannerist bronze sculpture for Duke Cosimo I between 1545 and 1554. Commissioned for the loggia, its location was specifically and very cleverly chosen.

THE STORY OF PERSEUS

This one comes from Greek mythology. Perseus was a regular guy who killed the evil sorceress Medusa. Medusa started out beautiful, but when she tried to seduce Zeus, his wife Hera put an ugly curse on her, turning her hair into snakes and making anyone who looked at her turn to stone. The God Mercury ordered Perseus to kill Medusa, giving him a winged helmet and winged sandals so he could fly. Athena gave him a shield so highly polished it was like a mirror. When Perseus encountered Medusa he held up his shield so that she saw her own reflection and turned to stone. He then sliced her head off with his sword and put it in a bag. Perseus then used Medusa's head as a weapon to kill his next monster, pulling her head out of the bag and holding it up to the monster who upon looking at it, promptly turned to stone.

THINGS TO LOOK FOR

While looking at the absolute perfection of this sculpture, also look for the winged sandals and helmet, the angle at which Perseus holds Medusa's head, and her body beneath him, still spurting blood.

Now look at the location of the statue. On either side of the entrance to the Palazzo Vecchio stand the two symbols of the Florentine

Republic, David who beat Goliath and Hercules defeating Cacus. The message is that with God's help they defeated something much bigger than themselves, symbolizing the people of Florence overcoming their rulers and becoming a republic.

Now, observe David's eye-line and that of Hercules. Both look directly at Medusa's head. The symbolism implies Medusa has turned David and Hercules (and therefore the republic) to stone. (So the Medici have turned their enemies to stone, and have turned Florence into a duchy, with them being the dukes. Clever, no?)

Lastly, look at the back of Perseus' head. If you inspect it closely you will see a hidden self portrait of Cellini himself, between the wings of the helmet with Perseus' hair as the sculptor's beard.

2. *The Rape of the Sabine*

This is one of the most well recognized works of sixteenth century Italian art, yet was created by one of the least famous sculptors (although once you know where to look you will see his work all over Florence). French born Jean du Boulogne moved to Florence around 1552 and became known as Giambologna. He became one of Cosimo I de Medici's favorite sculptors. Previously known for his small to mid-sized works, he started working on massive sculptures, including huge equestrian works such as the bronze Cosimo here in the piazza and later the bronze of Ferdinando on his horse in Piazza della SS Annunziata.

The Rape of the Sabine, also called *The Abduction of the Sabine,* stands more than four meters tall and was the first in European sculptural history to depict a group of figures without a dominant point of view. From any angle this sculpture is perfect, and from any angle it still tells its story. It has neither a front nor a back.

Although the subject is traumatic, the work itself is beyond beautiful. One thing I always point out to my tour groups is the indentation of the fingers pressing into her buttocks.

WHAT'S GOING ON HERE?

So what is going on in this 360 degree drama? First you should know the latin word *rapito* became the Italian word *rapirer* which translates to kidnap or abduct. This work is about abduction, not rape. It is a tale of *very* ancient Roman history, supported by the writings of both Livy and Plutarch.

After Rome was founded in 750 BC they needed women to make Roman babies, and keep the lineage going. The Romans weren't successful negotiating with the neighboring town of Sabine so they devised a scheme to abduct their women during a summer festival. The sculpture shows the moment when a Roman has captured a Sabine woman. He is marching over a Sabine man who is cowering in defeat. Livy's writing indicates the event wasn't about sexual violence, instead there were a variety of enticements by the Romans to show the Sabine women how they would be treated as wives.

When the sculpture was unveiled in Florence no one could find fault with it – it was deemed perfect.

I like to compare this work with another multi-figured sculpture nearby to show just how innovative and genius this one is. If you look over at *Hercules and Cacus* you will see it is heavy and bulky and all the action happens from the top down. Both figures are trapped there for eternity. Now look at *The Rape of the Sabine* and you see it looks like the work starts at the bottom and spirals upward. Your eye is drawn up instead of down. And there is every chance that if she can just push harder or wriggle out of his grip the Sabine woman may still escape. This sculpture conveys movement, aggression, fear, defeat, and triumph. I love the spiral motion of the figures as the Sabine man twists upward, the Roman follows that arc by twisting away, and the woman completes the spiral as she twists back and up. It's genius.

The Rape of the Sabine was installed in the loggia in 1583 at the request of Francesco I de' Medici, son of Cosimo I.

Michelangelo's Graffiti

While we are here with *Hercules* I want to point out something from **Chapter 13: Unusual & Interesting Things**. I get a huge kick out of showing this to my tour travelers as there can be a thousand people in the piazza blithely unaware, and only we will know to check out this random yet fantastic detail! This is definitely one of Florence's cool secrets: *L'Importuno di Michelangelo* or Michelangelo's Graffiti. We can't be certain he did it, but it is fun thinking he did, and legend says it's his. On the right side of the front wall of the Palazzo Vecchio, behind Hercules' bottom, one of the old Tuscan stones has the caricature of a man's face carved into it.

There are three alternating stories about the face:

1. Michelangelo carved it on a dare, using a kitchen knife, with his back to the wall. Not only breaking the law but showing off his genius by carving a perfect face without looking.
2. Michelangelo was often seen standing here, cornered by an acquaintance who was chatty and a bore. One day out of boredom, with his hands behind his back, he etched the man's face on the wall, the chatterbox being none the wiser.

3. Michelangelo was so disturbed by an execution he witnessed in the piazza, he immortalized the man's face, carving it into the wall. Ask around enough and you will hear that Michelangelo recognized the man about to be executed as being his own debtor, and carved his face into the wall.

We will never know the real story, but it is fun to find the face on the wall.

The Vasari Corridor

From the corner of the Palazzo Vecchio look up to see a covered bridge connecting the Palazzo with the Uffizi Gallery. This is the beginning of the walkway known as the Vasari Corridor, which runs for a kilometer from the Palazzo Vecchio across the Uffizi, where it makes a right hand turn, runs along the river to the Ponte Vecchio, then turns left and runs along the top of the bridge, ending at the Pitti Palace.

Florence was a dangerous place for the Medici. Other wealthy and noble families wanted them dead. Some conspiracies were successful (like the Pazzi conspiracy that killed Giuliano de' Medici) while others (like the Pucci conspiracy to kill Cosimo I) failed. Even with an escort of soldiers, walking about in the streets wasn't safe for the Medici. The local government offices were scattered around town, and if visiting several offices in a day your risk went up exponentially, so Cosimo I came up with a great idea. Why not move all the government and legal offices into one building? Furthermore, why not locate that building next to the city hall, further reducing the open air commute?

In 1560 Cosimo I commissioned Vasari to create the first office building, moving all the government offices to one location. It was named the Uffizi (*offices*). Vasari not only created the new building but also a corridor to access it, ensuring safe and secret passage from the Palazzo Vecchio (City Hall) to the Uffizi, across the Ponte Vecchio to an open viewing deck over the church of Santa Felicita', before reaching the Pitti Palace (which was the Medici home).

There were a couple of hiccups along the way:

1. The first problem was the Ponte Vecchio itself. The bridge was home to the butcher shops. They threw the blood and guts and waste over the side into the Arno River, making the view from the corridor gory and the stench grotesque. To resolve this problem, the butchers were relocated and jewelers were moved in. Some 450 years later the jewelers still remain on the bridge.

2. Another problem involved eminent domain. The corridor needed to pass through several medieval towers and buildings, which meant the owners were forced to give up space in their buildings. All agreed except for the Mannelli family. Cosimo could have steamrolled them but he appreciated their courage in standing up to him, so instead he instructed Vasari go around their tower. From the outside you can see the corridor wrap around the Manelli tower at the Oltrarno end of the Ponte Vecchio where it meets via Bardi and via de' Guicciardini.

When Cosimo I died in 1574 his son Francesco took over the work. It was finished in 1580 and the following year Francesco decided to use the corridor as his personal gallery, placing his collection of fifteenth century art, statues, bronzes and other pieces along the passageway.

MORE FACTS ABOUT THE VASARI CORRIDOR

- The entrance to the Vasari Corridor is a nondescript door on the first floor of the Uffizi. Most of the Uffizi's two million annual visitors have no idea of the treasures housed behind this blank door as they pass by!

- On May 26, 1993, the mafia destroyed part of the Vasari Corridor when they set off a car bomb next to the Torre dei Pulci, between the Uffizi and the Arno River. The bomb killed five people (including a six-week-old baby), injured 48 more, and destroyed works of art. The paintings were pieced back together and rehung in their damaged state to serve as a reminder of the attack.

- During World War II, Mussolini had the windows over the central part of the Ponte Vecchio enlarged to further enjoy the spectacular view over the Arno to Ponte Santa Trinita'. The windows were ready in time for Hitler's visit to Florence. Hitler was so impressed with the corridor and with this view that he ordered the bridge be spared. The Germans bombed all the other bridges as they made their retreat.

- At the time of writing this book the Vasari Corridor is closed to the public, scheduled to reopen in 2021.

The Ponte Vecchio

9.

The Ponte Vecchio

After the Duomo this must be the second most famous site in all of Florence. The Ponte Vecchio is beautiful and I think it's important to see the bridge more than once while you're in Florence. Even when I'm visiting Florence for weeks, I make sure I see the bridge more than once each day.

The Bridge

Ponte Vecchio is the oldest bridge in Florence, hence the name. Built in 966 it was the only bridge crossing the Arno in Florence until 1218. It was rebuilt in 1345 after the great flood but no one seems certain by whom. Some think it looks like the work of the Dominican monks, while Giorgio Vasari attributed it to Taddeo Gaddi. Regardless, it started out not only as a means of getting to the other side but also as part of the city's defense. The creamy colored structure with the square windows, tiled roof and triple arches in the middle is the Vasari Corridor.

Since the thirteenth century the Ponte Vecchio has housed shops and merchant stalls. In the early days there was a mix of everything including butchers and fishmongers. Between the refuse they created and the industrial waste run off from the tanneries lining the waterfront down to the Santa Trinita' bridge, the water flowing below the Ponte Vecchio (and the bridge itself) stunk to high

Heaven. Therefore the Medici had to smell it as they moved back and forth from their palace to the City Hall. Eventually the tanneries were moved up the river beyond Santa Croce and the Medici moved all other retailers off the bridge, deciding that only goldsmiths and jewelers could have shops here. To this day they still have all the shops along the Ponte Vecchio.

JEWELRY

I never see local Florentines buying jewelry on the Ponte Vecchio. I see the cruise ship passengers and big bus tour travelers. Locals tell me that much of the jewelry on Ponte Vecchio is neither handmade nor from Florence. I recommend window shopping along the bridge for fun, but let the cruise ship hordes buy their trinkets there. You, my friend, should take your business across the bridge to the little jewelry workshops in the Oltrarno, where the jewelry *is* handmade and where you can take home a genuine piece of Florentine craftsmanship.

If you cross the bridge at night or in the early morning you will see the fantastic old wooden shutters that make up the doors of the shops. They've been repaired and replaced over the years but they still look centuries-old.

PHOTOGRAPH STRATEGY

During the bulk of the season Ponte Vecchio gets packed with tourists from about 10am until evening. (And when I say packed I seriously mean *packed*).

When I base my Glam Italia tour groups in Tuscany we come to Florence for a day trip, arriving by 8:30am. We make it through

Piazza Duomo, Piazza della Signoria, Piazza Uffizi and over the Ponte Vecchio just slightly ahead of the crowds. But by the time we cross the bridge the masses are not far behind us. My tour groups and I normally stroll over the bridge to the Caffè Maioli on the Oltrarno side. Grab a spot upstairs, beside the huge windows overlooking the bridge. There we sit back with our cappuccinos and breakfasts and watch the hordes of tourists stream across the Ponte Vecchio. It's unbelievable how many there are. Maioli is totally a tourist joint, but the view from the upstairs windows makes it worthwhile.

If you're coming to Florence for a day trip, perhaps come to Ponte Vecchio *first* and work your way backwards through the other big sites. Just get here as early as possible. At the midway point on the bridge there are open areas where you will get the best photos. If you get here early, you'll have space to take those fabulous photos from both sides of the bridge. The photo from the Ponte Vecchio looking towards Ponte Santa Trinita' is pretty iconic and after coming all the way to Florence you might as well get your own! If staying in Florence, I recommend walking the Ponte Vecchio at 8am when the stores are still closed and you can see the wonderful old shutters. The light at that time is lovely so you'll get wonderful photos.

You should also see (and photograph) the Ponte Vecchio from the walls along the river banks. In the mornings I like to photograph it from the east side to catch the best light. Walking to the river from the Uffizi there are several great spots along the wall to lean out and get a great photo, but there will be loads of tourists trying to do the same thing. If the crowd is too large, walk away from the bridge toward Ponte alle Grazie. You can take some great shots from the Ponte alle Grazie bridge, and from the Oltrarno side of the river bank.

Crossing the Ponte Vecchio in the evenings is fabulous too, especially once the cruise ship and bus tours have left the city. You still see lots of travelers on the bridge but in more manageable numbers. There will often be musicians playing and in the soft Florentine light the ambience is gorgeous. In the evenings we often go to Piazzale Michelangelo to watch the sunset. It's always crowded, but the view is totally worth it. On the way back we cross the river at Ponte alle Grazie and spend ages at the midway point on the bridge taking photos of the Ponte Vecchio with a pink-orange fireball sun setting behind it.

After sunset I recommend taking photos from the Ponte Vecchio looking down towards the Ponte Santa Trinita'. The view of the night sky over the bridges of Florence is stunning.

Pickpockets

If I were a pickpocket in Florence my ideal places to hang out during the day would be: the Piazza Duomo, the Piazza della Signoria, and in first place with a gold star, the Ponte Vecchio. These three places get the highest volume of tourists, and when you see how packed the bridge gets you'll understand why it's pickpocket Heaven.

Be hyper-vigilant. Women should wear a cross-body bag, kept zipped or fastened closed, and with a hand on it at all times. Men should keep wallets in their front pocket with a hand on it. Pickpockets are quick and good at what they do. You might think you would feel if someone was stealing your watch or lifting your wallet, but trust me, you won't.

You will see plenty of tourists not paying attention to their belongings, setting themselves up as easy targets. If you are clearly alert to the situation and do what you can to make it difficult for them, pickpockets are likely to leave you alone and stick to the easy marks. At all times but especially in a crowd, be aware that there are pickpockets around and be smart with your belongings.

10.

The Pitti Palace

As with many stories in Florence, the story of the Pitti Palace involves the Medici. It starts with the construction of the Medici Palace (now called the Medici-Riccardi Palace). Wealthy Florentine banker Luca Pitti loathed his rival Cosimo de' Medici (the elder) and decided to outdo him by building a bigger, grander palace on the south side of the river. He wanted each window in his palace to be larger than the door at Cosimo's, and his courtyard to be so big that you could fit the entire Medici palace inside. However, in 1464 Pitti ran out of money and construction stopped.

A century later in 1549, Eleanora of Toledo, the Spanish blue-blood wife of Cosimo I, decided the Medici Palace and the Palazzo Vecchio were too small and too provincial for someone of her standing. So she bought herself the biggest private home in Florence and moved her family away from the hustle and bustle and political intrigue that came with life at Palazzo Vecchio. At that time the palazzo was only the center section of the current structure (roughly the center seven windows). Cosimo enlarged the palace, more than doubling its size. I'm sure old Luca Pitti rolled over in his grave at the thought of his enemy taking over his palace, even if it was 100 years later!

No other palace in Florence had a massive courtyard like the Pitti Palace. If you look at all the other big Florentine palaces you'll see they dead end into the street, so this huge space in front (now the Piazza de Pitti) must have seemed incredibly grand. And once the ruling family was living in the Oltrarno it became the chic place to be, so other noble and wealthy families moved over here too, breathing new life and money into what to this day is still one of the coolest neighborhoods in Florence.

The Pitti Palace maintained its luster as a royal palace for centuries. When the Medici dynasty ended in 1737, the House of Lorraine-Habsburg took over, followed by the Kings of Italy House of Savoy from 1865 to 1871. The Bourbon-Parma family had it next, then Elisa Bonaparte who briefly ruled over Tuscany.

Today this magnificent old palace houses a series of Florence's best museums, and overlooks and includes the Boboli Gardens.

The Palatine Gallery

The entire first floor of the palace is occupied by the magnificent Palatine Gallery. The collection of more than 500 Renaissance paintings was once part of the Medici collection. It includes the world's largest collection of Raphael, as well as works by Caravaggio, Titian, Rubens and Tintoretto. The Lorraine-Habsburgs curated the collection, which completely covers the walls in lavish frames. It's quite something!

PLANET ROOMS

The Planet Rooms have sensational Baroque frescoes by Pietro da Cortona painted between 1640–47 for Grand Duke Ferdinando II de' Medici. The furnishings throughout are fabulous too, sculptures and tables with inlaid semi-precious stones, and vases arranged in typical seventeenth century style.

The paintings throughout the palace aren't displayed chronologically or in accordance with a particular theme or school of art. Instead they hang in the rooms they were intended for, so it feels like a private collection rather than a traditional art museum.

SILVER MUSEUM

The Silver Museum gives insight into Medici daily life through their household treasures and silverware. Their dinner parties must have been epic!

ROYAL APARTMENTS

The Royal Apartments show you how they lived, although these have mostly nineteenth century furnishings rather than the sixteenth century furnishings of Cosimo I and Eleanora. Even so, they're fascinating, opulent and a bit overwhelming – which I love.

GALLERY OF MODERN ART & PORCELAIN MUSEUM

The top floor houses the Gallery of Modern Art (nineteenth and twentieth century Tuscan art) and in the garden (Boboli Gardens) is the Porcelain Museum.

MUSEUM OF COSTUME AND FASHION

The Palazzina of the Meridiana houses the Museum of Costume and Fashion, formerly called the Costume Museum. Founded in 1983 this was Italy's first State Museum dedicated specifically to the history of fashion and its social importance. It traces 300 years of fashion, underwear, accessories and jewelry from the eighteenth century to today. There is a permanent exhibit of the restored funeral garments of Cosimo I, Eleanora and their son Garzia. Check ahead to see if there are any temporary exhibits or if it will be closed for a new installation. If you have an interest in the history of fashion (like pretty much every wardrobe stylist I have ever worked with) this museum is not to be missed.

The Pitti Palace does get tourist traffic but only a fraction of what you see at the Ponte Vecchio, Piazza della Signoria and Piazza del Duomo. When I bring my travelers here I always find it manageable and enjoyable.

The Boboli Gardens

I love looking out of the high windows of the palace at the gardens as a precursor to walking through them, possibly because this is how I always tackle Versailles. (I like to give the Versailles reference because the Boboli Gardens were in fact the inspiration for the gardens at Versailles, as well as many other European Royal Gardens.) The view from up high gives you a better visual introduction to how sensational these gardens really are.

Niccolo Tribolo did the first design of the gardens but died shortly after Eleanora bought the property. The work was completed by Medici court architects including Ammannati (who we met at the Fountain of Neptune in Piazza della Signoria), Buontalenti and Vasari.

There is plenty to see here, including the amphitheater, the grotto, the cavaliere and the viottolone pathway through the trees.

A guided tour of the gardens takes about 90 minutes and is a great idea if you have time. There is so much here that you would otherwise overlook, especially given that this garden was a 400 year production. I particularly enjoy gleaning every detail I can about the time that Cosimo and Eleanora lived here, and the guides are always more than happy to indulge me. The Boboli Gardens are the largest green space in Florence, offering a welcome break from the crowds, and even without a guide they are glorious to walk through and explore.

Address: Piazza de Pitti

What's Nearby: The palace is opposite Caffè Pitti, and a one minute walk from Le Volpe e L'Uva. Ponte Vecchio is a two minute walk, Piazzale Michelangelo is a 20 minute walk from here.

11.

Piazzale Michelangelo

Come up here for an amazing view over the city of Florence. It's breathtaking. Because it is both up high and south of the river, the view captures the entire city. You get the full, perfect view of the Duomo as well as the towers of Piazza della Signoria, Badia Fiorentina and the Pazzi Chapel. Beyond being the ultimate photo opportunity in all of Florence (in my opinion), you can see how small this medieval city really is, how beautiful it is, and you can wonder at how a city this little could have been home to so many of the world's greatest artists, who in turn produced some of the greatest art in the history of the world.

THE HISTORY OF THE PIAZZALE

Despite the name, this space does not actually date back to Michelangelo's time. In fact it wasn't created until 1869 when architect Giuseppe Poggi was doing a major restructuring of the city walls. His gorgeous terrace was intended to be a showcase for copies of Michelangelo's masterpieces. The original plan was to not only have a copy of *David* up here but also copies of the sculptures that commemorate Lorenzo the Magnificent and Giuliano, situated in the Medici Chapel.

Poggi also designed what was supposed to be a loggia behind the terrace, to be a museum for Michelangelo's works. The museum never eventuated but instead in that space there is La Loggia coffee bar and restaurant, open daily from 10am until midnight.

DAY AND NIGHT

When my tour groups stay in Florence we come up here to watch the sunset on at least one evening. On the rare occasions that I get up on time, I walk up here to watch the sunrise (as fabulous as the sunrise is, I'm seldom up that early). Of course, it's gorgeous any time, and you see people up here at all hours of the day, but sunset from here is especially sensational.

It is also *packed*. Expect to find half the world up here with you. Somehow it all works out and you can see everything *and* get postcard-perfect photos.

When it's super crowded I slip down to the roadway immediately below the terrace, from where you also get a great view. There are stairs at either end of the terrace to take you down to the roadway.

HOW TO GET HERE

There are several ways to get here: you can drive, (if you are crazy enough to have a car in Florence) take a taxi, catch the number 12 or 13 bus (which depart from the train station), or you can walk. A word to the wise – the walk is steep. If you are a pro basketball player or an Olympic athlete it'll be no big deal. If you are only moderately fit (or less) chances are you will feel the burn. (I look at it as earning dessert or gelato, or maybe burning off a bowl of pasta!)

I like to come here after an aperitivo at Le Volpe e L'Uva or one of the other spots in the Piazza de Pitti/Ponte Vecchio area, in which case it's a walk along the river to Piazza Poggi and the Porta San Niccolo'.

If coming from the far side of the river, cross the Ponte alle Grazie and walk along the river to the Piazza Poggi and Porta San Niccolo'.

(This is the castle-like tower standing guard midway between the Ponte alle Grazie and the next bridge, the Ponte San Niccolo'.) From there you will see plenty of signs directing you up the roadway or the stairs. Both options are steep but worth it.

After you've captured the sunset, take the stairs back down and walk along the river to the Ponte alle Grazie. The views from the midway point on the bridge are legendary. You can get gorgeous photos of the Ponte Vecchio with the sun behind it, or if the sun is all the way down, the night view is equally breathtaking. While you're at it be sure to walk to the midway point of the Ponte Vecchio too. You can get sensational photos looking toward the Ponte Santa Trinita'. I take the exact same photos every single time, and they bring me no end of joy *every single time.*

Address: Piazzale Michelangelo

What's Nearby: San Miniato is just up the hill. You pass the Rose Garden on the way up here, and midway between Piazzale Michelangelo and the Pitti Palace is the Forte di Belvedere. The streets weaving all through this area are definitely worth exploring. There are endless eateries and places to grab a glass of wine, and vastly fewer tourists than on the other side of the river.

Museums

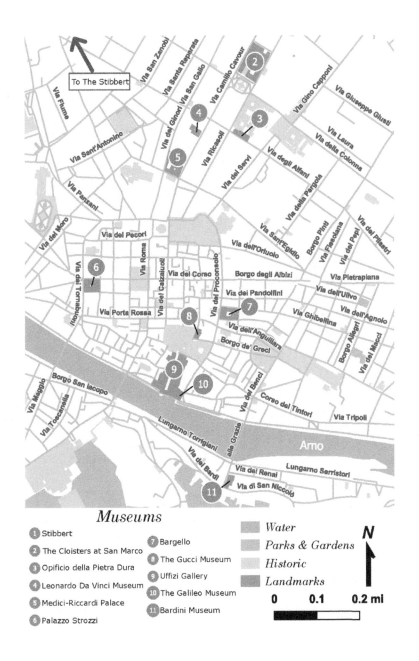

Museums

12.

12 Fascinating Museums in Florence

1. The Cloister at San Marco
2. The Medici-Riccardi Palace
3. Palazzo Strozzi Museum
4. The Bardini Museum
5. The Bargello
6. The Uffizi
7. Palazzo Davanzati
8. The Opificio della Pietra Dura
9. The Galileo Museum
10. The Stibbert Museum
11. The Gucci Museum
12. The da Vinci Museum

There are museums scattered all through this book. For example, the Opera del Duomo is in **Chapter 4: Piazza del Duomo...**, the Museo Ospedale degli Innocenti is in **Chapter 5: Piazza SS Annunziata**, the Accademia is in **Chapter 22: A Walk with Michelangelo**. Ideally you will find the museum in question either in context of its location (found in a piazza we are looking at), or in context of a person we are following. The recommendations in this chapter are for stand-alone museums that don't obviously fit into other chapters (though you'll still spot a few repeats).

On one of my tours last summer there was torrential rain in Florence, so we spent more time in the museums. We avoided the crowds outside the Uffizi, Duomo and Accademia and instead walked straight into some of the museums I'm going to tell you about in this chapter. I hadn't spent much time in these museums for a while and was wowed by how fantastic they are – and by how few people were visiting them! It felt like we had them to ourselves though the city was actually packed with tourists. Even though they didn't normally visit museums, my tour group *loved* it.

Many museums are closed on Mondays, so check ahead when planning your trip.

None of the following museums need advanced booking.

The Cloister at San Marco

This church also appears in **Chapter 13: Unusual & Interesting Things** (technically this cloister could have been put in the **Churches** chapter too), but as it is referred to as a museum, here we are.

If you love frescoes and Renaissance art, this place needs to be on your radar. The cloisters and convent of San Marco hold the largest collection of, and perhaps most beautiful works by, the painter Fra Angelico.

The complex holds many interesting stories too, from wayward monks, to my favorite Medici (Cosimo), to Florence's most illustrious fanatic (Savonarola). Leave the crowds to look over each other's shoulders in the Piazza Duomo and take the eight-minute walk to San Marco.

A LITTLE BACKGROUND

In the twelfth century this was a Vallombrosan monastery. In the 1200s the Sylvestrine monks took over. Below what is now the ground floor, traces of frescoes date back to that time. In 1418 the Sylvestrines were accused of '*laxity in their observance of the Rule*' (whatever that means. It's probably something completely benign but I prefer to think of it as monks behaving badly. Much more entertaining!) They were asked to leave but it wasn't until Pope Eugene IV and the Council of Basel intervened that they finally vacated the premises in 1437.

Meanwhile Cosimo de' Medici returned from exile in 1434 and wanted to get an order of Dominican monks established in Florence, so these buildings were passed on to the Dominican monks from nearby Fiesole. The place was in such a state of disrepair that the Dominicans spent the next two years living in damp cells and wooden huts. (Doesn't that make you want to know exactly what the Sylvestrines were getting up to?) The Dominican monks appealed to Cosimo, who was living nearby at the Medici Palace, to fund the renovation of San Marco. Cosimo had his favorite architect, Michelozzo, rebuild the entire structure in the perfect Renaissance design.

Honestly, the architecture alone is worth the visit.

FRA ANGELICO

Work began in 1438 and the church and convent were consecrated by Pope Eugene IV in 1443. In 1439 Cosimo commissioned a Dominican friar who had taken the name Fra Giovanni da Fiesole (Brother John of Fiesole) to paint the frescoes. Fra Giovanni became known as Fra Giovanni Angelico, (Angelic Brother John) which was shortened to Fra Angelico. One of the greatest painters of the Renaissance, Fra Angelico lived at San Marco for years, creating his greatest works.

The frescoes are exquisite. You don't want to race through them – allow yourself a decent chunk of time to enjoy them. The frescoes are in the cloisters and in the monks' cells. There are many and all are stunning, but I want to draw your attention to one in particular...

THE ANNUNCIATION

At the top of the staircase leading to the monks' cells is a huge painting of *the Annunciation*. Some consider this to be Fra Angelico's masterpiece. It is achingly beautiful. The fresco is 4.5 feet off the ground and the figures are life-sized, which gives it a certain immediacy. It is unusual to be able to get so close to such an important work. Perhaps it's these factors combined that make the experience so jarring.

An art historian guide taught me some cool things to look for:

- Normally Mary is depicted with symbolism (for example, a pot of lilies symbolizes purity, reading a bible symbolizes reverence and virtue). Neither of these are here because the monks already knew the story and didn't need the visual prompts required by regular parishioners.
- Like the monastery, the area Mary occupies is bare. Look closely and see how her surroundings resemble the loggia in San Marco. The hallway next to the painting leads to the monks' cells, with an undersized doorway every 10 feet or so. If you look at the doorway behind Mary, it too is

exaggeratedly low. Maybe Fra Angelico was suggesting that she was close by?

- From the top of the staircase the vanishing point in the painting looks a little off, with the floor angling up and away from you. However if you go down a few stairs and look back up into the painting, it makes sense. (I quite enjoy going up and down the stairs looking at it from different angles.)

- Mary and the Archangel Gabriel are both too large for the space they occupy. If Mary stands up her head will crash through the ceiling.

- Notice the way Gabriel's wing sparkles at you as you walk past. Fra Angelico must have used some form of mica or something similar when he created the paint, and almost 600 years later, we still catching the glimmer as we pass by.

Of course there are multiple frescoes here, and they are all astounding. Be sure to look for Ghirlandaio's *Last Supper*.

THE MONKS' CELLS

The Dominican order were into austerity and deprivation. These cells must have been *freezing* in winter. Each is very small, but has its own beautiful fresco for the monk to look at and pray to.

Two of the cells are particularly interesting:

Cosimo kept a cell here to pray and meditate in. I love mapping out walks of where the various artists and Medici worked and lived their lives, so I sometimes walk from the Medici Palace to San Marco, imagining what Cosimo might have looked at as he made his way to his meditation cell.

Savonarola also had a cell here. This was his parish for a while, and he was even the prior here for a time. Thankfully, when he was having his lunatic bonfire of the vanities he left the frescoes alone.

THE LIBRARY

Cosimo's library, completed in 1444, can be found inside this museum. This was the first public library in Florence. Although not like a modern day public library (the average servant or worker couldn't grab a book for the weekend), it did allow those who weren't priests or kings to interact with books. This was before the invention of printing presses, so each book was created by hand.

Priceless manuscripts belonging to the Medici are housed here, as well as collections belonging to Mirandola, Poliziano and to Niccolo de Niccoli. Niccoli's will stipulated that his collection was not to be sold or removed, and was not to be limited to the exclusive use of the monks, but was to be made available to all who held interest.

Lorenzo the Magnificent worked on the enrichment of this library. For years the library at San Marco held more books and manuscripts than the library of the popes. Owning books was the ultimate sign of wealth, knowledge, education and power. Plenty had wealth but few had books, let alone an entire library.

The Museum at San Marco is in the busy Piazza San Marco, which is full of buses and bus stops and locals making their way to and from work. Stepping through the entrance and into the cloisters catapults you into a different world, suddenly peaceful and quiet.

The entrance fee is only €4 which seems ridiculously low.

Address: Piazza San Marco, 3

What's Nearby: San Marco is one city block from the Northeast entrance to Piazza SS Annunciata (the church end), and is diagonally opposite the Accademia. It is two large city blocks from the Medici-Riccardi Palace and Piazza San Lorenzo. From the Duomo it is a 5–10 minute walk up via Ricasoli.

The Medici-Riccardi Palace

When his arch rival Rinaldo degli Albizzi died in 1442, followed by an orchestrated defeat of Milan in 1444, Cosimo's influence and power grew exponentially. So much so he decided he needed a new place to live. He had Brunelleschi design him a palace, and then shelved the plans saying they were too grand. He then had his favorite architect, Michelozzo, design something less ostentatious. (This was probably his plan all along, with the Brunelleschi part just a ruse tricking the public into believing he didn't want anything too opulent.) The resulting building had a fortress-like exterior with no windows on the ground floor, only arched gateways, so from the outside it looked imposing but not sumptuous.

In those days if you were building a new house or palazzo you would build onto something that already existed. Cosimo's plan was different. He razed the site diagonally opposite the Basilica San Lorenzo and built his new palace from scratch. Therefore, the Medici Palace is the first purely Renaissance building in Florence. It has three distinctly different floors topped with a huge cornice, and is incredibly elegant.

Beyond the entranceway (out of public view) he built a beautiful courtyard with an Italian-style garden. Donatello's *David* originally stood here as well as his *Judith and Holofernes*.

Construction was completed in 1460 but by 1517 it underwent renovations, including adding Michelangelo's *Kneeling Windows* onto the ground floor.

Excluding the years spent in exile, the Medici Palace was home to the Medici family until Cosimo I de' Medici moved to the Palazzo Vecchio in 1540. From then on minor members of the Medici clan lived here, until 1659 when Ferdinando II sold the palace to the Riccardi. The new owners enlarged and modified the palace, adding the large hall frescoed by Luca Giordano, considered one of the most important examples of Baroque frescoes in Florence.

A must see inside the palace is the Chapel of the Magi. Three walls, frescoed in 1459 by Benozzo Gozzoli, tell the story of the procession of the Magi (except that really they tell the story of the parade of the ecumenical Council of Florence in 1439). The faces of the people in the frescoes are important folks of the time, as well as all the Medici.

Now a museum, the Medici-Riccardi Palace is open to the public most days. As well as temporary exhibitions, come here to see the Chapel of the Magi, the frescoed large hall, Fra Filippo Lippi's beautiful *Madonna and Child,* and the marble room housing the Riccardi family's ancient marble sculptures.

Address: Via Cavour, 1

What's Nearby: The palace is diagonally opposite the Basilica San Lorenzo, so is a one-minute walk from the Medici Chapel and the San Lorenzo Market. It is one short city block from the Baptistery and Piazza del Duomo.

Palazzo Strozzi Museum

This is another secret hiding in plain sight.

Until exiled in 1434, the Strozzi were one of the wealthiest and most powerful families in Florence. And they loathed the Medici.

While in exile Filippo Strozzi worked hard to rebuild his fortune and regain his power, so when finally able to return in 1466 he did so with a vengeance. The Medici Palazzo, huge and ostentatious, was the first of its kind, so Strozzi decided to build one like it but bigger and more bombastic. He bought the land around his existing home and (hilariously) got permission from Lorenzo the Magnificent to build the new pad. There was some drama with the other wealthy families but in 1489 he broke ground. Construction on the palace was finished in 1538 and the palazzo remained in the family until their last heir died in 1937.

Although the interior has seen changes over the centuries, the exterior has remained the same for more than 500 years. The perfect example of a fifteenth-century palazzo, it looks like a fortress, is built to a symmetrical rectangular format and is three stories high. The bottom floor is made of heavy, rough-hewn blocks, and with each subsequent floor the stone gets smoother.

The inner courtyard is perfection, surrounded by a stone arcade of exquisite arches and columns. Under the arches the *Strozzi Café Colle Bereto Winery* opens at 8am and is a gorgeous spot for a snack or a meal. I seldom see tourists here, or if I do they are few and far between, so it is a fabulous place to watch local Florentines, who somehow always manage to look effortlessly chic as they go about their days.

The Strozzi palace is considered one of the finest examples of a Renaissance home. Walk around the exterior and examine the details, such as the wrought iron candelabra, torch holders, flag holders and the rings to tie up the horses, some even look like winged dragons. All were custom made by fifteenth-century Florence's master blacksmith, Niccolo' Grosso.

Quite apart from the Palazzo Strozzi being a wonderful place to enjoy a cappuccino, this is Florence's largest space for temporary art exhibitions, focusing on modern and contemporary art. The Fondazione Palazzo Strozzi wants to make Florence a dynamic, contemporary city, so have volunteered the rooms and huge halls to display all kinds of art. Exhibitions have included the Peggy Guggenheim collection, Cezanne in Florence, Botticelli, and Gustav Klimt. The Cezanne exhibit was the most visited exhibition in Italy in 2007, the Botticelli was the most visited in 2004. Check online to see what will be on while you're in Florence. There are three or four exhibitions each year.

PALAZZO STROZZINO – THE MOVIE THEATER NEXT DOOR

This is random but interesting. Diagonally opposite the huge Palazzo Strozzi is the much smaller Palazzo Strozzino. Housing the Cinema Odeon (screening English films) since the 1920s, it is also home to the British Institute of Florence Language School.

Formerly known as the *Palazzo delle Tre Porte* because of the three ground floor doorways, it was the Strozzi home prior to the big palace. When Palla Strozzi was exiled in 1434 he handed the property to his cousin Agnolo and Palla di Novello. They had Michelozzo renovate it and design a beautiful internal courtyard with portico, both of which were destroyed to build the movie theater.

More of the palazzo was destroyed in 1865, when many medieval buildings were ripped out to modernize Florence and create the Piazza della Repubblica.

Address: Piazza degli Strozzi

What's Nearby: Piazza della Repubblica, and in the opposite direction via de' Tornabuoni, the Salvatore Ferragamo Museum, and Ponte S. Trinita'. You are three minutes from SS Ognissanti.

The Bardini Museum

I always recommend this one to art lovers who have previously spent time in Florence. When you visit most museums in Florence, you go to see something specific, some world-renowned masterpiece. At the Bardini you come to appreciate the whole astounding private collection.

WHO WAS STEFANO BARDINI?

To understand this collection you need to understand Stefano Bardini, brilliant art connoisseur, restorer and collector – the Prince of Art Dealers. He had a different way of viewing the past and his somewhat avant-garde way of doing things would influence how museums would restore and exhibit works for decades to follow.

Bardini developed new techniques for preserving antiquities, detaching frescoes and restoring them. Some were controversial, including a technique known as *pastiche,* where fragments from varying origins were mixed together to create a 'whole' piece, which of course would sell better. However, it is worth noting that he didn't restore the frescoes in his own collection, preferring not to mess with their integrity.

Bardini was commissioned to break up and sell off private collections, while fattening the catalogues of several important museums. His ability to recognize beauty was uncanny. He had an astute eye for treasures that had been missed and hidden away, some of which are here in his museum.

He also had a brilliant understanding of how to stage a collection to make each piece visually appealing, revolutionizing the way antiques were exhibited.

Bardini realized most buyers were more interested in how a piece would look in their homes, rather than its importance historically, so he mixed and matched visually complimentary pieces together, regardless of era. You might find a Roman artifact positioned with something from the Renaissance, or an ancient sarcophagi placed with thirteenth century armor.

THE BUILDING

Bardini restored and renovated the building which is quite eclectic, although Renaissance in style. Built as a convent in 1273 by Pope Gregory X to celebrate peace between the Guelfs and Ghibellines, its original name was San Gregorio alla Pace (St Gregory of Peace). In 1775 it became the Palazzo de' Mozzi. The Mozzi family orchards and vegetable gardens are now the Giardini Bardini.

THE COLLECTION

The Bardini Museum collection doesn't follow any chronological order. Bardini rarely labeled items or recorded their provenance when he acquired them. Some of the items here are *pastiche*, comprised of several things put together to create his ideal visual.

The audio guide (€4) will help you understand how Bardini changed the way we view art and how his work impacted museums all over the world. The museum map will direct you to the more celebrated pieces and help you organize your visit.

Enjoy the large open spaces, natural light and the genius of the blue walls. This new concept became a Bardini trademark, demonstrating his approach to staging a scene. The free space allows you to appreciate the individual pieces, while the blue walls increase the brilliance of the white marble, making it glow.

When the collection was donated to the city after Bardini's death, the new curator painted all the walls white and arranged the pieces in chronological order. Using a huge catalogue of photos, the collection was recently restored to Bardini's original vision. His aesthetic was designed to let you lose yourself in the beauty, appreciate the craftsmanship and be mesmerized by the individual pieces, rather than focus on *who* created it, *where, when* and *why*.

Some items in this collection will surprise you. As you enter the building, an enormous Bernardo Daddi crucifix more than four meters tall completely overwhelms you, no doubt exactly the effect Bardini intended.

Bardini's sharp eye paired with perfect timing (of Florence selling off iconic items during its urban renewal) created an auspicious opportunity for a collector. For example: *Il Porcellino*, Florence's iconic boar (the replica of which is at the Mercato Nuovo or what I refer to in this book as the *Porcellino Market*) should never have made it into private hands! Luckily it went to someone who took care of it and willed it back to the city after their death. In the same room is a noteworthy sculpture by Giambologna, the Mannerist sculptor mentioned multiple times in this book. (How did a private collector acquire this?) Look for two Donatellos, including a terracotta bust of the *Madonna della Mela.* Also a wooden statue of a fourteenth century woman, busts dating back to the Greek and Roman eras, fifteenth century Tuscan wooden chests, and more – the collection is way more extensive than you would expect.

I can lose myself here for hours, but as much as there is to immerse yourself in at eye level, don't forget to look up. The ceilings are incredible too!

The museum opens 11:00am–5:00pm, Friday, Saturday, Sunday, Monday. Closed on Tuesday, Wednesday, Thursday.

Both the 12 and the 23 buses stop close by.

Address: via dei Renai, 37

The Bargello

This tremendous museum should be on the list of every art lover, especially fans of Donatello and Michelangelo.

The imposing building has an illustrious history. Built around 1250 it predated the Palazzo Vecchio as the seat of government, then became a prison, with executions taking place in the courtyard. Once restored in the nineteenth century to its former grandeur, it then became a museum.

Entering via the executioner's courtyard, visit the Michelangelo room on your right, or the Donatello room up the old staircase. It's easy to get lost here, as the layout of the rooms is more akin to an ancient palace than a modern art museum, but I think that adds to the magic.

There is plenty to see at the Bargello, but these are my favorite pieces:

DONATELLO'S *DAVID*

I would come to the Bargello for this piece alone. This bronze statue was incredibly controversial. Unlike Michelangelo's *David* (a big, brawny fellow sculpted more than 60 years later), Donatello's is effeminate and a little incongruous. For some reason this fellow is naked except for a hat and boots (or, depending on how you approach it, this naked fellow is wearing a hat and boots).

Created for Cosimo de' Medici for the courtyard of the Palazzo Medici, it was discovered during restoration that the hair, hat and boots were originally gilded, so they would have sparkled in the sunlight out there in the courtyard.

MICHELANGELO'S *BACCHUS*

Michelangelo created this sculpture in 1496 in Rome, when he was 21. It is one of only two surviving sculptures from his first time in Rome.

This piece is fantastic because, rather than the big strong bodies we associate with Michelangelo's sculptures, Bacchus is fleshy, almost womanly, and is obviously drunk. Bacchus, the god of wine, is leaning against a tree, being supported by a satyr. You can anticipate that he's about to trip and fall, a trick Michelangelo created by giving him a high center of gravity.

Michelangelo didn't give a god-like reverence to his Bacchus, instead making him look shallow and vapid; a human wearing a wreath of ivy leaves. (Ivy was sacred to Bacchus.) It's brilliant.

MICHELANGELO'S *PITTI TONDO*

This is another of my favorite Michelangelo works in Florence. *Tondos* (round formats) were considered a domestic art form and were typically created for private homes rather than churches.

The *Pitti Tondo* is is one of two tondos Michelangelo made for families in Florence in 1503–05. It features the Madonna and Child. Look for Mary's exquisitely lovely face. I love the way her head comes out of the frame. The intimacy between the characters is palpable. It's as if we're sneaking a glimpse of a real and relatable moment in their day, seeing them as human rather than the untouchable, ethereal figures we usually see.

THE BRONZE DOOR COMPETITION PANELS

In the Duomo chapter we talked about the competition to create the Baptistery's second set of bronze doors. Competitors submitted a bronze quatrefoil panel depicting the *Sacrifice of Isaac*. The panel (which you will see was quite small) had to include the father and son, an altar, a donkey, two servants, a tree and a hill. Huge skill was required to fit so much into such a small space.

All the submitted panels were melted down and reused, except for those of the winner and the runner up. (Some think the runner up only lost because his panel used a heavier bronze, making his doors more expensive.) The winner was Lorenzo Ghiberti, the runner up Filippo Brunelleschi. The two panels are on display at the Bargello, and should be on your *must-see* list. Without reading the signs first, see if you can guess which won and which was runner up!

Funnily enough, the consequences of this competition changed the face of Florence forever. Brunelleschi, so incensed at losing, turned his back on the craft forever. He focused on architecture instead, giving us the innovative dome of the Duomo. Had Ghiberti not won Florence may have never had its beautiful dome, or any of the other magnificent architecture created by Brunelleschi in his lifetime.

Address: Via del Proconsolo, 4

What's Nearby: The Bargello is opposite the Badia Fiorentina and next to Palazzo Vecchio.

The Uffizi

Each day thousands of visitors come to the Uffizi, Italy's most visited art museum. Many aren't art lovers but come to cross *The Birth of Venus* and *Primavera* off their bucket lists. As a result, during the main travel season, art lovers might not get to enjoy much quality time along that stretch of the museum. So here's the secret – crowds who file past those two Botticellis tend to not venture much into the rest of the museum. If you are here for the art then hang tight – there is much to see and the huge crowds tend to stay in one place. (If you've been to the Louvre in Paris you will understand. The walk to the *Mona Lisa* is packed beyond belief, but venture past her and the crowd disappears, letting you spend all the time you want with the pieces that speak to you.)

When the Uffizi reopened after the Coronavirus Pandemic the number of visitors allowed in at any given time was reduced. This may change again once the world gets back to normal, or finds a new travel normal.

Outside the main travel season it's an entirely different scenario. Recently I came in December and there was hardly anyone here. I had some sections all to myself and shared others with no more than a dozen fellow art lovers. It was wonderful!

THE HISTORY OF THE BUILDING

As I explained in **Chapter 8: Piazza della Signoria**, Cosimo I had Vasari build the Uffizi to house the local government offices in 1560, and creating the Vasari Corridor – the passageway from Palazzo Vecchio to Palazzo Pitti. This is why the Uffizi gallery has such an unusual floor pattern for an art museum.

RENOVATIONS

The gallery has undergone massive renovations and reorganization over the last few years and at the time of writing this there are more renovations to come. If you visited before 2016, you will find it an entirely new experience. The grouping of paintings, the displays and the lighting all have been modified, and it is fantastic.

STRATEGY

You need a good strategy when approaching a museum that gets as much human traffic as the Uffizi, and I recommend the following:

- Study a map of the museum ahead of time so you know which pieces are displayed where. Things have moved recently and there are more changes coming.
- Identify which art works are most important to you, to avoid missing seeing them as you move through.
- Get the audio guide.

- Don't go with a group. The crowd here moves like lemmings so it's easier to get around and slip through them when there's just one or two of you.
- Book tickets online, well ahead of time.
- Tickets are booked with a timed entry. Book *the earliest time possible*, ideally right when it opens. Last September, some friends booked the last time slot of the day, thinking the cruise ship crowd would be gone. It was an absolute zoo. When I met them afterwards at Caffè Pitti they were completely frazzled. The crowds had been overwhelming and it had been impossible to see anything clearly.
- Get the big attractions out of the way first, especially the Botticelli room. You will enjoy the experience much more when you're not trying to look through a crowd of people.

Address: Piazza degli Uffizi

What's Nearby: Piazza della Signoria, the Bargello and Badia Fiorentina are all right here. From the Uffizi, it's just a two minute walk to the best sandwich in the world at Al Antico Vinaio.

Palazzo Davanzati

This was the home of a Florentine nobleman from the late 1500s and it is glorious. After changing hands multiple times during the twentieth century, in 1995 the palazzo closed for 10 years of major renovations, including securing the building (it was in serious disrepair), lifting up and redoing the floors, and restoring the frescoes.

THE HISTORY

In the mid-fourteenth century the Divizzi family joined several houses together to make this palazzo. The property combines the closed, vertical style of a medieval tower house with the beauty of a spacious Renaissance palazzo, built around a central courtyard. In 1578 it was sold to Bernardo Davanzati, a wealthy merchant, intellectual and famous historian.

The front façade has large wooden gates which at one time were an open loggia used as a playground for children, a meeting place, waiting area, and commercial trading space.

A stone staircase leads to the first floor, then wooden staircases to the upper floors where the family lived.

The living spaces are fantastic. The walls are decorated with frescoes that were covered by heavy tapestries in the winter months to keep the cold out. Some rooms have walls entirely covered with frescoes, some telling stories, others with geometric designs, almost precursors to wallpaper. Look up and see painted arched loggia with views of imaginary gardens.

The bedroom *Camera della Castellana* has an incredible fresco cycle telling the love and death story of Chastelaine de Vergy. This story of a French romance gone wrong was popular in fourteenth century Florence. The frescoes were painted in 1350 to commemorate the marriage of Paolo Davanzati and Lisa degli Alberti.

THE KITCHEN

The kitchen is on the third floor. This ensured the family weren't bothered by heat, while mitigating the fire risk to the art and treasures below. The servants' quarters were up here too.

A guided tour of the kitchens shows interesting items, including pots and pans, cauldrons and cooking utensils, to everyday life things like spinning tools, and a loom. It's fascinating seeing simple items such as corkscrews, grain mills and dough kneaders. There is even an eighteenth century churn for making butter. (Book your tour ahead of time.)

The bathrooms have zinc and copper baths, jugs and buckets, and each floor has toilets, which were a novelty at the time and show just how wealthy the family must have been. The palazzo has an internal well and a hidden door on each floor, behind which water could be drawn up through a hole in the wall.

THE FURNITURE

As the original furniture was sold off a long time ago, the current furniture comes from donations and acquisitions from antiques markets, to give visitors an idea how the home would have looked in its time.

This museum gives fabulous insight into the lives of the noble families of Florence. While interesting for all ages, frankly *I would have died* to have seen this as a child or teen, and probably would have gleaned more from this palazzo than from a royal palace. If you're traveling with children this would be a wonderful addition to your Florence itinerary.

Address: Via Porta Rossa, 13

What's Nearby: Palazzo Davanzati is one minute from the Porcellino Market, close to SS Apostoli, two blocks from Piazza della Repubblica and less than five minutes from Piazza della Signoria.

The Opificio della Pietra Dura

Operational for more than four centuries, the *workshop of semi-precious stone* has evolved from a production workshop to the world's greatest restoration workshop. They restore everything, from stone to tapestries, paintings, archeological finds, paper and parchment to… everything.

The Opificio della Pietra Dura (OPD) is part of the Medici family legacy. Although marble inlay existed long before the Medici, in 1588 Grand Duke Ferdinando I created this workshop to specialize in marble inlays and semi-precious stone mosaics.

I recommend this museum to those who have already spent time in Florence and want to visit something different, as well as those with a specific interest in inlaid marble and restoration. If this is your first trip to Florence you may prefer to visit one of the other museums on the list.

WHAT'S INSIDE

The museum isn't large and you won't need a lot of time here, but it's really quite cool. The ground floor is divided into seven sections taking you through the evolution and progression of this art form.

Medici fans will enjoy seeing the history of Cosimo I's fascination with beautiful stonework through Grand Duke Ferdinando's construction of the Medici Chapel at San Lorenzo (which is *full* of inlaid marble). You can even see unused items from the chapel, including panels for the huge altar.

You'll learn how flowers and still life were inspiration for stone inlays and see how inlays were created. The ground floor takes you from the 1500s to the 1800s, seeing everything from the skill of *intarsia* to *scagliolia*, which is particularly interesting to know and recognize as you go through the palaces and historical sites in Europe.

The upper floor shows the craftsmen's techniques and tools, and the production phases when creating intarsia floors and inlay work.

The restoration areas of this museum are scattered across the city and are not open to the public. You can however visit the workshops with a private guide. I haven't yet done this, but it is on my neverending list of things I want to do in Florence.

Address: Via degli Alfani, 7

What's Nearby: Basilica San Lorenzo, the San Lorenzo Market, and the Palazzo Medici-Riccardi are all close.

The Galileo Museum

All roads in Florence seem to lead back to the Medici, and this is yet another.

Galileo Gallilei (1564–1642) is known as the Father of Science, the Father of Modern Physics, and the Father of the Scientific Method. He was an astronomer, an engineer, and a physicist. Branded a heretic by the Roman Inquisition in 1615 for saying the Earth revolved around the Sun, he was sentenced to house arrest for life, and ultimately he was forced to recant. When he died in 1642 the Pope banned Ferdinando II de' Medici from burying Galileo in Santa Croce. It took 100 years before he was moved to his rightful place in the basilica.

The Galileo Museum used to be the History of Science Museum. The 1000 core items come from the personal collections of the Medici family and their successors, the Lorraines. Both had enormous interest in mathematics and the sciences.

Cosimo I began collecting scientific instruments, keeping them in the famous cabinets of the Map Room in Palazzo Vecchio. His son Ferdinando I built up the collection, transferring it to the Mathematics Room at the Uffizi. Grandson, Ferdinando II, was infatuated with the sciences and with his brother, Leopold created the Accademia del Cimento at the Pitti Palace, furthering scientific research and the invention of laboratory instruments. Then Grand Duke Peter Leopold Habsburg-Lorraine moved everything next door to the Museum of Physics, which became the Specola Museum. They built an observatory and added more items to the collection, including some of Galileo's belongings, such as his telescopes.

Curated over 500 years, all of this has become the heart of the Galileo Museum.

Address: Piazza dei Giudici, 1

What's Nearby: The Galileo Museum is next door to the Uffizi, one minute from the Palazzo Vecchio and a two minute walk from Al Antico Vinaio.

The Stibbert Museum

This one is quirky but cool, especially for anyone interested in warfare, arms and armor.

Most of the Stibbert collection is comprised of more than 16,000 pieces of armory and weapons of European, Islamic, Oriental and Japanese origins, from the fifteenth to nineteenth centuries. The Cavalcade room alone has 14 knights on horseback and 14 foot soldiers, all dressed in sixteenth century armor. The Samurai collection contains more than 80 suits/costumes and hundreds of swords. Although best known as a warfare museum, there are also paintings and tapestries, furniture, porcelains, Tuscan crucifixes and even some Etruscan treasures. The paintings include an exquisite Botticelli, two Giordanos, and a Bronzino.

The Stibbert Museum has an interesting story behind it. Frederick Stibbert had an Italian mother and a British father. The family's fortune was created by his grandfather Giles Stibbert, Commander in Chief of the British East India Company in Bengal, and governor for several years. When Giles died, 21-year-old Frederick inherited it all. Frederick never worked, instead devoting himself to collecting treasures. He turned his 57 room villa into a museum, and when his collections outgrew that home, he had architect Giuseppe Poggi, painter Gaetano Bianchi and sculptor Passaglia, add on more rooms. (Poggi also created the lovely English gardens on the property, which you can walk through.) When Frederick died in 1906, he willed his collection and home to the city of Florence.

Address: Via Frederick Stibbert, 26

What's Nearby: The Stibbert is in the Refredi district, making it too far to reach on foot. Take a taxi.

The Gucci Museum

The Gucci Museum opened in 2011, to celebrate the 90th anniversary of the fashion house. Covering three stories of the Palazzo Mercanzia (a 600-year-old palace next to the Palazzo Vecchio in Piazza della Signoria), this museum tells the history of the Gucci brand.

The permanent collection is a mix of the brand's most iconic pieces, from clothing, to accessories including handbags, and of course, luggage. There is a contemporary art space, a boutique and the fabulous Osteria Gucci, a restaurant collaboration with three-Michelin-star chef Massimo Bottura.

The Gucci brand began in Florence in 1921. Founder Guccio Gucci loved the luxurious luggage carried by the well-heeled clientele at London's Savoy Hotel where he had worked. So back in Florence he set up a workshop with his sons and began making high-end luggage. In the 1930s the brand's wealthy, aristocratic clientele wanted items reflecting their equestrian hobbies, and some of Gucci's most iconic signatures emerged: the horse-bit styled bar with double rings and the saddle-girth-inspired green and red weft tape.

The museum rooms are arranged by theme rather than chronologically. Along with Gucci items, you'll find cool pieces from the archives, like old ad campaigns. The Travel Room contains iconic Gucci trunks and suitcases and international jet set memorabilia from the 50s, 60s, and 70s. There is also a nod to style icons such as Princess Grace for whom the Flora collection was created.

Fashion lovers will enjoy the Gucci Museum and the osteria is wonderful.

Address: Piazza della Signoria

What's Nearby: This is next to the Palazzo Vecchio, a block from the Bargello.

The da Vinci Museum

This museum has reconstructions of Leonardo's machines.

Amongst all the other brilliant things he did, Leonardo da Vinci (1452-1519) wrote more than 4000 pages of notes, studies, sketches and things he found interesting. These pages were later made into books, or codexes, two of which were the *Flight of Birds* and the *Codex Atlanticus* (both are in Milan). From these codexes it was possible to recreate some of Leonardo's inventions, and this is what you'll see here. There's nothing old in this museum, but it is cool to see the amazing inventions da Vinci thought up 500 years ago. Each display is well explained and some are interactive.

This small museum has a €7 entrance fee, making it quite expensive for what you get. I'm including it here because if you're traveling with children, they will find it interesting. Although we never came to this one, my son would have *loved* this between the ages of 7 and 12 (but perhaps not so much beyond that age).

Address: Via dei Servi, 66R

What's Nearby: The da Vinci Museum is midway between the Duomo and Piazza SS Annnunciata.

Mentioned Elsewhere in this Book

Here is a short list of some other museums, and where in this book you'll find more about them:

- **The Accademia** is in Chapter 22: A Walk with Michelangelo, as is the **Casa Buonarotti Museum.**
- **Casa Dante** is in Chapter 23: A Walk with Dante (and *Inferno*).
- The **Pitti Palace Museum** is in Chapter 10: The Pitti Palace & Boboli Gardens.
- The **Palazzo Vecchio Museum** is in Chapter 8: Piazza della Signoria.
- The **Ospedali degli Innocenti Museum** is in Chapter 5: Piazza SS Annunciata.
- The **Specola Wax Museum** is in Chapter 13: Unusual & Interesting Things.
- The **Salvatore Ferragamo Museum** is in the Shoes section of Chapter 16: Shopping.

Unusual & Interesting Things

13.

20 Unusual & Interesting Things

1. Galileo's Middle Finger
2. L'Importuno di Michelangelo
3. The Secret Side Door of Palazzo Vecchio
4. The Remains of San Per Scheraggio
5. Michelangelo's Hidden Graffiti
6. The Relic of St Antoninous
7. The Specola Wax Museum
8. Dante's Plaques
9. The Rose Garden
10. Fly with Leonardo
11. Clet Abraham's Street Signs
12. The Face of Berta
13. The Wine Windows of Florence
14. The Bull of Santa Maria del Fiore
15. The Tabernacles of Florence
16. The Devil's Wind
17. The Strangled Artist of the Duomo
18. The Madonna of the UFO
19. The Giardino Bardini
20. The Astrological Instruments of Santa Maria Novella

In any city it's fun to track down its odd and unusual things. Ancient cities and medieval cities tend to have no end of fascinating peculiarities. Highly touristed cities can leave you feeling overwhelmed by crowds, so it's good to have places to duck away to. This list of 20 unusual and interesting things to find in Florence gives you a blend of the weird and the wonderful as well as some escape hatches. You'd be surprised how few tourists know to look for these!

Galileo's Middle Finger

The Galileo Museum is in **Chapter 12: Museums**, but this particular exhibit is definitely unusual.

Galileo Galilei was a brilliant scientist, physicist, engineer and astronomer. One of his inventions was the thermoscope – the precursor to the thermometer. Another was the spyglass, invented in 1609. With it he discovered the moon wasn't smooth but instead had mountainous ridges and depressions.

Using his spyglass/telescope Galileo studied Saturn's rings, the phases of Venus and the four moons orbiting Jupiter. His studies of the planets and solar system paired with his mathematical genius convinced him that Copernicus was correct in his theory of heliocentrism, the Earth did in fact orbit the sun. The problem was, that didn't align with the story the Catholic Church was preaching. The Church was adamant the sun orbited the Earth. So, with zero tolerance for dissenters, scientists and mathematicians, the Inquisition declared Galileo a heretic, and threatened him with torture. On April 30, 1633, Galileo was forced to recant his scientific findings and was sentenced to life imprisonment. As he rose from kneeling in front of his inquisitors, after being forced to say the sun revolves around the Earth, he murmured '*e pur, si muove*' ('and yet, it moves'), which was basically giving them the finger.

Now, almost 400 years later, you can visit said middle finger, venerated and enshrined like a saintly Catholic relic, in an egg-shaped glass. Ninety-five years after Galileo's death a fellow named Anton Francesco Gori snapped off his middle finger. The finger was passed around for a couple of hundred years before it made its way to Florence's History of Science Museum. (Oddly enough, two other fingers of Galileo and a tooth disappeared in 1905. They resurfaced in 2009 and were returned to the museum.)

So now the question is: is Galileo's middle finger pointing to the sky, his discoveries and his beloved planets, or is he quite magnificently posthumously flipping off the church?

E pur, si muove...

Address: Galileo Museum of Science, Piazza dei Giudici, 1

What's Nearby: This is next to the Uffizi, Palazzo Vecchio and Piazza della Signoria. Ponte Vecchio is less than five minutes away.

L'Importuno di Michelangelo

Known as *Michelangelo's Graffiti*, this one is also in **Chapter 8: Piazza della Signoria**. There are several stories and they all involve Michelangelo standing with his back to the wall making the sketch (see Chapter 8 for the stories in detail).

On the right hand corner of the front wall of the Palazzo Vecchio, one of the old Tuscan stones has the caricature of a man's face carved into it. It's fun to try and find the face on the wall. (Behind the statue of *Hercules and Cacus* to the right of the main entrance to the palace, look for the ledge running parallel to the top step. Count four stones up and two stones from the corner, and there he is!)

Not only is this one great for kids, but every adult I show it to also gets a huge kick out of it. You can walk past it a million times and be completely oblivious, but once you find it, is impossible not to see every time you pass by. Though we can't be certain that he carved it, legend says he did.

Address: Palazzo Vecchio

What's Nearby: Palazzo Vecchio, Piazza della Signoria and the Uffizi are all close.

The Secret Side Door of the Palazzo Vecchio

From the front corner of the Palazzo Vecchio, turn left under the Vasari Corridor and walk along the wall. Before you reach the big door you will see the secret small door, set down low in the wall. I don't know how many times over the years I've walked past this and never noticed it. One time I rented an apartment just down the road from this secret door and passed it multiple times per day, none the wiser.

A few years ago I did the *Secret Passages* tour of the Palazzo Vecchio for the first time (I take most of my groups on the tour now). The guide explained that the Medici were always under threat of assassination, and couldn't just stroll out the front door of the palace, so they needed a secret exit. They would escape through the secret passageways in the walls, one of which led down an internal staircase to a secret doorway. The guide brought me out through the doorway onto via della Ninna. I was shocked that I had never noticed it before! Now I always show it to my Glam Italia tour travelers, but only after we have walked past it a couple of times and no one has spotted it!

What's Nearby: Ponte Vecchio is beyond the Uffizi to your right. Follow via della Ninna until it becomes via dei Neri and find the best sandwich in the world at Al Antico Vinaio.

The Remains of San Pier Scheraggio at the Uffizi

Opposite the secret door in the wall of the Palazzo Vecchio, there are a series of arches and columns built into the exterior wall. These are remains of the Romanesque church of San Pier Scheraggio.

The church was built on top of the foundations of a nineth century church (which was built on Roman ruins). San Pier Scheraggio was consecrated in 1068 and for the next three centuries was a church and meeting place for municipal councils until 1313. Writers including Dante and Boccaccio hung out here too. When the Palazzo Priori (now Palazzo Vecchio) was being enlarged and extended along via della Ninna, most of the church was demolished. In 1560 what remained was incorporated into the Vasari factory for the Uffizi. The central nave still stands today and was restored in 1971, but from the outside all that remains are the arches and the pieces of the columns.

Address: Via della Ninna, 5

What's Nearby: The Uffizi Gallery, Palazzo Vecchio, and the Loggia de Lanzi are close.

Michelangelo's Hidden Sketches

In 1975 a secret chamber was discovered below the Medici Chapel. The walls of the chamber were coated in lime, but as the lime was removed something staggering was revealed – the walls were covered in 400-year-old sketches by Michelangelo! So what was Michelangelo doing down there, and why did he graffiti the walls? *Of course* the story involves the Medici, politics and intrigue.

In 1527 the Medici were exiled (again) and Florence became a republic. Michelangelo was fed up with his former patrons, so he stayed behind, aligning himself with the new republic. He was not only a great artist, but was also a specialist in fortifications. In 1529 he became general governor and procurator of the fortifications, basically shoring up Florence's defenses against the Medici. But not for long.

The Medici pope, Clement VII, sent Spanish troops to overthrow the republic and install his 19-year-old illegitimate son Alessandro as the first Duke of Florence. Florence became a hereditary monarchy, and Alessandro became the western world's first black head of state. The city surrendered in August 1530, and things got a little hairy for Michelangelo.

The Medici sought revenge on everyone who supported the republic, including Michelangelo, so the artist had to disappear. He hid right under their noses in a secret chamber below the Medici Chapel in San Lorenzo. He was the architect for the chapel, so he not only knew of the space but had probably designed it himself. Michelangelo hid in this one windowed cell for between 30 days and 3 months, no doubt bored silly and terrified of being discovered. While down there, he spent his time sketching on the walls with charcoal. The sketches include a group of bodies resembling the Last Supper, later painted on the wall of the Sistine Chapel, and a hand pointing outward, which may have been a study for the Hand of God reaching out to Adam on the Sistine Chapel ceiling. He sketched David, (by now the symbol of the Florentine Republic) and a haggard man, hunched over scribbling on parchment, which may have been a self-portrait. He drew a man's knees, which looks like the sculpture he later made of Giuliano, in the chapel above the chamber.

In the end it turned out okay for Michelangelo. Pope Clement VII, who wasn't such a bad guy and had been a brother to Michelangelo for several years in the Medici Palace, wrote a letter pardoning him and ordering him back to work on the Medici Chapel.

At the time of writing this book, Michelangelo's hideout is not accessible to the public, but you can see the sketches on touchscreen monitors in three places: the Sagrestia Nuova in San Lorenzo, the Accademia, and the Bargello. The secret room is supposed to open to the public in 2020/21, so keep an eye out for it.

Address: San Lorenzo, 9

What's Nearby: The Basilica San Lorenzo, Laurentian Library and Medici Chapel, the San Lorenzo market and the Medici-Riccardi Palace are close.

The Relic of Saint Antoninous

These sorts of things give me the creeps but I got to see lots of them when traveling in Italy with my (then) 12-year-old son. Boys that age seem to have a quirky fascination with creepy things, and enjoy scaring themselves silly watching horror movies or looking at skeletons and ancient dead bodies behind glass. As such, my boy's radar was finely tuned, and he managed to find multiple Italian churches with relics in them, including this one.

San Marco shows up a few times in this book, as most stories in Florence seem to weave in and around each other. I've talked about the beautiful frescoes in the Cloisters (**Chapter 12: Museums**), Cosimo's library (**Chapter 3: The Medici**) and Savaronola's hangout (**Chapter 8: Piazza della Signoria**). Now we're back again to see one of the inhabitants of the church, San Antoninous, former Archbishop of Florence.

Antoninous was a much-loved fellow who enjoyed the deprivation of a monk's life. In fact, he didn't want to be Archbishop, but the pope threatened to excommunicate him if he refused. So he accepted the position but did it his own way, living the minimalist life instead of enjoying all the trappings that came with the position of pope. When he died his only possessions were some simple pieces of furniture and a mule. St Antoninous died in 1459 and his body stayed exposed (but clothed) for eight days, after which he was buried in full archbishop regalia, in a glass coffin in the Chapel of St Antoninous where he remains today. His mummified body still looks fresh and somewhat perfect – it hasn't decayed or discolored and the flesh hasn't withered away. It isn't a skeleton you see through the glass, (somewhat alarmingly) it is his body, showing no signs of having been there for roughly 560 years.

For me this is the stuff of 1000 nightmares, but for normal people and young boys, seeing old Antoninous in repose can be quite something.

Address: Basilica San Marco, Piazza San Marco

What's Nearby: San Marco is close to Accademia and Piazza SS Annunciata. The Duomo is only a 10 minute walk away.

La Specola Wax Museum

I find this one even more creepy than the doll hospital I told you about in *Glam Italia! 101 Fabulous Things To Do In Rome*.

Full of totally bizarre exhibits, La Specola became one of the first natural science museums open to the general public 250 years ago. It contains many oddities, including stuffed animals from around the globe (even a stuffed hippo that was a Medici family pet), but the really creepy exhibits are the lifelike wax models, spilling their innards.

Anatomists dissected dead bodies, in some cases actually flaying them, and wax specialists made intricate and perfect wax models of everything inside. La Specola has wax brains and lungs and hearts, but more than that, there are entire dissected bodies, each one anatomically perfect. Flayed heads show every nerve, artery, and vein (I can't even name all the parts in there), while women with their insides falling out show perfect reproductions of everything inside of us. There's a guillotined head lolling on its side with skin pulled back, giving you a three-quarter view. If you are in the mood for 10 years of nightmares, there is a reclining skeleton, still juicy-looking and colored as though the meat had only just been sliced off the bones.

I think the Renaissance women are the creepiest exhibits, especially when you look at their facial expressions. One is reclining with her hands in her hair, looking like she's in ecstasy, right up until you see her guts all spilling out.

These three dimensional models are legitimately used by medical schools, giving students a much better knowledge of the inside of a body than they get slicing up a cadaver. The precision with which the wax modelers recreated the insides of the human body is remarkable.

I recommend googling this before going, as visitors have been known to faint. La Specola is a paradise for medical students and serial killers, and is about as quirky and unusual as you can possibly get. If you have the stomach for it a visit here will be unforgettable.

Address: Via Romana, 17

What's Nearby: The Pitti Palace and Boboli Gardens, Ponte Vecchio is 2 minutes away, and if you need a stiff drink after your visit, it's close to Le Volpe e L'Uva.

Search For Dante's Plaques

One way Florentines have preserved and stayed connected to their magnificent history is by attaching plaques to the walls. As you walk the streets of the city, keep an eye out for these commemorative plaques dating back to the thirteenth century, especially those pertaining to Italy's most revered poet, Dante Aligheri. In all there are more than 300 plaques adorning city walls in Florence, 40 of them with lines from Dante's masterpiece *The Divine Comedy*.

The Dante plaques are in the historic city center. For example, on the façade of the Badia Fiorentina just below the Margrave coat of arms, you will find a plaque with lines from Dante's *Paradise*. Now find the other 39!

Once you start looking, finding them becomes quite fun.

The Rose Garden

'You should go up to the Rose Garden and just breathe.'

One of the fun thing about having friends living in your favorite cities is that they have wonderful ideas for things to do while you're in town. My friend Jimmy is a constant source of great ideas, and years ago after I had been buzzing around the city at warp speed, I dropped by his shop to see if he had any suggestions for me before I flew home the next day. There was a breeze blowing that afternoon, so he sent me up to the Rose Garden where I did indeed, just stop and breathe.

The Rose Garden sits behind an inconspicuous gate just below Piazzale Michelangelo, on the hill of San Miniato. Only occupying one hectare (2.4 acres), its verdant slope is home to 400 varieties of roses, a Japanese garden, and other plant life including lemon trees, totaling around 1200 plants in all. This is the kind of chill space where you can bring a book, stretch out on the grass and escape the crowds, all the while taking in the view and breathing in the delicious fragrance of roses and lemons. It really is lovely.

The garden was designed in 1865 by Giuseppe Poggi, who also designed Piazzale Michelangelo and the gardens at the Stibbert Museum.

What's Nearby: This is just below the Piazzale Michelangelo, and San Miniato al Monte. The Bardini Museum is also close by.

Fly with Leonardo

In 1506, Leonardo da Vinci experimented with the concept of flying. He climbed the hill of Monte Ceceri above the town of Fiesole (20 minutes by bus from Santa Maria Novella station) with a set of wings and a volunteer, and put the theory to the test – well, actually the volunteer did. With the wings strapped on, he leapt outward to soar through the sky, but ended up in a heap with a bunch of broken bones.

Although you don't want to try jumping yourself, you can still go up there, take in the view, and find the sign that marks the spot.

Address: Monte Ceceri, Fiesole

Clet Abraham's Street Signs

Keep an eye out and you'll notice some unusual street signs in the heart of Florence. French artist Clet Abraham uses stealth moves to alter common street signs with innovative stickers. A one way street sign becomes Pinocchio's nose, a Do Not Enter sign becomes a bar carried away by *David*, another becomes *Carabinieri in Love* as an officer bends over the bar kissing it. A Dead End sign becomes a crucifix. They are brilliant and funny and irreverent and cool. Before you get annoyed at the desecration know that these are easily removable stickers, and that Clet and his buddies go out at night to apply them, sometimes getting caught in the act and fined. They are fun to stumble upon and definitely warrant a photo.

Clet also has a studio shop in Oltrarno where you can purchase decals, stickers, T-shirts and more.

Address: Via dell'Olmo, 8

What's nearby: The shop is near the Rose Garden, Bardini Museum and Piazzale Michelangelo.

The Face of Berta

Look up at the exterior wall of Santa Maria Maggiore church, and the stone head of a woman embedded in the bricks will be looking down at you. This is Berta, another of Florence's mysteries and the source of some good folk lore about why she is up there, frozen in time.

The first tale dates back to 1326 when an astrologer named Cecco d' Ascoli was paraded through the streets enroute to being burned at the stake for witchcraft. As the procession passed by here he stopped and asked for water. Berta, watching from a little window above, called down a warning to the crowd. She knew he was a wizard who had made a pact with the devil that if anyone gave him water he wouldn't die on the stake. Ascoli was so furious he immediately turned her to stone, trapped forever in the window.

The second story says that Berta was a greengrocer who donated a bell to the church to alert the citizens to the opening and closing of the city gates. The Florentines were so grateful they made a bust of her and put it on the wall of the church.

In all likelihood Berta's head is actually taken from a Roman statue. In the Middle Ages remnants from roman statues were used to decorate buildings. Mind you, other than on via Belle Donne nearby, you don't see too many heads poking out of buildings like this, so maybe it was the curse of Ascoli?

Address: Viccolo di Santa Maria Maggiore, 1

What's Nearby: The Duomo is one block away. Also close are Fiaschetteria Nuvoli for an aperitivo, Basilica San Lorenzo, Medici Chapel, Jimmy's Leather Collection, and San Lorenzo Market.

The Wine Windows of Florence

While walking around Florence keep an eye out for wine windows on the exterior walls of the old palazzi.

In 1559 Cosimo I de' Medici decreed that noble families could sell the wine from their vineyards out of their palaces in the city. Of course nobles didn't want the local riffraff walking into their courtyards, so they thought up a clever alternative – the wine window (*Buchetta del Vino*). These little windows are also called *wine tabernacles*.

Wine windows were at street level on the exterior wall of the palazzo, close to the wine cellar. Instead of glass, they have little wooden doors, so no one could peep inside. The customer would knock on the little door and a servant would get them a glass of wine or a *fiasco*, which was a wicker wine bottle. Some would allow a customer to bring their own bottle to be taken downstairs and filled. The wine was exchanged for cash and everyone was happy. It is fun to think this was just a normal part of everyday life!

Unfortunately, when most of the palazzi were turned into hotels and apartments, the wine windows became a thing of the past. Most are sealed now, but you can still find them around the city. Some have signs saying *Vendita di Vino* on the wall above them, and are still in good condition.

There are 150 wine windows in Florence. The Palazzo Neroni on via dei Ginori has a sealed up *buchetta del vino*. I show my tour travelers the one at the Palazzo Bartolini Salimbeni (via del Giglio, 2) between the Medici Chapel and via dei Banchi. It still looks perfect and has the *Vendita di Vino* sign above it. It makes for a fantastic photo!

Funnily enough endless streams of tourists walk past without even noticing it.

Once you have spotted your first wine window in Florence you will start noticing them all over, especially in the Oltrarno.

The Bull of Santa Maria del Fiore

This is a fun secret to look for on the exterior of the Duomo. The Duomo is covered in decoration, statues and stone masonry. There's so much to see that even after a lifetime of studying the exterior at every possible opportunity I'm still finding new things. If you've already been to Florence and looked at the cathedral, I can almost guarantee you won't have noticed this interesting detail!

On the north side of the cathedral, find the Porta della Mandorla (the door to the dome). Look to the left above the door, and up high on top of one of the columns you will see a bull's head. There are two stories about the bull. The first says it commemorates the oxen that worked during the construction of Brunelleschi's dome. (Nice touch.) The second says that one of the stonemasons working on the cathedral was having an affair with a wealthy merchant's wife. When the cuckolded husband discovered the betrayal he filed a complaint with the ecclesiastical court and ended their affair. The heartbroken stonemason got his revenge by sculpting the bull's head and positioning it so that the animal's horns pointed at the shop of the husband, an eternal reminder of who the wife truly loved.

It can take time to find the head of the bull. I suggest googling it first. It is higher up than you think, but once you have spotted it you will notice the bull every time you walk by!

The Tabernacles of Florence

You will notice religious shrines on the walls all over Florence. Some have frescoes or paintings, some hold statues. Some are huge, others very small. Many celebrate the Madonna, some John the Baptist. Most have glass covering them but even those that don't are still in good shape. These are the tabernacles and there are around 1200 of them in Florence.

Tabernacles date back to the Roman era when little pagan temples to the gods decorated the streets to ensure prosperity, health, and protection of the people. When Emperor Constantine got on board with Christianity, the shrines evolved into images of saints and the holy family.

In Florence, they really got going in the 1200s. Towns and villages took patron saints, Florence choosing the Virgin Mary and Saint John the Baptist. The Cathars and the Waldesians were challenging the doctrines of Catholicism so the church began hunting down heretics. A tabernacle on your wall of the Virgin or Saint John was a great way to show you *weren't* a heretic.

When the plague arrived in Florence in 1348, reducing the population from 120,000 to 50,000, the tabernacles served two purposes. Firstly, the shrines were a comfort to devotees who filled them with candles, prayers and offerings begging the saints to save them. The second purpose was more practical. Priests, fearing that parishioners sitting close together in church would speed the spread of the plague, moved mass to the tabernacles outdoors. There the congregation could stand in the street in the open air, or lean out their windows from safe inside their homes. It must have been a terrifying time.

During the Renaissance, tabernacles became symbols of status. Wealthy homeowners hired the best artists and sculptors to make theirs more beautiful than the neighboring piazza. The less wealthy neighborhoods competed against one another too. An impressive tabernacle with the family name on it could elevate the status of a middle class family. A great example is the gorgeous church of Orsanmichele, in the heart of the historic center. Each guild was given a large niche to decorate with sculptures, and the wealthier guilds hired Donatello, Ghiberti and Verrochio to create theirs. The resulting building is exquisite.

Today some of the city's tabernacles still contain their original art while others have replicas, with the originals held by museums or private collections. Either way, they are lovely to stumble upon and are a beautiful aspect of a city that has more art per square kilometer than any other city in the world.

The Devil's Wind

Walking across the south side of Piazza del Duomo near the via della Studio you may find yourself in a vortex that feels like anything from a cold breeze, to an intense winter wind, to a full on whirlwind. This is the *Rifrullo del Diavolo* (the Devil's Wind), a meteorological phenomenon that of course, has its own legend.

Folklore says centuries ago the devil chased a priest through the streets, trying to steal his soul. (Another version has the priest performing mass outside the cathedral and the Devil showing up in the form of a whirlwind, scaring the crowd away.) Telling the Devil he needed to pray one last time, the priest slipped inside cathedral via the Porta dei Canonici (by the Campanile), and escaped through a door on the other side. Meanwhile the Devil got bored waiting and began to snore, creating the breeze that comes up the via della Studio. When he woke and realized he had been hoodwinked by the priest, he flew into a fury, his breath becoming a whirlwind.

Since then the Devil's Wind has never stopped blowing. You can judge his level of anger on any given day by whether you feel a breeze, a cold wind or a full on whirlwind!

The Strangled Artist of the Duomo

An interesting item hides on the monumentally huge bronze doors of the Duomo. The right hand door was sculpted by an artist named Giuseppe Cassioli. As you look at this incredible door, search for the head of a troubled young man with a snake wrapped around his neck.

During the 10 years it took Cassioli to complete his doors he suffered enormous harassment and criticism, partly for the work itself and partly over the amount of time it was taking to complete. But Cassioli had the last laugh. He sculpted a self-portrait on the door (the troubled young man) immortalizing his detractors in the form of the snake, squeezing the very life out of him.

The Madonna of the UFO

This one involves a little extraterrestrial intrigue in the Hall of Hercules at Palazzo Vecchio. Look for a large tondo measuring about a meter across, featuring the Madonna and Child with Saint John the Baptist. It's quite lovely, right? But there may just be a little more to this painting than meets the eye. Firstly we don't know who painted it. Alternately attributed to Tondo Miller, Bastiano Mainardi and

Arcangelo di Jacopo del Sellaio, no one knows for sure who's work it actually is.

At first glance it looks like any other Renaissance Madonna and Child with Saint John the Baptist. She wears a red dress with a dark cape and he is helping her with baby Jesus. Ho hum. But look over Mary's shoulder and things get interesting. Behind her in the countryside, find the shepherd with his small flock and his dog. Look closely at the shepherd and dog. His hand is raised to his forehead in awe as both he and the dog look up to the sky. Follow the line of their gaze and see what appears to be a B-movie-style flying saucer – a grey, oval object hovers in the sky, emanating golden rays as if moving. Could it really be a UFO? The painting dates to 1510–1520, a time which predates flying machines. Leonardo worked on his ornithopter around 1485 but the skies over Italy in those days were occupied only by birds. So what exactly was going on there?

UFOlogists swear this proves there were UFOs during the Renaissance. Some art historians say the grey object is an angel appearing as a cloud. (I don't see it – they were *realllly* good at painting angels back then, and none of them looked like grey ovals.) Historians also say the shepherd is shielding his eyes from the light of God.

If you visit this painting let me know what you think – a grey-blob angel or the artist's record of seeing a UFO?

Address: Palazzo Vecchio

The Giardino Bardini

Far from the tourist crowds, yet close enough to walk to, the Bardini Garden feels like a gorgeous, secret discovery. This is a great place to seek if you've been to Florence before, or if you're here for several days. I've never seen a crowd here, in fact I've only ever seen a handful of other visitors.

Many tourists know the Boboli Gardens but fabulously few know about this more intimate four hectare space. Here you find little grottos, statues, six fountains decorated with mosaics, a floral explosion of colors, a Wisteria tunnel and a lovely, grand Baroque staircase working its way up the slope to the Kaffeehaus, from which you get a snack accompanied by sweeping views across the city. The staircase was added in the seventeenth century, the statues toward the end of the eighteenth. This is a wonderful spot to sit for a while and catch up on your travel journaling.

AN INTERESTING HISTORY

Although now an oasis of blooms, this greenspace dates back to 1259 when the garden belonged to the Mozzi family. At that time gardens served a purely functional role, providing food for the family. The Mozzi owned much of the hillside, and this particular area was a fruit orchard. The Mozzi lost the property for a while then gained it back in the 1500s and they kept it in the family for more than 300 years until the last family member died in 1880. While they owned it they kept modifying the gardens, adding the staircase, statues and flowers. At one point they bought an adjoining property, adding the Kaffeehaus and its manmade *grotta* (cave).

When the last of the Mozzi died, the property was acquired by Carolath Benten, who transformed it into a Victorian garden. In the early 1900s Stefano Bardini bought the land and its villa, developing them into their present shape. The medieval aspects were lost, but Bardini created a masterpiece of interweaving styles, even including an Anglo-Chinese garden. Bardini added the Belvedere loggia, connecting the two buildings of the Kaffeehaus, running stone pillars from Pistoia along the front, creating a suitably dramatic finale to the grand staircase. When he died his son inherited the garden and turned it over to the city. The Bardini Gardens fell into neglect and disrepair, untouched, overgrown until a massive restoration project in 2000 resurrected the grounds to their current glory.

WHEN TO VISIT

The gardens open each day at the odd hour of 8:15am. If you take an early morning walk through the city (highly recommended), cross the river at the Ponte alle Grazie and come up here at opening time. Enjoy a beautiful view of the city as it comes to life, before the tour buses arrive.

During the summer the Bardini Gardens close at 7:30pm, right around sunset.

THE ENTRANCES

The easiest entrance is via dei Bardi, 1, by the Bardini Museum and Ponte alle Grazie.

The ticket office is in a stone building from where an elevator takes you up to the gardens. When exiting the elevator, look behind you and across the grand sweep of the terracotta rooftops of Florence.

The Costa San Giorgio/Villa Bardini entrance is next to the Fortezza Belvedere and the Boboli Gardens exit.

Address: Costa San Giorgio, 2 OR via dei Bardi, 1

What's Nearby: The Bardini Museum, Piazzale Michelangelo, and San Miniato al Monte are near, and it's not far from the Pitti Palace and the Ponte Vecchio (20 minute walk).

The Astronomical Instruments of Santa Maria Novella

Did you know that the calendar we use today is the product of a Dominican monk from Santa Maria Novella and Cosimo I de' Medici? What's even more interesting, is that to create this calendar they had to eliminate 10 entire days!

To understand this phenomenon we need to go back to the Julian calendar, created in 45 BC by Julius Caesar. Caesar decided a year would be 365 days, 5 hours, 48 minutes and 46 seconds long. This became the basis for the calendar used worldwide for more than 1500 years. Then along came a monk named Ignazio Danti. Danti came from a family of mathematicians and scholars. His grandfather was interested in astronomy and his father made astrological instruments and surveying instruments. He had uncles and an aunt who were incredibly accomplished in mathematics and literature, and his brother Vincenzo became a famous sculptor. (Vincenzo's most famous work is the sculpture of the *Beheading of John the Baptist* up the street at The Bapistery.)

Growing up, Ignazio learned the fundamentals of architecture and astronomy, painting and literature. He spent time in artist's studios and read manuals on the mathematical theory of perspective. His family had a substantial library themselves and published much literature. He too published nine important works. While at the monastery of Santa Maria Novella Ignazio worked on maps for

Cosimo I de' Medici, sharing his astronomical theories with him. Cosimo I funded Ignazio's construction of two astronomical quadrants, placed on either side of the main doors of the Basilica Santa Maria Novella. (They are still there.) With these he determined the length of the year and the equinoxes, which became the basis of the Gregorian calendar, the one we use today.

Danti calculated that the Julian calendar was off by 11 minutes per year. Using his astronomical quadrant and the armillary sphere affixed to the front of the church, he figured out when the spring equinox really occurred. The start date of the Gregorian calendar was October 4, 1582. On this date, 10 days were dropped from the previous system, making the second day of the new calendar October 15, 1582. This corrected the accumulating 11 minute error from Julius Caesar's calendar.

Ignazio Danti's astrological instruments are still on the front façade of Santa Maria Novella, although most people have no idea what they are and just walk right on past! We have many things to thank the Medici for, but who knew the calendar would be one of them?

Spectacular Churches

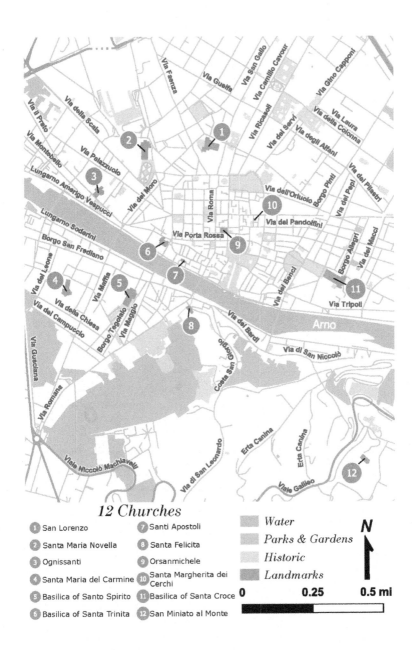

12 Churches

1. San Lorenzo
2. Santa Maria Novella
3. Ognissanti
4. Santa Maria del Carmine
5. Basilica of Santo Spirito
6. Basilica of Santa Trinita
7. Santi Apostoli
8. Santa Felicita
9. Orsanmichele
10. Santa Margherita dei Cerchi
11. Basilica of Santa Croce
12. San Miniato al Monte

Water
Parks & Gardens
Historic
Landmarks

N

0   0.25   0.5 mi

14.

11 Spectacular Churches in Florence

1. Basilica Santa Croce
2. Santa Maria Novella
3. Chiesa di Ognissanti
4. Santa Trinita'
5. Santo Spirito
6. Santa Maria del Carmine (and the Brancacci Chapel)
7. Santa Felicita'
8. Basilica San Miniato al Monte
9. Santi Apostoli
10. Santa Margherita dei Cerchi
11. Orsanmichele
12. Basilica San Lorenzo

Florence has many churches, and as much as Santa Maria del Fiore has no equal in *exteriors,* I believe many have more interesting *interiors.*

People often tell me they aren't Catholic, aren't religious, or don't want to spend time in churches. I talk to people of opposing faith or no faith who also don't see the point in visiting churches. I tell everyone the same thing: it doesn't matter your faith or lack thereof, visiting the churches in Florence isn't an attempt at religious conversion. It is a cornerstone component of learning, experiencing and understanding the culture and history of this spectacular city. So you should visit at least a couple.

Through church art, you can track the movement of fashion across the centuries, from colors, styles and fabrics worn, to the changing hair styles and representations of beauty. When the average resident of Florence couldn't read or write, this art was a visual representation of the stories of life here. Yes, they were telling Bible stories, but look a little deeper and you will discover the human history of Florence.

Florence and her churches have been intertwined since the beginning. This is a city of beauty and art indivisible. Much of that art and beauty lives inside the churches, and you need to see it.

TIME MANAGEMENT

When traveling most of us have limited time in any given place. Chances are you may have only a day or two in Florence, so maximizing your time is essential. When I see lines of people wrapped around the Duomo waiting to get in, I see it as a colossal waste of time. Not to disparage the Duomo, but *spending ages in a line to anything* seems crazy to me, especially when there are so many other equally impressive places you could visit.

Even crazier is that the staggeringly beautiful churches on the list below, with the sole exceptions of Santa Croce and maybe San Lorenzo, generally have no line at all. I have never waited more than 15 minutes to get inside Santa Croce.

Obviously, entire books have been written about each of these churches and the art within. So here, I'm aiming to introduce you to them, hopefully entice you to pop into some (or all), and direct you to a handful of things to look for while you're there. Some have pamphlets to guide you, others don't. All are operational churches, so may have services happening when you arrive.

One of my absolute favorite churches in Florence, the church of SS Annunziata, is not on this list only because it is in **Chapter 5: Piazza SS Annunziata**. I consider it a *must-see* in Florence.

Some churches on this list are quite small and don't require much time. Others, such as Basilica San Lorenzo, really do require a decent investment of time. By reading through this chapter you can figure out which ones will work with your schedule and then you can plan your time accordingly. There will be churches on this list you probably haven't heard of before, but trust me, they are well worth visiting.

The Basilica Santa Croce

If you only go inside one church in Florence, let this be the one. This is my favorite church in Florence, and one of my favorite churches anywhere in the world. I tell anyone who will listen that Basilica Santa Croce has the best church art in all of Tuscany. (Just between you and me, I haven't actually been inside *every* church in Tuscany so there is a chance I'm wrong, but it gets the point across – this church is phenomenal.)

The Basilica Santa Croce is the largest Franciscan church in the world, and may have been founded by Saint Francis himself. The original structure dates back to 1212, when Saint Francis visited Florence with his followers, setting up shop outside the city walls on a pretty inhospitable stretch of marshy land. The current structure was built on top of the old one in around 1294. It takes the shape of the tau cross (or Egyptian cross), the symbol of Saint Francis. The church wasn't consecrated until 1442.

Chapels in churches like these were bought and paid for by wealthy families as a way to show off their largess and importance. In a single move they could let the world know they were dirty rich *and* appease God for sins they never stopped committing. Santa Croce has 16 sensational frescoed chapels, plenty of them painted by Giotto and his students. What could be better than hiring the pre-eminent painter of the time to glorify and eternalize your family name? Most of these frescoes date back to the late 1300s.

Allow yourself time to wander the little chapels and look at the frescoes. Some have recently been restored, some are faded, some are irreparable. Plaques explain the art but I always end up googling more info on my phone too.

CRUCIFIXES

There are a couple of significant crucifixes to look for. In the Bardi Chapel at the far left of the chancel is Donatello's fantastic *Farmer's Crucifix* (1406). Brunelleschi said the rustic, peasant-like face looked like a farmer. I love it because while religious art looked so perfect and untouchable, this piece looks so down to earth. I wonder if parishioners back then could in some way identify with him?

In the refectory you'll find Cimabue's achingly beautiful crucifix from the 1280s. Largely destroyed by the flood of 1966 it will never be returned to its former glory, but still is a *must-see* for art lovers. The weight of Christ's body drops away to the side, causing a tension in his outstretched arms so palpable you can feel it. Be sure to google images of the crucifix before the flood. Somehow the weight of the wood swelling in the flood and the paint it lost make it even more dramatic, and the strain on Christ's body even greater.

THE NIGHT CREW

Basilica Santa Croce is the final resting place for some pretty significant characters in Florentine history. If the ghosts get up at night and have dinner parties, the conversation must be fascinating! For starters, Michelangelo is here, as are Rossini, Galileo and Macchiavelli. The city tried to bring Dante's bones back here but he is still buried in Ravenna so his sarcophagus remains empty.

THE PAZZI WERE HERE

The villainous Pazzi family have a freestanding chapel here at Santa Croce, built to show their wealth and power, second only to that of their arch rivals, the Medici.

Construction on this early Renaissance masterpiece began in 1442 and was completed in 1443. Thought to be the work of Brunelleschi, this space is magnificent. The chapel was built within existing walls so instead of the usual square shape, it's a rectangle. There is a very geometric feel to it, almost a classic Roman style. Instead of frecoes the walls are cool, clear *pietra serena*, giving a calming quality to the space. It has a hemispheric dome with an oculus and little side portal windows, that allow a really lovely light to stream into the chapel. The chapel was originally a chapter house, where monks came to learn and have lectures. With that in mind the serenity and clarity of the space make complete sense. It is ordered and rational, made more so by the geometry you see all around you.

The tondi of the apostles are by Luca della Robbia, whose work is also seen in the porch cupola. It is also thought that Donatello may have done the roundels of the Evangelists.

THE BARONCELLI CHAPEL

My Glam Italia Tour travelers who have watched the Medici TV show always enjoy seeing the Baroncelli Chapel inside the Basilica.

The chapel is renowned for Taddeo Gaddi's incredible *Life of the Virgin*. Gaddi (1290–1366) used what were then experimental architectural backgrounds, which we now call *still life*. The artwork is gorgeous and not to be overlooked.

However, perhaps the more exciting claim to fame is its namesake. The Baroncelli name is connected to one of the most heinous crimes in all of Florentine history, the murder of Giuliano de' Medici. (I talk about this in **Chapter 3: The Medici**.) In short, the Pazzi and the pope decided to murder Lorenzo the Magnificent and Giuliano de' Medici at Easter, and Guiliano was stabbed and killed by Bernardo Baroncelli inside the Duomo. In Italy, Easter is the holiest and most revered holiday, even more so than Christmas, so committing murder inside the cathedral at Easter took crime and barbarianism to an entirely new level.

The murder happened a long time after the Baroncelli chapel was created, but even so, if you are a follower of Medici–Pazzi history, you'll find the Basilica Santa Croce fascinating.

OTHER INTERESTING THINGS

- You must walk through the cloisters at Santa Croce. They are beautiful and peaceful. When the tourist crowds get too much for me in Florence this is one of my hideouts. It is also a lovely spot to escape the midsummer heat and enjoy the breeze and some shade.

- The polychrome marble façade of Basilica Santa Croce was added in 1863, and paid for by English benefactor Sir Frances Sloane.
- The 78-meter-tall bell tower, located in the cloister to the right of the church, stood unfinished for more than 100 years. The original tower collapsed in 1512 but the build of the new one ran out of funds and wasn't finished until the 1800s.
- I have a list of private tour guides in Florence, some of whom specialize in the art inside these churches. You can download a copy of the list at **www.glamitaliabooks.com/florenceguides**

What's Nearby: The leather school is behind the Basilica. Palazzo Vecchio, the Bargello and my favorite restaurant, Francesco Vini, are all within a couple of blocks along Borgo dei Greci.

Santa Maria Novella

This church is, in my opinion, under-rated and under-visited – which makes it my kind of place! It also happens to be spectacular.

Dominican Friars built this church between 1279 and 1357. The striped marble façade was completed in 1470 making this the only church in Florence with its original façade still in place. (Other churches were completed centuries later with newer designs, and some, like the nearby Basilica San Lorenzo, ran out of money altogether and never received their marble façade.)

SIT IN THE PIAZZA

The piazza in front of the church is lovely. Over the past few years all the apartment buildings surrounding it became hotels, so you don't see as many locals going about their daily lives anymore. Still, be sure to take time to sit and listen to the street musicians while soaking in the beauty of the church exterior.

If you're interested in architecture you will find this fascinating:

The façade had been partially built when the church's patron, Giovanni Rucellai, brought in Leon Battista Alberti to complete it. Alberti had a classic aesthetic. He liked buildings to conform to the Roman and Greek ideals of beauty, displaying rational order, perfect geometry and a sense of proportion. So right off the bat he had a problem – this was a gothic church, and gothic architecture is anything *but* orderly.

So he created a Romanesque façade, similar to the Baptistery just down the street. (Look for the alternating white and green *serpentine* marbles and an orderly use of geometry.) Not only was the structure gothic, but a portion of the façade had already been completed in gothic style. We don't know exactly how much, but look for six small gothic arches along the bottom portion, these are actually tombs. Alberti created harmony by changing the façade into a square shape, or two squares on top of each other. He gave the lower half a Corinthian column at each end, squaring the edges with a striped pier. The original center door was smaller too, so the main door was widened and modeled on the Pantheon in Rome. On either side of the doorway are two smaller doors with pointy gothic arches above them, so we can assume the original main door was similar. Alberti softened the upper portion of the façade with what looks like a Greek temple – a triangular pediment supported by four pilasters. A horizontal frieze of 15 decorated squares separates the top from the bottom, creating harmony and making your eye look for an overall square shape. Alberti hid the high gothic nave of the church and joined the top and bottom by placing a swirling scroll on either side of the temple.

It really is ingenious. I love sitting in the piazza listening to the musicians, while searching for the shapes in the façade, seeing how cleverly it was put together. There is much more to look for on the exterior, including an item in **Chapter 13: Unusual & Interesting Things**, but assuming you don't have all day, let's go inside.

THE INTERIOR

Santa Maria Novella is huge. The nave is 100 meters long, the ceiling seems to burst upward, it feels incredibly high and quite austere. But it's not. This church is an absolute treasure trove of art. This church holds works by Giotto, Brunelleschi, Filippino Lippi and Ghirlandaio just to name a few. Art lovers should allow plenty of time to walk the chapels and take it all in.

I've come here before, planning to spend an hour, and somehow managed to lose an entire day. Other times I've stop in briefly – I would rather spend an hour here than miss out altogether. Although I know I'll be back in Florence again soon a part of my brain always worries that this might be my last chance.

If you don't have much time, or are not quite so art obsessed, these are the pieces you mustn't miss:

- **Giotto's Crucifix.** Suspended in space, 19 feet tall and surrounded by air, Giotto's Crucifix hangs in the central nave, a sobering reminder to parishioners that Christ died for their sins. This is one of Giotto's early works (1288–89) and is both beautiful and jarring, almost as if to ground your thoughts before your brain explodes with all the art in the rest of this space.

- **Brunelleschi's Crucifix.** This wooden crucifix is in the Gondi Chapel and according to Vasari was a direct response to Donatello's Crucifix in Santa Croce, which Brunelleschi said looked like 'a farmer on a cross'. Brunelleschi wanted to show Christ as a man, yet still majestic. Look for the beautiful inclination of Christ's head and the realistic musculature of his body. The piece is captivating.

- **Ghirlandaio's frescoes** and stained glass in the Tornabuoni Chapel. The scenes of the *Life of the Virgin* and the *Life of John the Baptist* feature prominent figures from Florentine society at the time.

- **Paolo Ucello's *Life of Noah*** in the Green Cloister.

- **Filippino Lippi's frescoes** and stained glass in the Strozzi Chapel from 1502 feature scenes from the lives of St Philip and St John the Evangelist.

- In 1565 Cosimo I had Vasari helm a restoration program at Santa Maria Novella. They rebuilt the **Gaddi Chapel** and had it frescoed by Alessandro Allori.

- **Masaccio's Trinity.** Located halfway down the left aisle this was the first painting to use linear perspective. This was a new style of painting and caused great excitement. People flocked to see the fresco that turned a flat wall into a chapel. A nail under the cross with strings running from it became Massaccio's vanishing point. You can still see the marks from both. Considered his masterpiece, the work depicts his patrons, the Berti family, kneeling on either side of the archway. Below them is a tomb with a skeleton and an epigram in latin saying:

I was once what you are, and what I am you will become.

THE CLOISTERS

When visiting churches in Florence I always make time to walk the cloisters. Beautiful and peaceful, they give your brain a break from the overabundance of art inside, but often you'll find more incredible frescoes out here.

These cloisters were built around 1340. They access the Refectory, the Spanish Chapel, the Large Cloisters and at one time the entrance to the pharmacy of the monks was from the south side of the cloisters. (Now the entrance is on Via della Scala.)

Turn right as you step out of the church into the Green Cloister (*Chiostro Verde*) named for the green clay the artists used. Here you'll see some of the greatest work by Renaissance master Paolo Ucello, *The Flood* and *The Sacrifice of Noah*.

The Green Cloister also accesses the Strozzi Chapel and the Choistrino dei Morti

THE SPANISH CHAPEL

Just beyond the Green Cloister is the Spanish Chapel. Built between 1345 and 1355 it was originally a chapter house built for tax collector Mico Guidalotti, who donated a huge sum for the walls to be covered in frescoes. He died before they were begun, but ten years later Andrea di Bonaiuto was hired to paint the frescoes, telling stories of Jesus, Saint Thomas Aquinas, and the Dominican monks. In 1566 Eleanora, the lovely wife of Cosimo I de' Medici, began using this exquisitely decorated space as a chapel for her Spanish court.

Look for the image of the completed cathedral – at the time it was painted, the Duomo was still under construction.

Don't miss a visit here – the artwork is astounding.

What's Nearby: Santa Maria Novella is opposite the train station and less than five minutes from San Lorenzo. Also nearby are the Officina Profumo Farmaceutica and Ognissanti. Take time to wander the streets here, there are endless wonderful little shops and eateries. Photograph the doorways and Renaissance streets and soak up this fantastic neighborhood!

Chiesa di Ognissanti

This church is incredible to visit anytime, but when Florence is bursting at the seams with tourists I love it even more because *there is no one here!* It never ceases to amaze me that one small city can get so over-crowded, yet have so many spectacular places with scarcely a soul inside.

In 1627 this Church of All Saints became one of the first examples of Baroque architecture to penetrate the Renaissance face of Florence.

But its history goes back well before the Baroque. Ognissanti was built in the 1250s for a religious order called the Umiliati. Instrumental in developing the wool industry in Florence, their order had learned the wool business and techniques for improving the quality and durability of cloth while they'd been exiled in Germany a century or so before.

By the early 1300s the Umiliati began amassing artwork in their otherwise simple church. In 1310 Giotto painted the *Madonna and Child with Angels* for the high altar (now displayed in the Uffizi) and during recent cleaning and restoration they discovered he also worked on the crucifix in the left transept.

In the fifteenth century, frescoes were painted by Ghirlandaio and Botticelli, who is buried here near his beloved Simonetta Vespucci. In 1480 the two artists completed works facing each other across the nave. Botticelli's *Saint Augustine in his Study* balances Ghirlandaio's *Saint Jerome in his Study*. This was the Vespucci family parish church. In 1472 Davide and Domenico Ghirlandaio painted the frescoes in the Vespucci Chapel, including the must see *Madonna of the Misericordia*. Under the Madonna's arm, next to a man in a red robe, the face of a young boy looks out. This is Amerigo Vespucci, the explorer, navigator and cartographer for whom America was named.

During the sixteenth century, the Franciscans took over the church bringing precious relics including a robe worn by Saint Francis.

THE REFECTORY

A side door accesses the cloisters and refectory. For 300 years the Umiliati took their meals in this room. Later, under Cosimo I's protection, the Franciscans ate here too.

The refectory contains Ghirlandaio's breathtaking *Last Supper*, painted in 1480. I would walk clear across the city just to see this fresco. Actually, frequently I do!

THE CLOISTERS

Once again, not to be missed. Recently I ran into a lady in the cloisters, cellphone in hand, tears streaming down her face. Thinking something must be wrong I offered to help her, but it turned out she was just completely overwhelmed by Ognissanti, the artwork, the cloisters and the fact that there were only the two of us out here wandering around, taking photos. This was only moments after I had texted my mother (in the middle of the night New Zealand time) with the exact same sentiment – how on Earth could it be that in a city bursting with tourists, I was here in this extraordinary place with almost no one else around?

Address: Piazza Ognissanti, 42

What's Nearby: Santa Maria Novella is close. Epoca vintage store is a block or so away, as is Ponte alla Carraia bridge and the famous gelato store. Ognissanti shares the piazza with the Westin Excelsior if you're in the mood for a rooftop aperitivo.

Santa Trinita'

This is an example of why you should duck into any church you walk by, just in case there is something magical inside. Years ago while wandering around here totally lost, I spotted this church and popped in for a quick look. I was and still am overwhelmed by the artwork I found. Since then I visit Santa Trinita' whenever I can.

THE BACK STORY

Santa Trinita' was founded in the eleventh century, by the Vallombrosan Benedictine monks. Back then it was outside the city walls, but when the second city walls were built in 1172–1173 the church was incorporated into the city. The Vallombrosans liked austerity and simple Romanesque churches. In the 1300s the church underwent a 100 year restoration, enlarging and gussying it up, Gothic style. You can see some of the original building on the back side of the front facade, as they only refitted the outside. The current, Mannerist exterior was designed by Bernardo Buontalenti in 1593.

The Strozzi palazzo is just up the street, and at one time this was their family church.

THE ART

Santa Trinita' has 20 chapels and I suggest walking them all. At a minimum, make sure you see the following:

The Sassetti Chapel

This is perhaps the most significant chapel of them all. Francesco Sassetti was not only independently wealthy, he was also director of the Medici Bank. Since the fourteenth century the Sassetti family had a chapel at Santa Maria Novella. The Dominicans refused Francesco's proposal to paint a fresco cycle of the life of Saint Francis, so in 1478 he *acquired* this chapel in Santa Trinita'. On December 1480 he hired Florence's most sought after painter, Domenico Ghirlandaio, to paint his Saint Francis story. Work didn't start until 1483 and was completed in 1486. These frescoes are said to be Ghirlandaio's greatest works. They are spectacular. The fresco cycle takes up three walls and tell six stories of Saint Francis. In a fun twist, many of the faces of the people in the frescoes were members of contemporary Florentine society at the time.

Sassetti and his wife's tombs are in the side walls of the chapel. Their portraits are painted kneeling on either side of the *Adoration of the Shepherds* altarpiece, she on the left and he on the right.

The Bartolini Salimbeni Chapel

This one has a Lorenzo Monaco fresco cycle of *The Life of The Virgin* from the 1420s. These are some of very few examples of International Gothic style frescoes in all of Italy. The cycle was commissioned by the Bartolini family and actually covers another set of frescoes by Spinello Aretino, thought to have been painted in 1390.

The Doni Chapel

This one has sumptuous frescoes by Bicci di Lorenzo.

The Spini Chapel

My favorite thing here is the life sized statue of Magdalene by Desiderio da Settignano. It is similar to Donatello's statue of *The Penitent Magdalene* in the Opera del Duomo Museum, except she doesn't look old or toothless. She does however look bedraggled and gaunt. This could be the Mary who legend says lived in a cave in Marseille after the crucifixion. It is a fantastic work.

What's Nearby: The Salvatore Ferragamo Museum, Strozzi Palace, and the Ponte Santa Trinita' are close. Piazza della Repubblica is a five minute walk.

Santo Spirito

Cross Ponte Santa Trinita', head up a couple of blocks, turn right at via dei Michelozzi and within moments you'll be in one of the coolest piazzas in all of Florence, Piazza Santo Spirito.

This is a great place to chill out on a hot day. Bars and eateries line the piazza, two weekends per month it becomes an outdoor market, and at the top end of the piazza there's an unassuming building, the church of Santo Spirito. This is one of the last Brunelleschi-designed churches. When he died, only one column had been raised.

Entering the church you notice how geometric it is, circles and squares in perfect order. It feels clean and clear, creamy white walls balanced with columns, cornices, and moldings of *pietra serena* green-grey marble. Everything is in proportion. You see Brunelleschi's love of ancient Roman architecture here, his columns are smooth instead of fluted but the style is classical. It reminds me of the Pazzi Chapel at Santa Croce, even the dome feels familiar.

MICHELANGELO'S CRUCIFIX

There is a great story that goes with this church. In 1489 Lorenzo de Medici moved young Michelangelo into the Medici palace, raising him as his own son. Michelangelo lived protected under his patronage until Lorenzo's death in 1492.

The Medici were then exiled from Florence and (depending on which biography you read) the 17-year-old artist was either left orphaned or returned to his father's house. One story, the one I'm going with, has him taken in by the monks, who let him live here in the convent of Santo Spirito. The monks ran the convent hospital and Michelangelo wanted to learn how the insides of the human body worked, so he made a deal – if they allowed him to spend his nights carving up and studying the dead bodies in the hospital, he would make them a crucifix.

The wooden sculpture features a completely naked Jesus. It's fascinating to see how 17-year-old Michelangelo rendered the human body. The musculature of his later work isn't yet present, Jesus' body is almost boyish. For Michelangelo this was just the beginning.

Michelangelo's Crucifix is suspended from the ceiling in a side chapel. Life-sized, and with suitably spooky lighting in a chapel with nothing else around it, it is haunting. And completely brilliant. Add Michelangelo's Crucifix to your must-see list.

THE CLOISTERS

Once again the cloisters are a lovely place to escape the crowds and the heat of summer as you wander and take in the frescoes. Of course, there won't be tour groups here either, it's just you and maybe a sprinkling of artists and like-minded travelers.

What's Nearby: Pitti Palace and Ponte Vecchio are each a five minute walk away. Giuliano Ricchi Jewelry is at the opposite end of the piazza, Palazzo Guadagni's rooftop bar is here in the piazza. Although it feels a world away from the tourist madness, Ponte Santa Trinita' is only one bridge down from Ponte Vecchio, so you're only five minutes from the masses.

Santa Maria del Carmine, The Brancacci Chapel

This is another church you'd walk right past if you didn't know about the treasure inside. It's unfinished unassuming façade reminds me of San Lorenzo, and like San Lorenzo it is surprisingly enormous inside. Santa Maria del Carmine has some of the greatest frescoes of the early Renaissance, so for art lovers it'll be a highlight.

THE HISTORY

The Carmelite were one of the four thirteenth century *mendicant* (begging) orders, along with the Franciscans, Augustines and Dominicans. All four founded large churches in Florence. Santa Maria del Carmine's construction began in 1268. There were three renovations between 1328 and the 1550s, then it caught fire in 1771. Most of it was destroyed, but by some miracle the Brancacci and Corsini chapels survived, although the frescoes were damaged.

INSIDE

In 1782 the interior had a Baroque renovation. I'm not a big Baroque fan but this is quite cool. I once read that the ceilings were 'vertigo-inducing' so of course had to go inside and look up. The ceilings are striking and enormous, and if you look at them for a long time – it's hard not to – you do feel a little off kilter!

THE BRANCACCI CHAPEL

If you love Renaissance frescoes I promise you this is something you need to see. These are among the greatest examples of early Renaissance painting in all of Florence. Commissioned in 1424 by Felice Brancacci (whose uncle Piero, a wealthy silk merchant, left the money to build the chapel in his will), the frescoes tell the story of Saint Peter, the uncle's name saint. (Saint Peter is the fellow in orange.)

Masolino began painting in 1424, joined by his pupil Masaccio the following year. He then went to Hungary for three years, leaving Masaccio to work on the frescoes alone. In 1428 Masaccio went to Rome, dying later that year at only 27. Work stopped on the frescoes from 1434–1480 while Brancacci was exiled for supporting his father in law Palla Strozzi. Strozzi, the wealthiest man in Florence, joined Rinaldo degli Albizi's plan to overthrow Cosimo de' Medici, the most powerful political figure in town. Cosimo was imprisoned then exiled, but returned a year later and had *them* exiled. Neither Albizzi nor Strozzi ever returned. (Strozzi's son did in 1480 and built the huge Strozzi palace.)

Meanwhile Brancacci's will instructed his heirs to finish the chapel's frescoes. In the interim, the chapel was renamed and the part of the fresco featuring the Brancacci family was destroyed. By 1474 the Brancacci family were back in good graces. Filippino Lippi completed the frescoes from 1481 to 1485. Not only did he complete Masaccio's work but he added his own, *The Crucifixion of Saint Peter* and *The Disputation with Simon Magus*.

THE DESTRUCTION

Mindbendingly, in 1746 Florentine painter Vincenzo Meucci painted over Masolino's ceiling frescoes and those immediately below, in the process destroying Masolino's *Evangelists*. (Meucci also 'restored' *The Marriage of the Virgin* by Rosso at San Lorenzo, totally jacking that work up too. His handiwork at San Lorenzo was finally fixed in 2014.) In 1746 the prior in charge of the Brancacci Chapel ordered a big marble altar be mounted on the back wall, over the 300 year old frescoes. He also had a window cut into the wall, destroying even more.

RESTORATIONS

In 1771 a huge fire destroyed the church. The Brancacci Chapel survived but had considerable damage. Frescoes were blackened by soot and the paints containing iron were damaged by the searing heat, making the colors shift. Large chunks of plaster fell to the floor. The frescoes were restored after the fire and then again around 1904. Regrettably they coated the paintings with an egg-based lacquer (which was common practice at the time as it was thought to add vibrancy to fading colors). Unfortunately this egg wash left a murky, cloudy film over the frescoes that not only molded but also attracted dust, candle smoke, cigarette smoke and, in time, pollution from traffic.

Around 1980 Professor Baldini began a major restoration. Convinced there were frescoes hiding behind the marble altar, now a 200 year old part of the chapel, he convinced the Ministry of Fine Arts to let him remove it. Baldini was correct. Behind the altar was the original gothic window with a vertical ribbon of painting on either side of the frame. Each ribbon had the head of a boy, one painted by Masolino and the other by Masaccio! He also found fragments of the lost *Crucifixion of Saint Peter*. The marble altar had protected these works from both the fire and the egg wash. Furthermore the restorers were able to see precisely which colors to aim for to get the restoration exactly right.

DON'T MISS THESE

The frescoes in the Brancacci Chapel are vibrant and radiant. The chapel is small but I suggest allowing time to take it in. Two paintings to look for are the serenely beautiful *Temptation of Adam and Eve* by Masolino, juxtaposed with the tortured, aching *Expulsion of Adam and Eve From Paradise* by Masaccio. There is something so haunting in Adam's pain as he covers his face while leaving Eden.

Address: Piazza del Carmine

What's Nearby: Close to Santo Spirito and the vintage clothing store Recollection by Albrici. Have an aperitivo at Il Santino, before wandering up Borgo San Jacopo to the Ponte Vecchio.

Santa Felicita'

While we're in Oltrarno I want to draw your attention to this little church. Thought to be one of the oldest churches in Florence, second only to Basilica San Lorenzo, Santa Felicita' was dedicated to a Roman widow martyred with her seven sons in 165 AD.

At some point in the second century Syrian Greek merchants brought Christianity to Florence and settled here on the south side of the river. The first church was built on this site in the late fourth century. It was rebuilt in the eleventh century and again in 1736. If you've been to Florence before you've probably walked right past it (in my case multiple times) not knowing it was there.

The Vasari Corridor runs across the façade of the church, connecting Palazzo Vecchio to Pitti Palace. On the inside this secret passageway had a large window with a grate that allowed them to attend mass without being seen. Some say it was so they didn't have to mingle with the great unwashed, but I like to think it was self-preservation. (Less than 100 years prior, Giuliano de' Medici was murdered at Easter mass in the Duomo, so churches weren't necessarily a safe place for the family.)

Entering the church immediately to your right is the Brunelleschi-designed Capponi Chapel, with one of the absolute masterpieces of sixteenth century painting, *The Deposition* by Pontormo. Don't be lulled into comfort by the pretty colors, stop and look more closely. Normally a deposition shows the cross, telling you Christ has been taken down from his crucifixion. Here the cross is absent, and in its place a frenzy of motion and grief. With no vanishing point, the eye doesn't know where to go, so gets caught up in the movement. The faces aren't ethereal or stylized, instead they are *anguished*. Look for Mary, so overwrought she looks to be reeling backward, about to faint. For me the eyes of the two boys supporting the body are haunting, their expression of grief and bewilderment both palpable and soul stirring. This is the chapel's altarpiece, but to its right is another Pontormo fresco, *The Annunciation*. Archangel Gabriel tells Mary she will carry the son of God. Again there's a swirling feeling, from the tilt of Gabriel's head and shoulders, to Mary's body turning back to him. They could almost be floating in a circle. The two paintings are bookends to Christ's life, but the placement is odd. Don't you think *The Annunciation* should precede *The Deposition* and be to its left? Visit this church and see for yourself.

In the eighteenth century the cupola was lowered, destroying other frescoes that lived here. You'll also find works here by Taddeo Gaddi and Francesco di Antonio.

What's Nearby: Ponte Vecchio, the Pitti Palace and Boboli Gardens are right here. To the left of the church is the Costa di San Giorgio, the street Galileo lived on (his house was #9). At the end of this road is the Porta San Giorgio, the oldest remaining gate in the city. From here you can head up to Piazzale Michelangelo and San Miniato Al Monte.

Basilica San Miniato al Monte

A short (but steep) walk from Piazzale Michelangelo brings you to one of the most beautiful churches in all of Florence, San Miniato Al Monte. Construction began in 1013 on the site of the shrine to Miniato, a martyred Armenian prince serving in the Roman army. In 250 AD Emperor Decius, while camped outside of Florence, had Miniato thrown into the amphitheater to be eaten by a panther. The panther wouldn't eat him, so Decius had him beheaded. Legend says Miniato picked up his own severed head and walked across the Arno to this very spot.

One of the finest examples of classic Romanesque churches in all of Italy, the grey-green and white façade of San Miniato has watched over Florence for 1000 years. No doubt the inspiration for the facades of Basilicas Santa Croce and Santa Maria Novella, San Miniato exhibits perfect geometry, perfect symmetry. The façade was begun in 1090 but the upper portion was completed later, possibly in the twelfth century. On top of the church is a huge eagle holding bags of wool in his talons, the symbol of the wool guild, who were responsible for the church from 1288.

San Miniato's interior is exquisite. The patterned marble floor dates to 1207 and the wooden ceilings have been repainted in their original colors. The space is dominated by a huge fourteenth century golden mosaic showing Jesus flanked by the Virgin on one side and Saint

Minias on the other, offering his earthly crown up to the heavens. The walls are covered with 800 year old frescoes depicting the life of Saint Benedict.

Inside, the church happens on three levels. The upper level represents the universe, the ground level is the Earth, and the crypt represents death. Built between 1018 and 1063 the crypt is mostly in its original state. The original high altar is still here along with relics of Saint Minias. Be sure to look at the seven marble panels on the floor. Roped off to stay protected, the panels date to the very early 1200s.

San Miniato Al Monte is a functioning Benedictine monastery. In summer, the monks sing the Gregorian chant each day at around 5:30pm (check times beforehand). Required to do manual work the Benedictine monks make artisanal products which they sell in the little shop here. From ice creams to cakes and biscuits (cookies), beeswax candles and honey, it's all made right here.

The beautiful cloister attached to the church, dates back to the mid-1400s. The bishop's palace was built in 1295 but over the centuries has been used as a hospital and as barracks. Michelangelo designed a defensive wall to protect the church during the siege, and in 1553 Cosimo I de' Medici expanded these into a fortress. The cemetery here, the Cimiterio della Porta Sante, is also worth a look.

What's Nearby: Piazzale Michelangelo, the Rose Garden, Iris Garden and Giardini Bardini are close. Chiesa San Salvatore Al Monte is worth visiting for the stained glass windows and (of course) the art. Walk down the hill to the river and be sure to explore the little streets of Oltrarno, enjoy an aperitivo or have a bite to eat. It is lovely over here.

Santi Apostoli

I found this one by accident several years ago, ducking down a side street to escape umbrella-waving guides leading hordes of tourists from the Porcellino Market to the Ponte Vecchio. This is one of my escape routes for my little group of travelers, if I haven't timed it quite right to avoid the arrival of the tour buses. From the Porcellino Market take your third right onto Borgo Santi Apostoli. Keep your eyes peeled walking this ancient *via*. It tells stories of the Romans, Charlemagne, Michelangelo, the Middle Ages, and the Crusades – loads of history waits silently to be discovered.

This stood outside the original city walls. With the land too unstable and close to the river and the Roman Baths, it was difficult to defend. Once filled in and solid enough to build on it was included inside the second set of city walls.

Legend says the church was founded by Charlemagne in the 800s, although historians attribute it to the eleventh century. Remodels happened in the fifteenth and sixteenth centuries, with Michelangelo intervening to preserve the church rather than rebuild it.

ROMANESQUE

Thanks to Michelangelo preventing its modernization, Santi Apostoli is one of Florence's best preserved Romanesque churches.

It follows the simplicity of the Romanesque floor plan, and has a tranquil, simple interior. Very intimate and a little solemn, this church makes a drastic change from the huge basilicas dotting the city. The walls aren't adorned with frescoes, but instead there are some individual artworks worth seeing, including a terracotta tabernacle by della Robbia. Be sure to look up – the wooden ceiling added in 1333 is richly and beautifully hand painted. The original mosaic floor has been restored and the green marble columns from Prato are topped with Corinthian capitals, probably taken from the Roman Baths nearby.

THE SACRED STONES

The church has several artifacts but the most revered, most deeply steeped in legend, are the *Pietre del Santo Sepolcro*, gifted by Pazzino dei Pazzi in 1101, on his return from the crusades. Supposedly these stones were used to light the lamps of the tomb when Jesus was buried. Each year they are used to ignite the fireworks display known as *Lo Scoppio del Carro*, the big Easter tradition in Florence that starts in the piazza in front of the church.

LEFT IN LIMBO

Notice the quiet of the little piazza outside the church, Piazza del Limbo. Named Limbo because this was a cemetery for babies and children who died before being baptized, and theoretically were floating in space, unable to enter Heaven. I have to wonder how many Catholic mothers were completely traumatized by the thought of their dead babies spending eternity in purgatory.

THE FLOODWATERS

Look left as you exit the church into the piazza. Between the window and the drain pipe a small plaque high on the wall shows the level the floodwaters reached in 1966. All things considered, it's amazing more of the city's spectacular artworks weren't destroyed in water that deep.

You don't need much time here, but it's a lovely respite, and a nice little church to visit. Lately the crowds of tourists in Florence have grown beyond belief, and getting caught in them can be quite overwhelming. However, they stay in straight lines between the main attractions, so if you find yourself needing to escape just duck down any of these side streets – you always find treasures like Santi Apostoli, more history than you can wrap your head around, and a quiet little piazza to rest your brain in.

Address: Piazza del Limbo, 1

What's Nearby: Ponte Vecchio, Porcellino Market, Piazza della Signoria, Palazzo Vecchio, Piazza della Repubblica and Museo della Davanzati are all close.

10. Santa Margherita dei Cerchi

This tiny church is of particular interest to fans of Dante Alighieri and Dan Brown's Inferno. I cover it in depth in the chapter **A Walk With Dante**. A moment away from Dante's house this church was an important part of one of the most enduring love stories of all time, that of Dante and Beatrice. The art in here is a bit kitchy but look for Beatrice's tomb and the basket of letters with it, all of which you can read about when we take our walk with Dante.

Address: Via Santa Margherita

What's Nearby: piazza della Signoria, Badia Fiorentina, The Bargello, Dante's House and Piazza della Repubblica.

11. Orsanmichele

This church hides right under your nose in one of the most highly trafficked areas in Florence, and it's fantastic. Diagonally opposite the Porcellino market you'll see a square building with statues in niches wrapped around its walls. You might not recognize it as a church, as from the outside there's nothing churchy about it. Most visitors have to loop around it a couple of times to find the entrance – heads up, it's in the back.

Of course there is a good story behind Orsanmichele. In 895 AD this was an oratory in the monastery of San Michele, surrounded by a garden (*orto*). Over time the name was shortened from Orto San Michele to Or-San-Michele.

The original structure burned down in 1239 and was rebuilt as a wooden loggia. The loggia had a column with an image of the Madonna on it, which was accredited with several miracles. The loggia then burnt down and in 1336 the Silk Guild rebuilt it as a grain market. Hence the odd shape – this building was originally a grain market with a grain storage facility on the upper floors. It made sense to have a granary in the middle of town as during times of sieges and wars you couldn't go to the countryside to get grain.

As an open loggia, in some ways the city flowed through it. Bernardo Daddi painted the *Madonna delle Grazie* to replace the painting lost in the fire. This one had miracles attributed to it too, especially during the plague of 1348. With miracles come pilgrims, and they came in such volume to pray at Mary's feet it became impossible to keep the space functioning as a market. So a new market was built across the way (the Mercato Nuovo/Porcellino Market) and this space was converted into a church.

Each of the city's guilds (unions) had to provide a statue of their patron saint for their niche/tabernacle wrapping around the building's exterior. The current statues are casts of the originals, now safely housed in the museum above the church. These weren't completed until the mid-fifteenth century, so benefitted from the genius of Renaissance sculptors such as Donatello, who carved the Linen Drapery Guild's exquisite *Saint Mark*.

Inside the church the gorgeous *Madonna delle Grazie* lives inside an incredible tabernacle created by Orcagna in 1348–59.

Two of the columns on the left side of the church have open grain chutes, once used to transport grain down to the market. Odd yet cool, you will probably be the only person noticing them. Beautifully frescoed ceilings show the original loggia shapes. Look for large metal rings embedded in the ceiling. These are not inquisition torture devices, but instead were for working the pulleys hoisting up heavy blocks of grain.

Again, you won't find many people here. Hundreds will be streaming up the street to Ponte Vecchio, yet in here is barely anyone. Personally, I think this church is beautiful and well worth a visit. You won't need much time here, although you can go upstairs to the museum too. Make time to wander around the outside and look at each niche. You can identify each of the guilds and the art is wonderful.

What's Nearby: This is in the heart of everything. Immediately nearby are Piazza della Repubblica, Porcellino Market, Ponte Vecchio, Piazza della Signoria, Palazzo Vecchio and the Uffizi.

12. Basilica San Lorenzo

Don't be fooled by the rustic exterior, not only is San Lorenzo a monumental complex, it is also home to many *firsts* in the worlds of art and architecture. Many of the churches on my list can be visited somewhat quickly, (although I can lose myself in them for hours) but this is one to reserve a chunk of time for. There is much to see here, especially for Medici fans.

RECENT CHANGES

For centuries (until 2015), the piazza in front of San Lorenzo was full of hustling, bustling market stalls – the San Lorenzo market. Gossip says the bishop of San Lorenzo told Mayor Matteo Renzi that if he moved the market back from the piazza then he would make sure Renzi became Prime Minister. Whether true or not who knows, but Renzi moved the market and became Prime Minister. Some of my Florentine friends don't like the change, but I enjoy seeing and accessing the basilica without having to navigate the market stalls. (Another Renzi change I'm a *HUGE* fan of was banning traffic in the Piazza Duomo.)

SO HOW OLD IS IT?

Several churches claim to be the oldest in Florence, and Basilica San Lorenzo is one of them. We *do* know it was consecrated in 393 by Saint Ambrose, one of the fourth century's most influential ecclesiastical figures. For 300 years it was the cathedral of Florence, until Santa Reparata, the current Duomo's predecessor.

BRUNELLESCHI, THE MEDICI AND SAN LORENZO

More than just a church, Basilica San Lorenzo is part of a much larger monastic complex, worked on by the greatest architects in Italian history: the Old Sacristy by Brunelleschi, the Laurentian Library by Michelangelo, the New Sacristy designed by Michelangelo, the Medici Chapels by Matteo Nigetti.

There were Romanesque renovations in 1059, then in 1418 Cosimo de' Medici initiated major renovations. This was the Medici church, so he hired Brunelleschi to turn it into a temple to the family. Work started in 1419, but construction slowed due to lack of funds. By the 1440s only the Sacristy (now known as the 'Old Sacristy') was completed, as it was the only part of the building financed by the Medici. In 1442 Cosimo took over financing the total renovation. Brunelleschi died in 1446, before it was finished, and it is disputed who replaced him, the top candidates being Manetti and Michelozzo.

The basilica was completed in 1459 for a visit from Pope Pius II (the Piccolomini Pope of Pienza), but the chapels along the right side were still under construction in the 1490s. The final construction didn't entirely correspond to the original design. Brunelleschi planned for the chapels along the sides of the church to be deeper, like the chapel in the transept. Regardless, you will see his hand here in everything.

The church is an overwhelmingly huge space, tamed by Brunelleschi's use of mathematical ratios, controlled proportions and geometry. Look for his classical Roman elements, grey-green columns of *pietra serena* with Corinthian capitols, the perfect balance in his shapes and use of spaces. The harmony in his design makes this the epitome of Renaissance architectural perfection.

EXTERIOR AND INTERIOR FAÇADES

Considering the majesty and beauty of the exteriors of the Duomo, Santa Maria Novella, Santa Croce and San Miniato al Monte, it is hard to conceive of a church as important as San Lorenzo being left with this rough, rustic façade. In 1518 the first Medici pope, Pope Leo X, commissioned Michelangelo to design a façade in white Carrara marble. He created a wooden model for a classically proportioned exterior, but money ran out and it was never made. Michelangelo did however make an *internal* façade for the church. Two huge columns hold up a balcony behind which three doors are bookended with pilasters wrapped in oak and laurel garlands. You can see it if you look back from the nave. (This was something I had missed for years. Now I make a point of turning around and looking at it whenever I'm inside this church.)

THE CLOISTER

You enter this church via the cloister, a peaceful green space hidden from bustling life in the piazza outside. The juxtaposition felt more extreme when the market stalls butted up against the church.

Known as the Cannon's Cloister, this space is defined by a lovely two story loggia – a round, arched arcade atop Ionic columns on the lower level and a squared architrave on the second level. The simplicity and harmony of the shapes and colors add to the peaceful feeling floating through this space. Although Brunelleschi's design, it was executed by Manetti, who also finished Brunelleschi's work at Santo Spirito. This was a living area with the kitchen and offices looking out over it. Brunelleschi designed a second cloister here which is closed to the public.

THE CRYPT

Technically not a crypt, but a cellar and museum for the church's reliquaries and liturgical paraphernalia, there are a couple of things to look for here:

- Donatello is buried here. His stone marker is close to the tomb of his friend and patron, Cosimo de' Medici.
- Of course Cosimo's tomb is not a simple affair. Look for a marble sarcophagus with a huge pillar. Cosimo is buried inside the column, symbolizing him being not only the pillar of the family, but also of this church. The pillar pushes upward directly in front of the altar in the church above.
- Inside the church a tomb slab is inlaid in the center of the crossing, in front of the altar. During mass, this space would have only been available to Cosimo, the patron of the church. Look up and you see it is directly below the oculus of the dome, making a clear line from his tomb pushing up symbolically to the space in front of the altar and floating up to Heaven. Body below, spirit above. In death he still shows us his power and influence.

THE OLD SACRISTY

This didn't earn the moniker 'Old Sacristy' until the new one started construction in 1510. From the main aisle of the church the Old Sacristy is on the left. You need to visit the Old Sacristy if for no other reason than that it marked the beginning of a new style of architecture based on proportion, the use of classic orders and the unity of elements. This is one of the most important monuments in early Renaissance architecture.

WHAT IS A SACRISTY?

Traditionally the sacristy is the little side room where priests put on their garments, but this sacristy was built to be a mausoleum to Giovanni di Bicci de' Medici. Renovations like San Lorenzo weren't funded by wealthy families simply donating cash and walking away. Instead each family bought and was responsible for an individual chapel. Giovanni di Bicci de' Medici dropped the most cash and got the biggest space, choosing to pay for the sacristy. He hired Brunelleschi who created for him the epitome of Renaissance architecture.

Instead of the soaring, aggressive shapes of gothic architecture, the Old Sacristy has an incredible sense of clarity and calm. This is a space built on the manageable geometry of a square, broken up with perfect circles. Inside the sacristy look for shapes: the room is a perfect square with a rounded dome on top. Circles and semi-circles create balance, symbolizing eternal life. Like God, the circle has no beginning and no end, it just *is*. Imagine the dome is Heaven and the square walls represent gravity and Earth, then see how Brunelleschi united the two with pendentives and half circles, embracing the square while rising up to but not quite touching the dome. The white spaces between the half circles create an ethereal feeling of lightness and space, rising up and out of the oculus at the top. Knowing this is a mausoleum, imagine the soul rising up, floating through the oculus and onward to Heaven.

The colors in the Old Sacristy not only create a sense of calm and balance but also direct your eye to the shapes. The cream stucco walls offset the grey-green *pietra serena* stone, emphasizing the geometry of the space. It is magnificent.

DONATELLO IS HERE

Not only is this remarkable architecturally, it is also artistically important. The artwork here, the tondos, lunettes and the pensives above the bronze doors, are all by Brunelleschi's friend Donatello. Donatello received the commission and started work without consulting Brunelleschi. This created a spat between the friends (and possible lovers). Brunelleschi planned on his pietra serena directing the eye to all the shapes, so the walls needed their creamy white anonymity. Instead, Donatello's colors *emphasized* the walls. When Donatello realized that Brunelleschi disapproved of his work he ran around town disparaging Brunelleschi. The architect wouldn't let the slight go, so he wrote a series of sonnets letting the world know he had nothing to do with the art, the bronze doors or anything else on the walls.

Their sniping aside, Donatello's work is, of course, incredible. Eight tondos tell four stories of John the Evangelist and four of the apostles. The Johns have the burden of being 12 meters high, on a concave surface. They are two meters in diameter but even so, much of the detail is hard to make out without binoculars, which explains his use of color. Interestingly the surface was prepared with wet stucco and nails, then worked with the hands. You can see fingerprints in the stucco, and the nails are still visible, especially around the pot John stands in.

DONATELLO'S BRONZE DOORS (1440–1443)

I find these bronze doors fascinating. Apparently Brunelleschi planned two archways with open passages, and the bronze doors didn't come until later. The left is the *Door of the Martyrs*. In the arch above it we see Saint Stephen with the stone on his forehead, talking with Saint Lawrence holding the grid he is to be burned on. The right door is the *Door of the Apostles.* Its arch shows the Medici patron saints, Cosmas and Damian. The heads and the way their hair is depicted are based on Roman busts.

The doors are comprised of 20 panels, 10 per door. The left door tells the story of martyrs and the right door has 10 panels of apostles. What I love about them is that each panel shows two figures reacting to one another. In each one someone acts and the other *re*acts. They are in conversation, in debate or argument, in movement. In all 20 panels everyone is doing something rather than just standing or sitting immobile, and the faces *interact*. Offset by empty space behind them, the message isn't blurred with landscapes, just the two figures in each panel. Smooth bronze backgrounds give clarity and depth. Each panel has a solid vertical and horizontal frame, but look closely and you'll see a foot or feet stepping out of the lower horizontal bar, as if the person is coming out to us. The bottom four panels also use this trick with their vertical bars as hands and other body parts reach out.

The doors are made of 25% tin instead of the usual 10%. This percentage was ideal for bells, so the doors were probably cast by bell makers. Not only was this more expensive, it was also much harder to work with – the more tin in the mix, the harder and more brittle it became, making it difficult to chisel and risky to hammer. Knowing this, now look at the drapery of the robes they wear. It is even more remarkable that Donatello was able to give us so much detail and definition.

These are just random details from a tiny section of an enormous church, but to me the tiny details are everything. Knowing about them makes me seek them out. Otherwise I would just see doors, the artist's name and some dates.

THE LAURENTIAN LIBRARY

Generally only open to the public when there is an exhibit happening, visiting the Laurentian Library costs extra. This was once the Medici library. At that time there weren't public libraries to go borrow a novel to read over the weekend. Books were rare, exotic things exclusively for the wealthy. Each was a handmade, prized possession. Owning a book made you special. So imagine owning an entire library! What a way to showcase your wealth, importance, education and power.

I view the Laurentian Library in pieces: Michelangelo's staircase and vestibule, and the library itself.

Michelangelo's Staircase

The staircase flows down from the library at the top like liquid chocolate. Pooling and oozing, gathering at the sides, but not gushing at you. It comes at you at a lazy, languid pace. Thought to be the first freestanding staircase in the world of architecture, narrow at the top, the staircase flows wider and wider as it descends, gathering momentum as it comes at you. Michelangelo planned the stairs to be made of wood, which would have warmed the room, but instead they were built from *pietra serena* stone. From the bottom looking upward they're almost overwhelming, because the distance between the first step and the wall opposite is short and abrupt. Within moments you could be swallowed up by this mass rolling down at you. The staircase is oddly magnificent.

Michelangelo's Vestibule

This space is really unusual. I'm hesitant to call it a room – a room would be more friendly. This vestibule is small, yet towering, domineering and very masculine. The colors are soft but cold. The walls are almost hard to find, not because they are covered in art – they aren't – but because there is so much going on.

At the lowest level, scrolled ornamental brackets normally used to support something above, are used as a decoration. Sitting in pairs of grey-green stone, they look muscular below embedded columns which start halfway up the wall, looking like they are being pushed downward. The brackets are oversized like a huge set of arms, and the bottom, where the wrists would be, are at head height if you are walking around. Filled windows reach up high, making the vestibule feel dark and somber. The pietra serena pilasters of these stone windows play an odd trick too, they taper downward ominously, with fluting only at their lower section. Their smooth upper section looks weighty and strong, again pushing downward. Above all this a second layer of real windows, way up high, to let in the light. The effect of this non-windowed then windowed space makes the lower portion of the vestibule feel gravity rich and lead weighted, while the upper portion where sunshine streams in feels dizzyingly light. Columns sink into the walls, pilasters, scrolls and corners feel like they'll crash into each other.

All these components working together make this space really interesting. Drama, mystery, power... perhaps a symbol of Medici dominance?

The Library

Juxtaposed with the heaviness of the vestibule below, this space is light, bright and airy. The library is long and narrow, with walnut stalls lining its flanks below long rows of bright windows on each side. This was clever, as five centuries ago there was no electricity, so any light would have had to come from candles. With a core collection of more than 3000 manuscripts every means to reduce the fire hazard of candles was wise. A coffered, wooden ceiling gives the room warmth, and after the drama of the vestibule below there's a sense of relief and tranquility up here. The light is bright, even on a cloudy day. Unlike the downstairs space, this is symmetrical, the mind can calm and study or reflect in this environment. There is balance, harmony and light.

Both Cosimo and Lorenzo the Magnificent contributed massively to the library's prestigious collection of Italian manuscripts. They had money and power, but weren't born noble at a time when that really mattered. Perhaps this library made them feel or look scholarly rather than just newly rich.

THE MEDICI CHAPEL

San Lorenzo is the resting place of the Medici, most of whom are buried in the Medici Chapel. The entrance to the Chapel is outside, at the back of the church. Giovanni di Bicci de' Medici was buried in the Old Sacristy in 1429, and Cosimo the Elder was buried in the crossing of the church. In 1520 Cardinal Giulio de' Medici (who became Pope Clement VII) had Michelangelo begin work on a mausoleum to glorify his family. He finished the architectural work by 1524 but worked on the sculptures until 1533.

The chapel is separated into three sections:

- The Crypt
- The Chapel of the Princes
- The New Sacristy.

The Crypt

You enter through the crypt. Once past the ticket office and X-ray machine, you walk into a low-ceilinged space of support arches and religious memorabilia. The minor family members are buried here. It wasn't prettied up until the nineteenth century, at which point numerous tomb slabs were added. Look around down here before heading upstairs.

The Chapel of the Princes

This octagonal space with its huge dome was built between 1604 and 1640 by the architect Matteo Nigetti, working to the designs of Giovanni de Medici, a semi-professional architect. By this time, the Medici dynasty was 200 years strong and this mausoleum was a celebration of them. Personally, I find it a bit bombastic, especially when compared to the simple lines and clarity of the Old and New Sacristies. But of course, that's half the fun of it. I love the Medici and everything they gave us, so I enjoy this space.

The Chapel of the Princes was designed to hold the bodies of the Grand Dukes. Stand in the center of the room and turn in a slow circle – every inch of the walls is covered in different colored marbles and semi-precious stones. Sarcophagi reside in niches in the walls, complimented with bronze statues. The inlaid marble and precious stones took centuries to complete. In fact, the intense craftsmanship required to create something this spectacular led Ferndinando I to create a semi-precious stone workshop, the *Opificio della Pietre Dure* (see **Chapter 12: Museums**). Artisans from the workshop worked on the Chapel of the Princes, but the high cost of the rare materials used and their limited availability meant it took a long time to complete. Though this room had been intended to overwhelm, the Medici ran out of money and power long before its completion. The plan had been to cover the interior of the dome in vibrant lapis lazuli, but it stayed bare until 1828 when Pietro Bienvenuti painted the frescoes we see today.

One thing I notice when visiting the Chapel of the Princes is that people leave an incredible resource here untapped: the docents working the room. It seems everyone who engages with them just wants direction to the toilets or the New Sacristy. Although not all are fluent in English, they all are walking talking encyclopedias of Medici knowledge. I never have fewer than a thousand questions to ask, and even those with the most studious faces just light up when I ask them. They take time explaining, pointing out things you hadn't noticed, telling you the stories of this fantastic place.

A recent Glam Italia tour group had all watched the Medici show on Netflix, twice. They *loved* it and consequently were in awe of everything Medici we saw in Florence. Now, if your brain is bubbling over with Medici info and you work in a place as remarkable as the Medici Chapel, spending your days directing tourists to the public toilets, your radar is going to start pinging when a little group of excited Medici fans walks in. I entered the chapel ahead of my travelers, and was able to stand back and watch as they came in. You could almost see sparks coming off them! As with everywhere Medici we went, their excitement was palpable. Not only did *I* pick up on it, but so did the docents. My group stayed in the Chapel of the Princes longer than I have ever done in all of my many visits here, and at all times they were asking the docents questions, or were being shown something or having something explained in detail. They loved it! Then, once we moved into the New Sacristy, one of my travelers kept going back and asking more questions, so one of the docents ended up coming with us and pointed out some really cool things. The experience was fabulous.

The moral of this little side-story is that if you are genuinely interested, polite and friendly towards the docents, a whole new world will opes up to you. Be sure to ask them more than just directions to the toilets!

The New Sacristy

This is my favorite part of the San Lorenzo complex. Not only is it the burial site for two of my favorite Medici (Lorenzo the Magnificent and Giuliano), it holds some of my favorite sculptures in all of Florence, and is a place where some of my favorite stories of Florence during the Renaissance converge. The New Sacristy combines Michelangelo's deep love for some of the Medici (Lorenzo and Giuliano) and his loathing for others (Giulio and Alessandro). Some of Michelangelo's most sensational sculptures live here inside his own architecture. It tells stories of two Medici popes, Leo X, son of Lorenzo and Giulio di Giuliano, who became Pope Clement VII.

So let's start with the architecture. Michelangelo designed this Sacristy to pair with Brunelleschi's Old Sacristy on the other side of the church. Work began in 1520 at the behest of then Cardinal Giulio de Medici, with the architecture completed in 1524, a year after he became pope. Michelangelo completed the sculptures in the 1530s. After the lavish swirling circle of the Chapel of the Princes, you step in here and experience a new sensation. The clean, clear lines Brunelleschi loved, the order of geometry, circles and pendentives up above. But Michelangelo didn't copy Brunelleschi, he balanced him and then added his own flavor to the mix.

I think of the New Sacristy as purgatory. Built as a square, the dense bottom level feels quite claustrophobic. It is grey and off-white, boxy and dark. The lower and mid-level windows are blind, allowing no light in and letting no souls out. You can imagine ghosts careening madly around this space, crashing into the walls before they realize they have to rise up, up, up into the heights of the dome and float out through the oculus. The height of the dome is a bit of an optical illusion. When you are inside the sacristy it seems incredibly high, but from the street it's not.

The New Sacristy was built 80 years before the Chapel of the Princes, and was never completed, the frescoes never painted. Michelangelo intended that a fresco of *The Resurrection* would be behind the altar. Maybe with paintings in place the sacristy would have seemed a little less maudlin, but I like it this way.

The New Sacristy appears in three chapters in this book so take a look at all of them to get a complete picture of why this place is so impressive (see **Chapter 22: A Walk With Michelangelo** and **Chapter 13: Unusual & Interesting Things**).

THE SCULPTURES

I absolutely love these sculptures.

First Giuliano, against the back wall, or the right as you walk in. Giuliano was murdered inside the Duomo in 1478 when he was 25. Michelangelo was 3 at the time. The Medici weren't handsome men, with the exception of Giuliano, who as we see here was beautiful – at least in Michelangelo's eyes. He sits here as a testament to power, strength and beauty, his neck alone being one of the most beautiful works of sculpture anywhere in the world, his face one of the most beautiful in all of art history. Although seated, he looks ready to leap out of the tableau, pushing off with his left leg, stepping out with his right, his upper body already in motion. Below him, sculptures represent Night and Day, two absolutes, both also in motion, turning away from us.

Opposite Giuliano is his brother, Lorenzo the Magnificent. Michelangelo has made Lorenzo contemplative, his ankles crossed, his left elbow resting on the arm of his chair, his thumb supporting his chin and his finger resting below his nose. Deep in thought, his visage remains in shadow for all eternity. Below him are Dusk and Dawn, those murky, undefined parts of the day that swirl around in the mist where the best thoughts happen. Unlike Night and Day who are in poses moving from us, with their heads moving away from each other, Dusk and Dawn lean into one another and look to the middle of the room. Another thing I adore here is that Lorenzo was incredibly charismatic, but physically quite unattractive, yet Michelangelo has made him beautiful. While here, look at Lorenzo's face. In Michelangelo's hands he is handsome.

Both sets of sculptures are magnificent. For a while Lorenzo was Michelangelo's family. Michelangelo lived with the Medici family in the Medici Palace across the piazza from this church. They ate meals together, hung out in the palace with the great minds of the time, and shared a deep bond. Lorenzo looked after the teenage Michelangelo, raising him with his son Giovanni (Pope Leo X) and Giuliano's orphaned child Giulio (Pope Clement VII). You can feel the sculptor's love and tenderness for Lorenzo and Giuliano in these works.

THE POEM

Part of Michelangelo's method and preparation for a new work involved writing poetry. His poem *Night and Day Speak* was written for his work here. You can feel the depth of his emotion at the loss of Giuliano, some 50 years prior to working on this sculpture.

Day and Night speak and say:

We with our swift course have brought the Duke,
Giuliano to death.

Is it just that he, the Duke, takes revenge as he does for
this, and the revenge is this:

That as we (Day and Night) have killed him, he, dead,
has taken the light from us.

And with his closed eyes, has locked ours shut, which no
longer shine on earth

What then would he have done with us while alive?

— Michelangelo Buonarotti

Buying Leather

15.

How to Buy Leather in Florence

Leather jackets are big business in Florence – *really* big business – as are leather bags, belts, wallets and shoes. You'll see leather jackets for sale everywhere, from street markets to big leather stores and small artisan workshops. Florence has been famous for its leather for centuries, and in my opinion this is THE place to buy yourself a really fabulous leather jacket.

But how do you know if you are buying good quality or something that will fall apart when you get home? Leather jackets are quite expensive. A mistake with the purchase of a belt, wallet or even a handbag in a market is not a huge financial loss, but making a mistake with a leather jacket could be costly.

Not Everything is As it Seems

- The same merchant may own a boutique or shop and also have market stalls. Sometimes the same item is vastly different prices at each place.
- The same leather worker might work for luxury designers *and* make pieces for some smaller businesses, bringing the same exquisite workmanship to both. A small shop or no-name brand does NOT mean low quality.

- The hides that are used to create designer jackets may be sourced from the same place that an artisanal shop purchases their materials from.

- On the other hand, a slick salesperson (anywhere) may talk you into what you think is a fantastic jacket but when you get back home you find you've massively overpaid for cheaply-made rubbish.

Whether you have time to go back and try on a jacket more than once before purchasing, or you have to make an on-the-spot decision, let this guide help you buy the perfect leather jacket in Florence.

About the Markets

You can find wonderful leather jackets in the markets but the associated distractions may stop you spotting a problem. Many market stalls will have a brick and mortar shop nearby, so if you find something you like tell the salesman you want to visit their shop. If they don't have one, keep moving.

In Florence, leather goods are available at every price point. All the big names are here: Gucci, Prada, Chanel, Louis – everyone. You will find mid-priced leather vendors, from the slightly unaffordable to the very affordable. You will also find inexpensive leather.

Unscrupulous vendors know that many tourists are only there for a day, or can only spend a short amount of time shopping and want to buy something quickly. If a tourist only has a couple of hours to shop they are less likely to be savvy shoppers, and more likely to unknowingly part with big money for a jacket that falls apart when they get home.

I'll happily buy bags, belts and wallets from market stalls, but for an expensive item like a jacket I prefer to step inside a shop. Inside a shop, the atmosphere will be calmer and more controlled, and you can allow your senses to help guide you through the process.

Jimmy

When I first started buying leather in Florence, I met Jimmy Ahmed, owner of the eponymous **Jimmy's Leather Collection** at Piazza San Lorenzo, 2.

When we met, years and years ago now, he was working for other leather merchants. Since the first time he helped me buy something (a beautiful honey-colored leather weekender bag and matching oversized tote that have traveled all around the world with me for years), Jimmy has been my go-to guy for all things leather. To me, Jimmy and Florence go hand in hand, always part of the same equation. I always drop in for a coffee as soon as I arrive in Florence and I stop to say arrivederci on my way out of town. Over the years we got to know each other's families and he has become one of my most trusted friends.

Jimmy opened Jimmy's Leather Collection around 2013. Most of the merchandise he sells there is his own design. He inspects every hide by hand, making sure it is perfect. Instead of using chemical dyes he uses non-toxic vegetable dyes that last forever and hold their color. They never bleed onto your skin or clothing (even when wet). There is nothing he doesn't know about leather.

Over the years, he has taught me (and my travelers) how to identify real leather or a cheap knock off. Here are his guidelines:

- **Price:** The price of a jacket is directly proportionate to the quality of three things: the hide, the workmanship, and the finishing.

- **Aroma:** What does the leather smell like? Leather should have a musky, natural aroma. Avoid anything smelling like chemicals. Chemicals are used to treat lesser quality hides.

- **Texture:** Quality leather feels soft, supple and almost buttery. It definitely shouldn't feel stiff or tough. Leather should have texture to it. Looking closely, you should see what looks like skin, with pores. If it's completely smooth it may be a bonded product or may be chemically treated.

- **Lining:** Lining is essential for a jacket to hold its shape, but not all linings are equal. Turn the jacket inside out and look at the lining. Ideally you want cotton, viscose, or a cotton mix – fabrics that breathe and aren't prone to holding odors. Polyester can make you sweat and can get smelly.

- **Finishing:** While looking at the lining, also look at the inner seams. Quality craftsmanship will have excellent finishing – it is a point of pride with Italians. Can you see loose threads or unfinished edges? If so, that jacket is NOT of Tuscan quality.

- **Stitching:** Stitching should be tight, precise, and straight, with small stitches sewn closely together. Italians are known for clean work and straight stitching, so if you see a looser stitch or if the stitching lacks precision, you can safely assume it is of poor quality. If a client sees a jacket they like, I immediately look at the exterior stitching. If it is off, we walk away.

- **Hardware**: Is the zipper durable? If there are any dome or snap fasteners, check the quality. No one produces a fabulous jacket with a high quality hide and excellent craftsmanship, and then uses a cheap zipper. If the hardware is cheap, it is probably not a quality jacket.

- **Fit**: How loose is the jacket around the arm holes? Cheap jackets are cut loosely so they'll fit more people. The underarm should be fitted with no bulk or excess space through the back.

- **Seams**: Look at the shoulder seams and collars. Are the joins thick and bulky, or are they streamlined? A badly made jacket is poorly joined and bulky in these areas. A quality jacket will have beautiful workmanship where the shoulders meet the sleeves, and where the collar meets the shoulders.

- **Alignment**: Check that the left and right front panels align perfectly. Low quality/sweatshop jackets often don't quite align. These jackets are thrown together quickly without attention to detail or clean work.

- **Coloring**: How is it colored? There are two main methods for dying leather. The mechanical way involves spraying the hide in a single process with a chemical/synthetic dye. The finish is shinier but less durable. You'll see this with cheaper jackets. Hand dyed jackets use vegetable dyes instead of synthetic or chemical dyes, and it takes a three-layer process to color the hide. The finish on the jacket is matte, not shiny. The patina of a jacket colored with vegetable dye will only get more beautiful as the leather ages. This non-chemical way of treating leather is a traditional Italian technique and is part of the 'Tuscan quality' you're looking for when buying leather in Florence.

- **Lamb vs Cow:** Most leather jackets sold in Florence are lambskin. Younger lambskin is ideal because it is thick and soft, while older lambskin has more lines on it, similar to older skin.

Don't be put off if some shops carry low-end merchandise as well as their high-end jackets. They need to be able to offer something to everyone. Plenty of travelers want something in the €200 range, which is not going to get them a top quality jacket, but they will still be super happy taking home a well-made leather jacket from Florence. What you want to avoid is paying €500 for a €200 jacket.

Beware of These Labels

Some terminology to be aware of when shopping for jackets:

- **Real Leather** just means the hide comes from an animal. It could be from a variety of animals; and it could come from China, the Middle East, Turkey, North Africa... anywhere.

- **Made in Italy** can also be a little disingenuous. Legally, 'Made in Italy' means at least 33% of it was made here, but the rest may have been made somewhere else. Or it could mean it was made in a Chinese sweatshop in Italy. Or it may mean that it was made in Italy to the highest standard by a master craftsman.

Obviously you want 'Real Leather', 'Made in Italy', but you need to ask more questions. Don't assume those words alone mean it is the quality product you are looking for.

- **Full Grain** (*pieno fiore/cuoio pieno fiore/pelle pieno fiore*). This is considered the best quality leather that money can buy. It typically hasn't been sanded, is durable yet supple, and its patina gets lovelier over time.

- **Top Grain** (*parte grano/cuoio di grano*). Top grain has been sanded to remove some of the natural imperfections but is still considered high quality leather.

- **Genuine** (*vera pelle/vera cuoio*). This is cut from the bottom half of the hide and doesn't necessarily show a grain. You see it everywhere, stamped onto bags, wallets and leather journals etc, but is perhaps not the leather you want in an expensive jacket (unless you're buying suede).

- **Bonded** (*cuoi rigenerato*). Beware! This material is factory-made from leather dust, scraps of leftover leather, shavings and general detritus, pressed together with glue, dye and chemicals. It is spray-painted to look like natural leather but the chemical smell should give it away. Technically this can have a 'Real Leather' label because it is made from leather bits, and may also wear a 'Made in Italy' too.

- **Imitation** (*semipelle/ecopelle*). This at least is honest. This is a great solution for vegans and vegetarians who don't want to buy animal products, but if you're shopping for authentic leather avoid *semipelle* and *ecopelle*.

Shopping

16.

Shopping

One of the joys of travel is finding cool and unusual things to bring home, AKA shopping! Florence has tremendous shopping, whatever your price point. I normally do a decent chunk of my Christmas shopping in Florence each summer, because there are so many fabulous and unique items available here.

Florence is *the* place in Italy to buy leather. The city has been famous for its leather production since the thirteenth century, when tanneries lined the Arno River in the Santa Croce area. Today, 700 years later, Florence is internationally recognized for the quality and beauty of its leather products. From belts to wallets, handmade shoes to handbags and jackets – everything you can think of is here. Even if you'll be travelling all around Italy, **do your leather shopping in Florence**.

Italian leather, and by extension Florentine leather, is different from leather you find at home. Pick up an Italian leather jacket and you will notice it feels like butter. Turn to the inside and see (in most cases) the beautiful stitching and quality craftsmanship. I have bought so many Italian handbags over the years and always find they are incredibly durable, hold their shape, and last forever.

If there was ever a place to buy handmade leather shoes, it would be Florence. If handmade is beyond your budget don't worry – there are gorgeous Florentine shoes at every price point.

I've been buying leather-bound journals at the San Lorenzo market for years. They occasionally become gifts (because people get so excited about them), but I always get one to be my travel journal for the following year.

But there is more to shopping in Florence than just leather and souvenirs. From home décor to jewelry, fashion and much more, Florence is a shopper's paradise.

Shopping and Me

I confess, I usually loathe shopping. At home in the US I would rather have teeth pulled than go shopping. But in Italy it's an entirely different experience. Merchants and salespeople here actually care that you are getting the right thing and that you are happy with your purchase.

One of my first shopping experiences in Florence started with what I initially thought was an insult from the salesperson. (It wasn't). I was perusing the racks and picked up an item to try on. The salesperson walked over, took it out of my hand and put it back on the rack saying, 'No – with *that bottom* this is definitely *not* for you.' My eyes filled with tears. I was mortified and about to bolt for the door when she pulled out three other items and said, 'These are perfect for you. They are perfect for your shape and will make your bottom look wonderful.' It was not an expensive shop, there were no big commissions to be made, the salesperson just wanted to make sure I had the right clothes for my shape and that I left the shop well cared for. While I tried things on, she kept coming back and styling me – try it with this belt, tuck this top in, pull that top out, etc. I left the shop with an array of fabulous pieces, feeling like a million dollars.

A similar thing happened several years later at my friend Jimmy's leather store. I was looking at sensible black and brown jackets that covered my ample derrière. Jimmy took them out of my hands and hung them back up saying, 'No, no, no – these are not you.' He then pulled out a red leather jacket that stopped at the hip – something I would never have considered in a million years. I didn't even want to try it on, telling him it would make my bum look huge. Jimmy wouldn't take no for an answer, so I slipped it on to appease him. I didn't think there was even a sliver of a chance it could possibly work on my curvy frame. But of course, he was right. The jacket was perfect. It is now my absolute favorite item in my wardrobe. I plan outfits around it and it travels all around the world with me. It's the Best Thing Ever.

Where I am going with this is that even if you don't like shopping, be open to the experience while in Florence. Chances are you will come away with something wonderful that you will treasure.

How to Understand Florence's Street Addresses

Florence is one of only two cities in Italy to use a black and red numbering system, which can be really confusing.

Let's start with the order of the words, which is fairly standard in Italian addresses. An address won't be written as 5 Rome Street. Instead the street name comes first then a comma, then the street number:

via Roma, 5

You might also see Roman numerals used in some street names, so instead of via 25 Aprile or 25th of April Street:

via XXV Aprile

In Florence, street names can change every block or two. For example, from the Santa Maria Novella train station the road that loops up through the Accademia and SS Annunziata, ending at Mercato San Ambrogio, changes its name every two major blocks, from via Guelfa to via degli Alfani to via de' Pilastri. Another little stretch from San Lorenzo to just beyond the Duomo starts as Piazza San Lorenzo, then via de' Pucci; three blocks later becomes via M Bufalini for one large block, before becoming via S. Egidio.

Red or Black?

Most of the time the even numbers will be on one side of the road and the odd numbers will be on the other. But not always.

If a big palazzo has been subdivided into multiple smaller homes with separate street entrances, each entrance may have its own letter, for example: *via Roma, 5D* and *via Roma, 5F.*

Residences and hotels get black or blue street numbers. Shops, offices and businesses get red numbers. The red numbers aren't always colored red, they may be in black but have the letter *R* after the number.

Just to make it more confusing, the red numbers won't follow the same sequence as the black and blue numbers. So walking down the street you will see 2, 4, 2R, 6, 8A, 8B, 8C, 8D, 10, 4R, 12. Sometimes the R numbers are really far away from their corresponding black numbers.

One time, a business address I was looking for was blocks away from the residential corresponding number. I got so confused and so lost that by the time I found the business, they had closed for the day.

Now if I'm looking for a business I always ask what they are close to, and I find that first.

Bring Your Passport

I don't actually carry my passport on me as I don't want to risk losing it to an enterprising pickpocket, but I do photograph the picture page with my phone and email it to myself. If you lose your bag and phone you can always log onto your email *somewhere* and retrieve that information.

In most cases, if buying an item costing more than €155 you can claim the sales tax back at the airport when you leave. Many shops have the paperwork on site and will fill it out for you, but they need your passport details.

Recently one of my Glam Italia tour travelers bought some Etruscan-style jewelry in Volterra. The shop filled out the forms for her and charged her the discounted price with the tax removed already. Sales tax is as much as 22%, so the rebate or instore discount can be significant.

Shops

HIGH STREET SHOPS

Like any major city anywhere in the world, Florence has high streets full of all the same international shops. Pick a price point, they're there. With few exceptions they all carry merchandise that you can buy anywhere. So why waste precious Florentine time on high street shopping? Unless you spot something in the window that you just have to have, keep on walking. Florence has much better than that to offer.

BOUTIQUE SHOPPING

Step away from the high streets of via Calzaiuoli, via del Corso, via Roma, and the upmarket via Tornabuoni, and you will find the real treasures of Florentine shopping: small, owner-operated boutiques. They are everywhere and they are fantastic. This is where you'll find the unique bits and pieces you'll love forever and that will always remind you of Florence.

From shoe shops to lingerie, home décor to fashion, vintage clothing to food stuffs, the boutiques of Florence are glorious. They are scattered all over the city, so the shop you want to visit may be on your way to some big site you are visiting.

My book *Glam Italia! How To Travel Italy* has an entire chapter on the ins and outs of shopping in Italy – which parts of the country are famous for which items (what to buy, where), how to get your sales tax back, useful phrases and translations, how to ship goods home, and much more.

Before I direct you to some of my favorite boutiques I have one warning:

Don't Buy Counterfeit – Ever!

Wandering the streets of Florence, you'll come across street vendors with the best knock-off designer handbags you have ever seen, neatly displayed on a sheet on the sidewalk, looking more inviting than you can imagine.

1. Firstly – don't even stop and look. These vendors will chase you down the street if they think you are interested.

2. Secondly – DO NOT BUY ONE. I am dead serious. **It is illegal to buy counterfeit designer goods in Italy.** There is no excuse, the authorities won't let you off and your embassy can't get you out of this one. There is an automatic fine of up to €10,000. If they don't catch you in the street, chances are they will pick you up at the airport. No counterfeit is worth the trouble you will be in.

My Favorite Shops in Florence (by Category)

These have been arranged for you by category rather than geographically. Florence is a really small city, so assume everything is within walking distance.

Buying Shoes

Florence is a glorious place for shoe shopping, in fact it has a fabulous history with the shoe. Since the late 1200s shoes have been an important fashion item in Florence. With its access to incredible leathers and superior artisans, footwear became a mega export commodity. By the late thirteenth century there were more than 2800 shoemakers in the city, mainly along the streets of via dei Pepi, Borgo Allegri and via Verdi in the Santa Croce area (home to the leather tanneries). In the Oltrarno there were 500 cobblers on via Romana alone! Shoes were big business.

Boots, shoes and sandals were made in a variety of materials, from leather to silk, some embroidered and adorned, others simple and functional. Shoes were handmade and made to measure until factories appeared in the mid 1800s. The craft was passed down through generations, so don't be surprised if you find a shoe shop is owner-operated with shoes made either on site or at their workshop nearby.

Here are some of my favorite shoe shops in Florence:

SASKIA SCARPE SU MISURA

If in the market for incredibly chic, bespoke shoes for men this is the place to go.

Fellow redhead, Berliner Saskia Wittmer, makes luxury, made-to-measure shoes for men. Saskia has been creating handmade shoes in Florence for her exclusive international clientele since 2000. Refreshingly, in a world where everyone posts selfies with or photos of their most celebrated customers, Saskia is discrete. She keeps the names of her clients secret – so secret in fact, that when I once photographed her beautiful store for a blog post she went through the images and removed any where a client's name was identifiable. After decades working in the entertainment industry, I love the privacy she affords the wearers of her shoes.

These are not off the rack shoes. Her client has an initial fitting and a *last* (or mold) is made of his foot, then styles and colors are chosen. The painstaking detail with which she works is remarkable. Each shoe is a work of art, designed to last a lifetime. The process of crafting each pair of shoes from start to finish takes five to six months. With their lasts stored on file, clients can order new shoes from Saskia from any corner of the world, and they do come from far and wide.

Saskia's shop is spare yet magical, with her exquisitely crafted shoes suspended from wires, as if dancing along the walls. The store shares space with her work room, which I found enthralling. From the wooden work station to the wood handled tools of her trade, the ceiling to floor shelves of client's lasts and the shoes in various stages of manufacture, standing here you know you are in the presence of a master craftsperson (in Saskia's case, a quietly, internationally renowned and highly sought after master craftsperson).

Address: Via di S. Lucia, 24R | Saskiascarpesumisura.com

What's Nearby: You're walking distance from Santa Maria Novella, close to the Westin Excelsior Hotel and the magnificent church of San Salvatore di Ognissanti.

FRANCESCO DA FIRENZE

Wandering around Santo Spirito I always discover something new and exciting. Whether I stumble upon a hidden jewelry shop, a hole-in-the-wall place for an amazing aperitivo, an antique store (or in this case a shoe shop), Santo Spirito is an area that keeps on giving. Some of Florence's greatest treasures can be found hiding behind unassuming storefronts, and this is one of them.

Francesco Laudato and his son Valerio make classic, fabulous, incredibly comfortable handmade leather shoes, sandals and boots for men and women. Choose from existing stock or order a custom pair. Made to order boots and shoes ship in approximately one month, made to order sandals are ready within a few days. Everything is made on site in the back of the shop, adding authenticity to the experience. Chances are you will find exactly what you are looking for on the shelves, but if not, a pair of shoes from Francesco is a pretty exciting package to receive in the mail when you get home!

Address: Via Santo Spirito, 62R

What's Nearby: Santo Spirito church is just up the street. Il Santino, a favorite spot for an aperitivo, is right here. Ponte Vecchio and Pitti Palace are a 5 minute walk.

TIP TAP

If you know any littlies, this darling children's shoe shop is an essential place to visit. Every pair in their extensive selection is made in Italy, and they are absolutely beautiful! Tip Tap has shoes for boys and girls, but the girls' shoes are *to die for.*

Everything comes in sizes from birth to size eight, and they have slip-ons, lace ups, sandals, slippers and boots in classic and whimsical styles. They also carry the iconic Friulane velvet slippers, from the Friuli region in the north. If you want to make an impact with a gift for a child back home this shop is an absolute win!

Even if you don't have any *bambini* to shop for, you should still stop and look in the window.

Address: Via della Spada, 50R | Calzaturebimbo.it

What's Nearby: Santa Maria Novella is close. Stop in at the Officina Profumo Farmaceutica and pick up Catherine de' Medici's signature fragrance. The beautiful church of Ognissanti is nearby too.

ANTICA CUOIERIA

This is one of my go-to shoe shops in Florence and a favorite for my Glam Italia tour groups. I only know about it because my Florentine friends buy their shoes here. They're still wearing shoes they bought here 20 years ago. These are classic, beautiful shoes, made from local Italian leather, by master craftsmen. You can't go wrong!

Antica Cuoieria makes shoes for men and women. Men get spoiled in Florence with shoe shopping – there are so many incredible options for them, so I love that this shop caters to women too. The styles here are *fabulous*. They are not bespoke, these are ready-to-wear shoes, so you will be walking out the door with them. Some merchandise changes with fashion, but they have classic lines too. These are not overly expensive shoes, more a middle price point. Their Chelsea boot for women runs around €110. They will also ship shoes home for you.

In all the years I've been shopping here, Gianni has run the shop. I doubt he would remember me, but by all means ask for him when you are there. He is incredibly knowledgeable and very helpful.

As an added bonus, they have a tiny outlet store around the corner. Walk down the alleyway next to the shop and on your left you will find their outlet with leftover stock from last year. This can be an absolute treasure trove. I've had clients come away with multiple pairs of super chic shoes from both shop.

Address: Via del Corso, 48R

What's Nearby: Piazza della Repubblica, Orsanmichele, the Porcellino market and Piazza della Signoria are in one direction, you're two blocks from the Duomo in the other.

SALVATORE FERRAGAMO MUSEUM

While we're talking about shoes, I need to tell you about the museum dedicated to Florence's most celebrated cobbler of the last century, Salvatore Ferragamo.

Ferragamo moved to Florence in 1927 after a successful run in Hollywood earned him the moniker 'shoemaker to the stars'. In Florence he had easy access to the best materials and the most skilled artisans, and as his empire grew he continued making shoes for the biggest movie stars in the world (including Audrey Hepburn and Marilyn Monroe). Since the 1930s his shop and atelier were housed in the fabulous Palazzo Spini-Feroni on the uber chic via Tornabuoni, so it is only fitting that this is the site for his museum. The collection covers his work from 1927 to 1960 and is an exciting destination for shoe aficionados and fashion mavens – and for anyone who loves the history of the silver screen.

Address: Via Tornabuoni, 2R

What's Nearby: This is midway between the Duomo and Santa Maria Novella, a couple of blocks from Piazza della Repubblica. Tornabuoni dead ends at Ponte Santa Trinita', only minutes walk from Santo Spirito immediately across the river.

Buying Leather

JIMMY'S LEATHER COLLECTION

See my chapter on **How to Buy Leather in Florence** for detailed guidelines about what to look out for if you're shopping for leather.

I send everyone to Jimmy's, and have done ever since he opened his store in 2013. Personally, I wouldn't go anywhere else. Jimmy and I have been very dear friends for years and years. I bring all my tour groups to meet him and shop here, and have sent readers of my blog and my books here for years. Everyone has a fantastic experience and most weeks I receive at least one photo or get tagged on Instagram by a reader visiting Jimmy's, holding up their shopping bags!

Jimmy's leather jackets are gorgeous. Most are his own design and the styles are beautiful – there is something for every body type. The lining, the stitching, the craftsmanship... everything is superb. Jimmy's staff are super knowledgeable, multi lingual and super fun. Jimmy speaks 21 languages (and in Florence he has often used 11 of them by lunchtime). The other staff average around 10 languages each. I always get a kick out of watching them flip seamlessly from one language into another.

When you come to Jimmy's be sure to tell them you read about them in my book. The folks at most of the shops and restaurants in this book don't know me from Adam, but everyone at Jimmy's has known me for years and will be thrilled to meet you.

Address: Piazza San Lorenzo, 2

What's Nearby: Jimmy's is in the Piazza San Lorenzo, opposite the Basilica and the Medici Chapel. The San Lorenzo Market begins 50 feet away, the Mercato Centrale is just inside the San Lorenzo market. The Duomo is two blocks from here, the Palazzo Medici-Riccardi is on the corner.

Buying Gloves

MADOVA

Florence is world-renowned for beautiful leather gloves, and Madova is one of the best known purveyors of Florentine leather gloves. They carry every length, size, color you can imagine and the staff are incredibly knowledgeable. They'll immediately know your size and style and are tremendously helpful.

Decades ago, on my first trip to Florence, I bought a pair of red leather gloves here. They were beautiful, soft and elegant. After a lifetime of wear they are still beautiful.

Address: Via de' Guicciardini, 1R

What's Nearby: Ponte Vecchio, the Porcellino Market and Orsanmichele are right here. You're a three minute walk to Piazza della Signoria and five minutes from Piazza della Repubblica.

Buying Lingerie

There is something special about bringing home a completely unique piece of lingerie from your travels. For centuries Florence has been known for its beautiful needlework and embroidery. The two shops I recommend visiting for exquisite lingerie also carry all kinds of embroidered/ needleworked items, including bedding, monogrammed towels, specialty table cloths and napkins, and even flower girl dresses. They both also carry lovely items to wear next to your skin.

LORETTA CAPONI

Anthony Hopkins once described this emporium as 'the finest store in all of Italy'. It's not hard to see why. Loretta Caponi's showroom in the wonderful Palazzo Aldobrandini, with its frescoes and highly polished floors, is a thing of beauty. Since 1967 Caponi has provided beautiful and romantic handmade embroidered items to the upper echelons of Italian society, as well as an exclusive international clientele. Famed not only for beautiful table linens and bedding but also for the most divine babywear, Caponi created trousseaux for clients including Princess Diana, European Royalty, Arabian Princesses and Madonna. Her beautiful wares can be found in the yachts, private jets and homes of the Kennedys, Rockefellers, Rothchilds and Gettys. Loretta Caponi also makes possibly the most beautiful nightgowns and bathrobes in the world. Nothing could be lovelier.

Address: Piazza Antinori, 4R

What's Nearby: Loretta Caponi is on via Tornabuoni, near all the designer shops, only a couple of blocks each way from the Duomo and Santa Maria Novella.

LAURA NUTINI

I discovered this beautiful shop completely by accident years ago, while in Florence with one of my best friends. We were walking aimlessly (which is when you find the best secrets and surprises), turned a corner and there it was, nestled between Piazza della Signoria and the Ponte Vecchio, hidden from the masses, yet only a stone's throw away.

This store has been in business for decades and is staffed with a team of expert artisan seamstresses making beautiful, one-of-a-kind creations. Look for linens and nightgowns, an unusual pairing anywhere but here in Italy. The skill of their hand-embroidery is glorious. (On my next visit, I'm planning to get some of their hand-sewn monogramed silk pyjamas and pillowcases.)

Address: Via Lumbertesca, 8R

What's Nearby: Piazza della Signoria, Palazzo Vecchio and the Uffizi. Immediately nearby are the Porcellino market, Orsanmichele, and Ponte Vecchio.

QUERCIOLI & LUCHERINI

You will walk right past this store if you don't know to look for it! It hides a stockpile of fun underthings, this time for both men and women. I particularly love their pyjamas, especially the Hugh Hefner styled button up jammies for men. They are gorgeous.

They carry everything from bras to nipple covers to nightwear, but are renowned for their sensational selection of socks and stockings. These are not boring old fuddy-duddy socks. Think fun patterns, stripes and spots in bold colors and varying lengths, for men and for women, and incredibly cool tights and hose. The quality is tremendous.

This is a great place to find yourself something memorable, or to pick up some very cool gifts.

Address: Via Porta Rossa, 45R

What's Nearby: You're diagonally opposite La Grotta Guelfa, close to Porcellino Market, Piazzas della Repubblica and della Signoria.

Buying Vintage Clothing

I love finding really good vintage shops. Not the thrift store kind, but the ones with incredibly stylish pieces from by-gone eras.

EPOCA

This is a goldmine for shoppers seeking high end vintage pieces in mint condition. Gucci handbag? Check. Chanel sunglasses? Check. Designer shoes? Check.

The store is highly organized. Clothing is color grouped, items are *styled*. There's nothing haphazard here. Talking to the older gentleman who runs Epoca you quickly realize he knows every item in the store and exactly where it is. The shop itself is not large, yet you can lose yourself for ages in here. The merchandise (both designer and non-designer) is fantastic. Come here to find the perfect blazer, or 1960s statement blouse to pair with jeans. There are some American pieces here too, but mostly this shop holds a collection with a strong Italian and French fashion sense.

Address: Via dei Fossi, 6R

What's Nearby: Ognissanti, Santa Maria Novella are close. Santo Spirito is only a 5 minute walk. Stroll the little neighboring streets in the Santa Maria Novella area – there are so many tremendous little shops and eateries tucked away all through here.

STREET DOING

I found this one by accident relatively recently. This is a curated collection of Florentine designers (plus some Frenchies and Americans) held in multiple rooms of organized displays that almost feels like a museum, not a store. Who are the Florentine designers? Think Pucci and Gucci, Ferragamo, and Cavalli for starters. Everything here is in fantastic condition too: boots and shoes, handbags and scarves, clothes and accessories, even evening gowns! The store is unisex and has some fabulous menswear and shoes, but I am usually most interested in the costume jewelry, hats and sunglasses for women.

If you enjoy a classic blazer, Pucci dress, scarf, or a vintage Gucci bag – you will *love* this place!

Address: Via dei Servi, 88R

What's Nearby: Via dei Servi is only two blocks long. The Duomo is at one end, Piazza SS Annunziata at the other.

MOMO VINTAGE

Momo Vintage moved to this location in 2017 after 20 years in San Lorenzo. Away from the big crowds, this is a wonderful area to explore and observe Florentine life. Momo is another great spot where you'll find Chanel, Ferragamo, Celine, YSL – every major designer you can think of. The collection is nicely curated and items are in wonderful condition. If you appreciate the value in really great vintage clothing, bags, shoes, etc, you will love Momo Vintage.

Address: Via dei Serragli, 7R | Momovintage.it

What's Nearby: This is in Oltrarno, just beyond Santo Spirito, near Santa Maria del Carmine and the beautiful Brancacci Chapel, just moments from Santa Trinita' bridge.

RECOLLECTION BY ALBRICI

Alberto Albrici opened his antiques business on via dei Serragli in 1961. A curator rather than a dealer, he collects the stories that go with each piece, then finds it the right home. In 2012 he acquired the store next door to his antiques business and applied the same aesthetic to vintage clothing. But not just any vintage clothing. Albrici curates the finest moments in twentieth century fashion. There are one-off dresses, of course made in Italy, some bespoke, others representing the best in international designers. This isn't just a shop, it is a collection, so he cleverly named the store *Recollection*. It carries amazing fashion and accessories, vintage handbags, shoes and costume jewelry by the biggest names in fashion. They take a fabulous vintage piece and give it a modern twist.

Albrici says the items come from fascinating women who have stories to tell. The staff can regale you with who wore an item where, when and why and tell you the story to go with it. I live for this stuff! Plan to spend some time here listening to the stories and exploring the merchandise, and make sure you leave with something truly spectacular. This shop is *glorious*. The store was fittingly described by UrbanItaly.com as 'a spellbinding history of haute couture through the 1900s'. Not only do I love visiting the store, I also follow Recollection by Albrici on Instagram for a daily dose of fabulousness.

Address: Via dei Serragli, 22

What's Nearby: Recollection is close to Santa Maria del Carmine and the Branacci Chapel, Santo Spirito, Il Santino for an aperitivo, and Ponte alla Carraia for a gelato.

CELESTE VINTAGE

If you are serious about finding vintage designer handbags, come here. They do sell more than just bags, but Good Lord, *the bags*! As with any consignment/vintage store there is an ever changing selection of merchandise, but expect to find Ferragamo, Gucci, YSL, Celine – all the big names, in excellent condition. Designer shoes, accessories and fabulous clothes await you here. Happy shopping, and you're welcome!

Address: Piazza San Felice, 1R

What's Nearby: Celeste is opposite Pitti Palace, close to the Boboli Gardens and Caffè Pitti, less than five minutes from Ponte Vecchio.

Buying Linens

I've bought many tablecloths and linens from Florence and Tuscany over the years. They always make me happy and remind me of a fabulous trip. Admittedly I mostly seek out linens from merchants at local village markets, but for those interested in specialty Florentine linens, or specialty Italian linens, Florence has fantastic places to shop.

For hand-embroidered linens, there are Loretta Caponi and Laura Nutini (both mentioned above with the lingerie shops), but I have two other suggestions for you.

LISA CORTI

Milanese designer Lisa Corti spent her childhood in Africa, where she fell in love with the bright colors the women wore and the way the sunlight bounced off them. Later she spent time in India and discovered another visual banquet of bright colors and patterns, as well as weightless, magical fabrics. Her eponymous line is fueled and fed by all of these experiences and impressions, blended with a geometry that creates harmony.

From tableware to pillows, sofas, bedding, and home accessories (including aprons and the most unique pill boxes and hat boxes you'll ever see), this line is stunning. Colors are bold, the patterns make sense, and it is all incredibly beautiful.

Address: Piazza Lorenzo Ghiberti, 33

What's Nearby: You're close to the Sant' Ambrogio market, the church of Sant' Ambrogio (from **Chapter 13: Unusual & Interesting Things**). Piazza Santa Croce is a 10 minute walk, with Casa Buonarotti between the two.

LE TELERIE TOSCANE DI GIULIA

This boutique offers all manner of Tuscan linens, from bed linens to tableware, to monogrammed towels and much more. Giulia is a master craftsman and trained under Laura Caponi before venturing out on her own. The aesthetic is typically Tuscan and Renaissance-Tuscan. It is perfect not only for souvenirs but also for gifts. They have beautiful monogrammed sheets and towels too. In the gift category they have items for children, tableware, decoupaged trays and other kinds of easy-to-pack-in-your-suitcase things.

Address: Sdrucciolo de' Pitti, 15R

What's Nearby: Le Telerie Toscane is down a little side street opposite the Pitti Palace. It is just around the corner from the Caffè

Pitti and the Boboli Gardens and is a two minute walk from the Ponte Vecchio.

Buying Paper & Stationery

Florence has a long history of creating beautiful paper products and marbled papers. Hand bound journals and books from Florence make fabulous keepsakes and gifts. Trust me, watching a paper marbling demonstration is fascinating, and makes a wonderful addition to your Florentine experience.

ALBERTO COZZI

I learned about this place from an artist friend, Jill Seale. Jill loves the art of marbling paper and fabrics, and has spent considerable time in Florence learning the craft. When I asked her where to buy marbled papers, notebooks & journals, without hesitation she told me to go to Alberto Cozzi.

This store opened in 1908 and is a multi-generational family business. Considered an authority on Florentine paper and bookbinding, their products are sought worldwide. The company's bound books are used by libraries and businesses (like legal firms and notaries), who want items of value and beauty that will last forever.

Cozzi family members regularly host demonstrations creating these beautiful papers, where you can buy marbled papers and bound books. They have leather bound books, and will print your name or initials on them in gold leaf, using time-trusted techniques and instruments. They make some of my favorite souvenirs. They also sell picture frames and photo albums and all kinds of other wonderful things.

Address: Via del Parione, 35

What's Nearby: This is roughly halfway between Ponte Vecchio and Ponte Santa Trinita', just one block from the river, near the churches of Santa Trinita' and Ognissanti. The Museo Salvatore Ferragamo and Loretta Caponi are close by.

SCRIPTORIUM ATELIER

If you love calligraphy, handmade paper, sealing wax, blank books, inks and pens then this will be the place for you. You can order wedding invitations and restaurant menus and all manner of printed items on your choice of paper, or you can buy readymade items. Be sure to look at their *Contentitori Libri* (hollowed-out books to hide your personal treasures: money, secrets, jewelry). They make fantastic gifts.

Address: Via dei Pucci, 4 (inside the courtyard)

What's Nearby: Behind the Duomo before via dei Servi, Scriptorium is near the Opera del Duomo museum.

Buying Perfume

OFFICINA PROFUMO – FARMACEUTICA DI SANTA MARIA NOVELLA

This is the world's oldest pharmacy and is a treasured under-the-radar spot. It can be tricky to find so don't be surprised if you walk right past its unassuming storefront.

Founded by Dominican Friars sometime after their arrival in 1221, the monks made medications, salves and balms from herbs they grew in the monastic gardens of Santa Maria Novella. They used these to heal the sick and the dying in the church infirmary. When the Black Plague wiped out more than 70% of Florence's population in the fourteenth century, the monks famously made a distilled rosewater antiseptic to disinfect people's homes. You can still buy this exact product (*Aqua di Rose*) now sold as a toner and a perfume.

In the sixteenth century, the monks created a special perfume to celebrate the wedding of 14-year-old Catherine de' Medici to Henry II, the future King of France. Until this point, perfumes were suspended in oil, which quickly went rancid. The monks devised a method still in use today of suspending fragrance in alcohol. The fragrance created for Catherine (known then as *Aqua della Regina)* is still available, although it has been renamed *Aqua di Santa Maria Novella*. Its distinctive blend of bergamot and aromatic spices is still popular today. You can buy it as fragrance, bath products or candles.

REIGN

For ages friends told me to watch a Netflix show called *Reign*. It's the story of Mary Queen of Scots and her marriage to the heir to the French throne. I wasn't really interested, but when I finally decided to watch an episode to appease everyone, I ended up loving it, mostly because of Catherine de' Medici. She is played as ruthless, villainous and brilliant, and I kept watching the show just to see what she would get up to next.

I have no idea whether the real Catherine de' Medici was anywhere near as interesting as she is on TV but I guarantee if you watch the show you too will have an entirely different appreciation for the Officina Profumo!

Now when I'm in Florence, I always go out of my way to visit the Officina Profumo. I douse myself in the perfume of Catherine de' Medici and have bought everything they sell with that fragrance. In fact, as I write this book I have her fragrant candles burning on my desk. I buy them as gifts and I try to make people watch the show so that they will get as big of a kick out of the perfume as I do.

Catherine de' Medici's is just one of many fragrances available here. There also sell wonderful skin care products, bath products and home fragrances. Even if you're not interested in fragrance, still slip inside and have a look. The building itself, the frescoes and the rooms are worth visiting. The recently opened library here has frescoes by Mariotto di Nardo. You may spot something unusual with his *Last Supper*. (Normally we see them at a rectangular table but here they sit at a round table. A small detail but I find it fascinating.)

Address: Via della Scala, 16

What's Nearby: Of course, this is next to Santa Maria Novella. Tip Tap and Ognissanti are close by. San Lorenzo market, Basilica and the Medici Chapel are less than a 5 minute walk.

FARMACIA SS ANNUNCIATA

Chemist and herbalist Domenico di Vincenzo Brunetti opened this store in 1561. The same dark wooden cabinets have held his wares for more than 500 years! Here you will find the farmacia's exclusive line of all natural products, still made to the original recipe: skin care and hair care products for men, women and children, sage soaps and toothpastes, body gels, aftershave, and suntan oils, all wrapped in the store's simple signature black and white packaging. They also have their own fragrance line. Everything is handmade, so you can bring home something unique and lovely, with a history spanning centuries.

Address: Via dei Servi, 80R

What's Nearby: You're next to Piazza SS Annunziata. The Duomo is 500 meters away and between the two is vintage clothing emporium, Street Doing.

Buying Housewares

BARTOLINI

This is another shop found by accident while walking in Florence. (I swear you find the best things just by wandering around!) If you've ever dreamed of buying fabulous Italian kitchenware, tableware or barware, this is the place for you! I don't bring home electronics, but there are so many chic and modern kitchen items here, from espresso cups to vegetable cutters, and pasta machines to mokas. Bartolini has a tremendous collection of things you never realized you needed, but that will look gorgeous in your kitchen or on your table.

Address: Via dei Servi, 72R

What's Nearby: Bartolini is next to the da Vinci museum, four buildings along from Farmacia SS Annunciata, in the shadow of the Duomo.

IL PARALUME

If you are in the market for a new lamp, lampshade or chandelier, welcome to lighting paradise! Everything here from the lampshades to the lampstands is made by hand using exclusively Italian products. Lamp bases are made from wood or metal, lacquered, gold leafed or left au naturel. Some merchandise here has an old Tuscan feel, some is quite modern. They have lamps and mirrors in every size imaginable. (I am particularly enamored of their chandeliers and wall lamps.)

Il Paralume opened in 1952, and apparently their lamps are in the bar scene of the iconic Italian film *La Dolce Vita*. You can buy from their existing stock or have something custom made. And don't worry about fitting lamps or lampshades into your suitcase – Il Paralume ships worldwide.

Address: Borgo San Frediano, 47

What's Nearby: Il Paralume is in the Oltrarno, just beyond the Ponte alla Carraia, close to the Gelataria alla Carraia; also close to Santa Maria del Carmine (the Brancacci Chapel), and the less-visited San Frediano in Cestello.

CASTORINA

This is one of those fantastic family businesses you stumble upon wandering the artisan neighborhoods of the Oltrarno, where the secrets of master craftsmanship pass down through generations. The Castorina family are master wood carvers, who relocated from Sicily in 1895. Whether you're seeking massive furniture pieces for your home or small decorative items, curtain rod holdbacks, bookends, furniture legs or keyhole inserts, this is the place to come. At first it's overwhelming – there is so much here, but take a deep breath (inhale the fragrance of fresh wood) and start by looking at the smaller items. Everything is made by hand, even the small, perfect cupids (*putti*).

There are many small, packable items that make perfect Florentine souvenirs, so whether you're on a home decorating mission or just meandering through Florence looking at interesting things, add this one to your list.

Address: Via Santo Spirito, 15R

What's Nearby: Castorina is between Ponte Santa Trinita' and Ponte alla Carraia. You're two minutes from Piazza Santo Spirito, and down the street from Il Santino. Gelataria alla Carraia is three minutes from here, Santa Maria del Carmine less than five minutes.

PAMPALONI

The Pampaloni family silverware business began in a shop on the Ponte Vecchio in 1902. At the time the family lived above the shop and workshop, but now, three generations later, Pampaloni is on via Porta Rossa. Here you'll find everything from €10,000 candelabras to small pieces of incredibly cool jewelry, all made in silver. Decanters, pitchers, trays in all sizes, frames and cutlery make incredible gifts, especially for weddings. This is a great place to buy yourself something special that will last a lifetime. It is easy to get caught up in the larger homeware pieces, but be sure to check out the jewelry too. The *Human Metal Forx* bracelet is one of the coolest pieces I've seen in a long time.

Address: Via Porta Rossa, 99R

What's Nearby: You're one minute from Basilica Santa Trinita', just over a block from La Grotta Guelfa restaurant and three blocks from the Porcellino Market.

Buying Jewelry

On my first trip to Florence, while exploring the town we wandered across the Ponte Vecchio into the Oltrarno. My friend Andrea and I stumbled upon a tiny shop, not much more than one window wide, where the owner sat behind a wooden bench, hunched over his tools, making jewelry. I bought a pair of earrings that were like nothing I had ever seen before. They became my favorite earrings, for years worn only on special occasions. Several massive moves around the world later and I now have no idea where they are, but this brings me to some important words of advice:

- Seek out the artisan workshops in the Oltrarno and buy your jewelry there. I was not much older than a teenager when I bought my earrings, so they can't have been expensive.

- If possible buy yourself a piece of jewelry when you travel. It doesn't have to be expensive, but you will treasure it forever and it will always remind you of where you were when you bought it.

- Don't save things for special occasions! Wear what you love all the time. Maximize your pleasure. Life is too short to keep your favorite things tucked away.

CARLO CECCHI/ GIULIANO RICCHI

This is one of the best kept secrets in Florence. In 1962, aged 15, Giuliano Ricchi began his apprenticeship under goldsmith master Carlo Cecchi, creating works of art in 100% sterling silver and 18 karat gold in the way of the masters. Giuliano is considered a national treasure, being one of the very few remaining 'smiths' in all of Italy who not only designs his pieces but manufactures them from start to finish, following the tradition of the Renaissance master, Cellini.

Suffice to say, he is a really big deal, albeit a humble one. You would never guess that this lovely, unassuming gentleman is highly sought after by, and designs for, major international fashion houses such as the House of Dior and Nina Ricci, and also for European Royalty. His products are sold in stores in Italy and all around the world (including the upscale department store, Nieman Marcus, in the US).

Don't be thinking this is out of your price range – although he designs for the biggest names in the world, he also creates for regular folks. Expect to find exquisite treasures here, including jewelry, pill boxes, key chains, and business card holders. Apparently President Clinton was a big fan of his Post-It Note holders. Everything is handmade in a multi-step process of molding, shaping, engraving, and electroplating. Most of Ricchi's designs are cast in brass then dipped in gold or silver. All of his designs are special and I particularly love items that are specifically Florentine, such as the fleur-de-lis.

Giuliano doesn't have a big, flashy showroom on a big commercial shopping street. Instead his operation is low key, with essentially no store front. If you don't know where to seek him out, then, like most travelers to Florence, you'll miss out. Giuliano Ricchi's atelier is in Piazza Santo Spirito. When you visit, you'll not only get to see his merchandise but also his workshop, which like the man is totally unassuming. Here you can watch the master at work and buy pieces at below retail price.

The workshop is in a palazzo at the far end of Piazza Santo Spirito (number 12). Ring the doorbell marked 'Ricchi and Carlo Cecci', and either Giuliano or his wife Maria will come and get you.

Address: Piazza Santo Spirito, 12

What's Nearby: You're close to the church of Santo Spirito, my favorite apertivo spot, Il Santino, and one of my favorite rooftop bars, The Palazzo Guadagni.

A Traveler's Best Kept Secret – The Prada Outlet

There is an outlet center just outside Florence, but I found it uninspiring. HOWEVER, there is a *fabulous* outlet experience a short train ride from Florence – the Prada Outlet in Montevarchi.

This is Prada's largest store in the world and is unlike any outlet store. It is *madly chic*. Doormen greet you in Prada suits, and everyone working here wears sleek black Prada pants and a crisp white Prada shirt. They are multi-lingual and all look like perfect Prada specimens, groomed to the nth degree, their hair and makeup understated perfection. This is fashion nirvana. On arrival you are given a numbered ticket and as you wander around the store, everything you want to purchase is applied to your ticket number and awaits you at the cashier's booth when you are ready to leave. This is a sleek operation. You don't carry around armfuls of clothes, shoes and bags like it's the Macy's sale, and there are no bargain basement shopping carts. They have everything here, glasses, sunglasses, bags, shoes... everything you see on the runway. The men's section is enormous too. Huge flat screen TVs play the latest Prada runway shows, the racks are not crammed, and you feel like you are in a big glam Prada store, not at an outlet.

Everything is 50-70% off the regular retail price, which at Prada is still not cheap, but is perhaps more accessible. (One of my Glam Italia tour travelers picked up a $3500 Prada handbag for $500.) If an item is at Nordstrom in the US, it will probably already be at the outlet in Montevarchi, so before I leave for Italy, I visit Nordstrom and try a few things on. Then I look for (and usually find) the same item at the Prada outlet at a fraction of the price. For example, I'd seen a pair of shoes at Nordstrom for US$980 and a week later I purchased the same pair in Montevarchi for €270 – AND I got the sales tax back at the airport (€59), so ended up spending around €210 euros or US$225. Major savings!

HOW TO GET THERE

Take the train from Santa Maria Novella to Montevarchi. Taxis run back and forth to the outlet all day long. Don't forget to bring your passport as they will fill out your tax forms for you at the cashier's booth. There is a Prada café here too, so grab a chic coffee and a snack before you leave.

17.

The Best Markets in Florence

I love exploring local markets when I travel. Whether shopping for leather handbags, housewares, gifts, treasures from old villas, or something to bring home for dinner, the markets in Florence have it all.

Florentine markets are great for treasure hunting or for buying local Tuscan breads, cheeses, wines and produce. Don't be surprised to find a street market with booths selling vintage Louis Vuitton, Prada and Chanel handbags next to a booth selling hot porchetta sandwiches, all while surrounded by Renaissance history. Markets in Florence are a visual banquet!

SAN LORENZO MARKET

This is Florence's original leather market. It's the place to score a killer deal on Italian leather handbags, wallets, belts and some pretty incredible Italian leather jackets. (Read **Chapter 15: How to Buy Leather** first.)

The market used to fill the piazza in front of Basilica San Lorenzo but recently moved back to the streets around the Mercato Centrale. Hundreds of stalls line the streets selling leather goods, leather bound journals, pashminas, jewelry, and ceramics. Buy souvenirs for yourself or do Christmas shopping for others. Handbags in the market selling for €35 show up in boutiques in the US for hundreds of dollars, so be sure you come to Florence with room in your suitcase!

In any market environment watch out for pickpockets and be smart while you're shopping. Although many of the vendors sell quality merchandise, there are some 'Made in China' replicas as well. Dodgy vendors know the average tourist won't have the time or the experience to tell the rubbish from the quality. My best advice is don't make any big dollar purchases in a hurry. If you don't have time to really look a piece over and make sure it is genuine, don't buy it. If you see a leather jacket for €150 there's a good chance it's not real Italian leather, but some type of imported hybrid.

Address: Piazza San Lorenzo

Hours: Open every day.

Mercato Centrale

In the late nineteenth century the Mercato Vecchio (old market) was pulled down to make way for the Piazza della Repubblica, so Florence needed a replacement covered food market. A city block behind San Lorenzo was selected and architect Giuseppe Mengoni (best known for the cast iron and glass Galleria Vittorio Emanuele II in Milan) designed the new market based on Les Halles in Paris. The new market opened in 1874, and although madly modern for its time, integrated beautifully with the neighborhood. The traditional design of the stone façade of the ground floor evoked Renaissance loggias, while the second floor was startling with its red cast iron frame and many windows.

The ground floor of the indoor market hall sells local Tuscan meat, fish and produce, much of which gets snapped up by local restaurants. Throughout the day you'll rub shoulders with Florentines doing their shopping. Pack your cash and your camera and stroll the aisles and booths. This place is fun whether you're shopping for a dinner party or a mid-morning snack.

The second floor is a Tuscan gourmet food court full of booths and stalls offering bottles of oils, jars of jams and readymade meals to eat there or take away. There is also a cooking school. There is a Chianti consortium here where you can try wines from multiple wineries and have them shipped home. This is a perfect option if you don't have time to visit a winery, or if you just want to stop somewhere for a glass of wine.

For the last few years my home in Florence has been an apartment in a palace next to the Medici Riccardi Palace, so the Mercato Centrale is only a five minute walk away. I often drop by the food court on my way home to grab something for dinner. My Glam Italia tour travelers love swinging by after a busy day of sightseeing, and choosing fresh pasta, cheeses, local jams, cold meats, prepared meals or items needed for the evening's antipasti. I love shopping here and hope you will find your way here for a meal, a snack or a quick look around!

Address: Piazza del Mercato Centrale

Hours: Open every day.

Mercato Nuovo (Mercato del Porcellino)

The Porcellino Market carries much of the same merchandise as the San Lorenzo Market but is a fraction of the size. In the sixteenth century, the Mercato Nuovo replaced the old market across the street at Orsanmichele.

This market is also known as Mercato del Porcellino thanks to its fountain of a wild boar, nicknamed 'the piglet' (*porcellino*). Legend says if you rub the boar's nose you will come back to Florence. Actually, depending on who you are talking to there are a variety of legends as to what fortune the nose rub will bring, but I would die if I couldn't come back so I rub that pig's nose every time I'm in town! The current porcellino is a replica of the bronze boar created by Pietro Tacca in 1634, which in turn was a copy of a Greek marble boar given to Cosimo I by Pope Pius IV. The marble boar now lives in the Uffizi. The original bronze boar is in the Bardini Museum, and this replica, with his shiny, well-rubbed snout, has been in situ since 1998. Rub his nose then put a coin in his mouth and see if it falls through the grate.

While in the crowd surrounding the porcellino, keep your hand firmly on your bag. This market is very crowded and therefore a pickpocket paradise. This past summer I watched a ring of gypsy girls trying to get their hands inside handbags, and brazenly reaching into the fountain retrieving coins as fast as tourists were dropping them in. Be sure to wear a cross-body bag, keep it zipped closed with the side that opens against your torso, and with your hand on it. The gypsies mostly disappear with the tour buses, so if you're staying overnight come back when the market closes. You'll have the piggie to yourself and no one trying to pick your pocket.

After the market closes, you'll also be able to see the beautiful loggia that houses it. With the hustle and bustle of a busy market and the incredible volume of people shopping here, it is impossible to see how gorgeous the building actually is until the crowd clears.

There is something else to see when the market closes: the *Pietra dello Scandolo* (Stone of Shame) is a circle of bi-colored marble in the middle of the loggia floor. The stone has a second name, *pietra dell'acculata* (stone of the bum punishment). During the Renaissance one punishment for not paying your debts was being chained to a post on this spot and having your naked bum paddled. Wouldn't that be mortifying? (There is a slang expression in Italian: *stare con culo a terra* – to have your ass on the ground, as well as a dialect word *sculo*, which means misfortune, both of which may have come from the naked bum-whacking in the loggia!)

Address: Piazza del Mercato Nuovo

Hours: Open every day.

Mercato Sant' Ambrogio

Few tourists find their way here, so it feels like an insider secret. This is an indoor-outdoor market selling fruits, vegetables and all kinds of foods. Come here for fresh prosciutto and cheeses, and also for knick-knacks, vintage clothes and general household items. The Mercato Sant' Ambrogio is a local market for Florentines. As with the San Cosimato market outside my front door in Rome and the village markets I love to visit all over Tuscany, it smells and sounds like the quintessential Italian market. It's such an authentic experience that even if you're not shopping, I recommend you make an effort to walk it, smell it, and enjoy it!

Address: Piazza Lorenzo Ghiberti

Hours: 7am–1pm daily.

The Ciompi Market

This antiques market happens on the last Sunday of the month in the Piazza dei Ciompi. From furniture to porcelain items, knick-knacks to design objects, this is a great place to shop for unique and interesting things for your home. Or you can just wander through and look. A handful of permanent stands open daily, selling all kinds of cool things (including a stand where I bought some chic old buttons to breathe new life into a coat).

The piazza is named for the Wool Guild (the Ciompi) who had themselves an uprising here back in 1378. The revolt was called the *Tumulto dei Ciompi*. Lorenzo Ghiberti's house is here in the piazza, as is a very beautiful loggia, which looks somewhat out of place. Back in 1565 when the Vasari Corridor was being built, the stinky fish market was moved from the Ponte Vecchio. Cosimo I had Vasari design this loggia in what was then the town marketplace (now Piazza della Repubblica). The Loggia del Peche was home to the fish sellers for the next 300 years. In 1885 when the old market was torn down to build the republic square the loggia thankfully was saved and moved here. It looks a bit incongruous, but by not blending in it does draw your attention.

The great flood of 1966 hit this piazza hard. Look for plaques high on the walls of the palazzi to see how high the flood waters reached.

On the northeast corner of the piazza, by the loggia, is a flower vendor. When I'm staying in Florence I love to buy fresh flowers here for my apartment. A little detail like fresh flowers can make your vacation rental feel deliciously homey.

Piazza Ciompi has some tremendous restaurants and eateries. On via Pietrapiana enjoy the ambience of the piazza with a coffee or a drink at Bar Plaz, or further down the road is the excellent Cibreo Trattoria, which has a line waiting outside every night for dinner.

Address: Piazza dei Ciompi

Hours: The last Sunday of every month.

What's Nearby: Piazza Ambrogio, Casa Buonarotti (Michelangelo's house) and you're a 5–10 minute walk from Piazza Santa Croce.

The Cascine Market

Easily the biggest open air market in Florence, stretching one kilometer through the Cascine park, and open every Tuesday from 8am–2pm, this is a place locals shop for everything including food, housewares, clothes and more. I haven't been for a couple of years, but I have brought disposable plates and utensils in a bag from home and picnicked here. I recommend walking the length of the market first and having a good look before you start buying things, as it's a long way from one end to the other lugging heavy shopping bags. Stop at the food stalls on your way back (they're at the front end of the market), buy your picnic items then go stretch out on the grass and enjoy a Florentine afternoon with great food and a good book, far from the madding crowd.

Getting There: The Cascine market is most easily reached by tram or bus. Both tram and bus tickets are bought in Tabaccaio shops around the station. Make sure you validate your ticket when you board.

- **Tram**: Take the tram from Santa Maria Novella in the direction of Villa Costanza, to the Cascine stop. Returning, take the tram in the direction of Alamanni. Trams run every 10 minutes.

- **Bus**: From Santa Maria Novella, take Bus 17 to Parco della Cascine, to the Cascine stop. Returning, take the 17 bus in the Viale Verga direction. This bus goes all the way to Piazza San Marco, which is handy if you are staying further into the city center than Santa Maria Novella.

Address: Viale dei Lecci, in Parco Cascine

Hours: Tuesdays, 8am–2pm.

Santo Spirito Flea Market

If you're in Florence on the second Sunday of the month, head over to the Santo Spirito Flea Market. Stalls selling everything from antique furniture to vintage clothing and accessories are fun to explore, and you might find some treasures to bring home.

The piazza has plenty of bars and restaurants to sit and people-watch. Florentines love this market, and I love checking out their outfits as they walk by. They always look so stylish even when perusing stalls at a Sunday market.

Address: Piazza Santo Spirito

Hours: The second Sunday of the month. The Santo Spirito market stays open until late.

Santo Spirito Artisan Market

On the third Sunday of the month, Piazza Santo Spirito hosts an artisans market selling organic, local and handmade products. Shop for honey, wine, candles, cutting boards made from olive wood, or jewelry made from recycled materials. This is a fabulous market to shop for gifts and also to sample some local flavors before lunch.

Address: Piazza Santo Spirito

Hours: Every third Sunday of the month.

Fortezza da Basso Antique Market

On the third weekend of each month, market stalls line the area around the pond and along the paths at the Fortezza da Basso. This market is for antiques, furniture, collectibles and more.

While you're there, check out the fort itself, designed for Alessandro de' Medici in 1530 by Antonio da Sangallo, and considered a masterpiece in military architecture.

Getting There: A visit to this market requires a special trip, rather than dropping by while in the neighborhood. By taxi it is five minutes from the train station.

Address: The garden at Fortezza da Basso

Hours: Every third weekend of the month, 9am–7pm.

Fiesole Vintage Market

Just outside Florence is the magical little town of Fiesole. Famed for its frescoes and Roman ruins, the town also has one of the best markets in Tuscany. On the first Sunday of every month, Fiesole's main square, Piazza Mino, hosts an amazing flea market where you can find antiques, collectibles, vintage clothes and all manner of rare and interesting objects.

Getting There: Bus 7 departs every half hour from Piazza San Marco for the 20 minute ride to Fiesole. Buses run into the night (double check before you go), so you can stay for dinner before coming back to Florence.

Address: Piazza Mino da Fiesole, Fiesole

Hours: The first Sunday of the month.

What's Nearby: I recommend visiting the Roman ruins first and having a good wander around town before shopping. Take time to enjoy an aperitivo or lunch with a view before heading back to the city.

Aperitivo Time

18.

Aperitivo Time

I absolutely love aperitivo time in Italy. There is something so gloriously civilized about stopping for a pre-dinner drink and nibble at the end of the day. I love the social interaction and the mini event it creates, I adore sitting outside somewhere fabulous with a gorgeous view and a glass of wine, especially in the summer months.

In Rome, I meet my Roman BFF at a simple little bar in the Trastevere, and sit out in the piazza with a gorgeous view of ochre-hued buildings, cobblestones and potted plants. Happy as a clam.

In Venice, I go to Bar Foscarini on the Dorsoduro with its view of the Grand Canal, or to one of the bars lining the Zattere. I love being outdoors overlooking the water.

In San Gimignano, I like to be at the wall with a glass of wine, watching the sun drop low over the vineyards and olive groves.

In Sorrento, I have a huge balcony with a view of Mount Vesuvius and the Bay of Naples. More than anything I love sitting up there at sunset with a glass of fiano and a bowl of olives. The fragrance of Sorrento lemons wafting up on the breeze from the hillside below is heavenly.

But in Florence, I go for a different vibe. I love slipping into tiny little bars with a neighborhood clientele. It's fun watching locals engage in their social rituals after work, often squished together at the bar, always madly chic and stylish. Aperitivo time serves an important social function in the local Florentine lifestyle. Unlike the meat market of happy hour in the US, this is a time of human connection. Sit back and watch them for a moment, everyone is making eye contact as they talk to each other, leaning in; the food and wine become social glue in this casual setting, keeping the bonds of the human experience good and strong. I dream about owning a slice of that life.

Before I tell you about my favorite places to have an aperitivo, let's talk about what you should expect: an aperitivo is a late afternoon/early evening glass of wine with snacks, maybe a selection of cheeses and olives, cured salamis, fresh figs with prosciutto (my personal favorite), and in Florence it is invariably with crostini.

CROSTINI

What are crostini? These are thin sliced rounds of fine textured bread, brushed with oil and toasted. Because they are small, they have intensely flavored toppings, making them the perfect little bites.

The snacks will vary based on where you go. Some come free with your drink, others you purchase. With the exception of two entries on this list, the most important criteria for perfect aperitivo time is the quality of the food and wine. Choose places offering boutique wines and where you can see that thought and care have gone into the food choices, rather than some *aperi-trash* all-you-can-eat buffet option.

Regardless of your dinner plans (if you don't drink alcohol you can do a lemon soda instead), I definitely recommend taking part in aperitivo hour while in Florence. You can also do aperitivo walking tours in Florence with a private guide. I have a list of guides for you at **www.glamitaliabooks.com/florenceguides**

Here are some of my favorite places for an aperitivo:

Piazza Duomo

Yes, it's touristy and over-priced, but who cares? It's unlike anywhere else in the world. If you're in Florence in summer, you *must* sit outside at one of the bars in the Piazza Duomo and have a drink, at least once. Because this is tourist central, hang on to your handbag, expect to pay more than necessary for a perfectly average bottle of wine, and consider yourself lucky if they bring you a bowl of chips.

What is important here is the view. Soak it in, let it burn its image into your brain. The view of the cathedral in that exquisite late afternoon/early evening light will become your default memory of Florence.

I prefer the south side, because of the way the light plays against the side of the cathedral – it's so incredibly beautiful. There's magic in the air, with street musicians playing violins and accordions and artists selling paintings. It's worth doing at least once.

Near the Duomo

FIASCHETTERIA NUVOLI

This is (yet another) of my accidental finds. On a day when Florence was full of tourists, I ducked down this side street to get a quick coffee before heading off to wherever I was going. I walked in here but it was empty and a guy was working in the kitchen, deep in thought, making what I later found out were crostini. There was no sign of a coffee machine, so I walked back out. He came flying out after me calling out, 'Hey! Hey! Come back!' I assumed he thought I was a shoplifter, so I went back to show him I wasn't and to avoid being arrested in a foreign language, which he found hilarious. Thinking I was offended when he didn't come speak to me at the bar, he had chased me down the street to make things right and to explain that he had been at an important stage in the making of crostini. It so happened that crostini is one of my favorite words, so I wound up sitting here at the bar with a glass of local red, sampling his creations, and chatting with him while he prepped for aperitivo time.

Fiaschetteria Nuvoli is small and gets packed every day, so plan to arrive a little early. Their wines are glorious and their food is fantastic.

Address: Piazza dell'Olio, 15R

What's Nearby: Here you're one block below the Baptistery, between the Duomo and Santa Maria Novella.

Near San Lorenzo

LA CASA DEL VINO

I've been coming here for years. I used to pop in for a glass of wine while waiting for my friend Jimmy to finish work nearby, and I still get a kick out of stopping here for an aperitivo. This area is full of bars and restaurants so you're spoiled for choice with hipster and chic options, but I recommend finding your way here for a more authentic experience. Casa del Vino is a standing-room-only wine bar dating back to the 1800s. With its carved woodwork and marble counter tops, ambience and rich history, this is a place locals frequent and tourists don't know about, despite it being in the middle of the busy street market!

The trick here is to stand at the bar and join in the conversation. Gianni and Nicoletta keep a lively multi-lingual chatter going, and before you know it you'll be chatting and rubbing shoulders (*literally* – the place is tiny) with local artisans, workers and artists who frequent this bar.

The wine selection is extensive and fabulous, yet surprisingly affordable. The food is wonderful. There are lots of options but I love the Tuscan crostini, the finger foods and cheeses. They also make fantastic panini, served wrapped in paper. A cross-body bag is a bonus here, allowing you to keep one hand free for your sandwich and the other for your glass of wine.

Address: Via dell'Ariento, 16R

What's Nearby: This is smack bang in the middle of the San Lorenzo market streets, close to Mercato Centrale, Basilica San Lorenzo, the Medici Chapel and Jimmy's Leather Collection.

Oltrarno District

IL SANTINO

Honestly, this one is probably my favorite. It's a tiny sliver of a bar on a street with no view of anything special, yet it is totally cool. Half the time it is too packed for me to go in, yet I come back to try again over and over. With only four tables and a handful of bar stools inside, in nice weather patrons spill out onto the street, wine glasses in hand. They're mostly regulars – this place really does fly under the radar. The staff are young, hip and knowledgeable. I've always found them friendly.

Il Santino specializes in natural wines and wines from small, boutique Tuscan wineries. They do give you a complimentary snack but I recommend ordering a *tagliere* plate of their incredible cheeses and meats, all of which arrive fresh from local farms, and/or some crostini.

Address: Via di Santo Spirito, 60R

What's Nearby: This is right by Santo Spirito, 5 minutes from Ponte Vecchio and the Pitti Palace.

LE VOLPI E L'UVA

The Fox and the Grapes is a darling wine bar just beyond the Ponte Vecchio in the Oltrarno. If you don't know to look for it you will miss it – if you get to Santa Felicita' church you have gone too far. The clientele is mostly locals and Italians visiting from other parts of the country, plus the odd straggler like me.

The wine list is ever-evolving. At any time there will be around 30 wines available by the glass, all from small, lesser-known wineries from all over the country. This is a great place to get involved with a crisp white from Alto Adige or a peppery red from Sicily. I love discovering boutique wines that will never be produced in supermarket-type volume. The staff will tell you about the slopes a wine was grown on and how the terrain dramatically changes the taste from the wines on the neighboring slope. I love that kind of wine chatter, especially when the wineries are small and family run. I'm all about the story that goes with anything.

One time a wine waiter acted out this dramatic story of a vine fighting to grow through the stones and rocks, with no irrigation, blasting sunshine and the onslaught of all the elements. He told me how the vine has to *struggle* in order to create a great wine and a vintage discernably different from the year before. I was all in. The wine, of course, was fantastic, and it marked the beginning of my love affair with Brunello, but it was the story and the passion with which he told it that had me enthralled.

One last secret about waiters and sommeliers telling you the story behind a given wine: they don't get impassioned about a mediocre or sub-standard wine. The more involved they get with the story, the more the hands get going, the more excited they are – and the more fantastic this wine will be!

The food here is fabulous. Order a *tagliere* platter of farm-to-table meats and cheeses – always a winner. Try their tiny truffle panini, or pretty much anything from the snack menu.

Address: Piazza dei Rossi, 1R

What's Nearby: You're two minutes from Ponte Vecchio, three minutes from the Boboli Gardens and Pitti Palace. On long summer evenings I love to stop here for an aperitivo and then burn it off walking up to Piazzale Michelangelo to watch the sunset over the city.

I suggest you wander all through this area. The little streets are full of shops and eateries and vastly fewer tourists than on the other side of the river. Around here, you get an authentic glimpse into Florentine life, and it is gorgeous.

Near Piazza della Signoria

IL LOCALE

This is the most expensive recommendation on my list and the only one you need to dress for. Everywhere else you can wander in with the after-work crowd and be totally casual, but Il Locale is an event and an experience, and you do need to be dressed for it (which means no shorts and trainers, no cargo shorts and no graphic T-shirts). Expect to rub shoulders with well-to-do Florentines and international elites here. Don't be surprised to see supermodels, movie stars and rock stars along with the gentry and the other rich and famous.

The ground floor has both outdoor and indoor bars. They are madly chic and quite expensive with cocktails running between €20 and €35. There is an extensive and impressive wine list, but this is the place to have a cocktail with some very elegant canapes. Don't order your Long Island or Moscow Mule, opt instead for something a little more refined. Ask the bartender for a recommendation or try a house specialty drink. The bartenders are mixologists (a label I'd find pretentious anywhere else), whipping up fabulous creations that fit this modernized palace perfectly.

There is so much history in this building. In the 1500s the Concini Palace was owned by Cosimo I's Prime Minister, Bartolomeo Concini. It was built on top of the thirteenth century Bastari family palace, part of which can still be seen in the basement. The wine cellar below that is part of an ancient Roman ruin that dates back to 30–15 BC. The whole place is extraordinary.

Il Locale also has a full restaurant. The cuisine is modern/fine dining. It gets rave reviews but again is very expensive.

Address: Via delle Seggiole, 12

What's Nearby: You're close to the Bargello, Palazzo Vecchio and Dante's house, and five minutes from the Duomo.

Near the Train Station

MANIFATTURA

This place is super cool. It's a newer bar that crafts chic cocktails from products only made in Italy. You won't find 7-Up or Coke here. It's all authentic, and did I mention cool?

The bar is contemporary but the white-shirted bartenders give it a very 50s retro feel. Instead of the faux international or American-style bars, I love that Manifattura holds tight to the legacy of Italian cocktails and Italian drinking culture. Everyone who works here loves it and seems proud of the place. Always a good sign! The snacks and appetizers are specifically paired with the drinks. Order your cocktail then ask the waiter or bartender what they recommend to eat with it – they will be specific.

This place is somewhat of a secret and the clientele is predominantly local, which is even more reason to go.

Address: Piazza San Pancrazio

What's Nearby: You're near Ognissanti, Santa Maria Novella and Epoca Vintage store.

CAFFETERIA DELLA OBLATE

Oblate makes the list for its fantastic view and laidback vibe. You can swing in here for a coffee in the morning or for an €8 drink and snack buffet in the afternoon/evening. I'm not a fan of buffets, but I do enjoy a good view and Oblate has one in spades.

The food is simple and nothing special, but good. The baked goods in the morning are organic, so the afternoon fare probably is too. A glass of wine is only €4–5, so it's not the type of place where you need to flash your diamonds and impress everyone with your handbag.

It also has some fun history. In May 2007 the Oblate library opened in the former convent of the Oblate, located between via dell' Oriuolo and via Sant' Egidio. It's a modern library and is popular with local young folk and moms. The former convent was commissioned by Folco Portinari in the 1290s. Folco was a pretty interesting character and was the father of Dante's beloved Beatrice. He built the hospital of Santa Maria Nuova in 1288 thanks to Beatrice's nanny, then built the convent of the Oblate to help sick women. The nanny, Monna Tessa, actually retired here. The Order of the Oblate lived here taking care of sick women until 1936. Because it was a functioning convent for 600 years it was never modernized, so it's like a time capsule. On the top floor of this thirteenth century convent is the Caffeteria della Oblate. With its glass walls, you can enjoy the view even when it's raining. It has a huge outdoor terrace with a panoramic view across the city, but the big draw is that you are up high, directly in front of the 'cricket cage' balustrade of Brunelleschi's dome.

Just between you and me, the Folco Portinari–Dante connection had me sold before I even arrived. It could have had a view of the men's toilets and I still would have been thrilled, just because I love the Alighieri-Portinari story! (See **Chapter 23: A Walk With Dante**.)

My first time here was with the city archivist I told you about in the chapter on the Duomo, so I associate this place with cool local 30-somethings with fascinating jobs in the city and endless stories about Florence, dating back to Julius Caesar.

Caffeteria della Oblate is a little tricky to find, but that means the tourist crowd can't find it either, so walking around in circles trying to get here is worth it. And of course, there's that view…

Address: Via dell' Oriuolo, 26

What's Nearby: This is right behind the Duomo. Also very close to Piazza SS Annunziata, and also not far from Casa Dante.

19.

Rooftop Bars

If you enjoy an aperitivo with a fabulous view, Florence has some tremendous rooftop options. The following is a list of eight rooftop bars that I have personally enjoyed. My advice would be to time your drink-with-a-view for late afternoon/early evening. Especially in the summertime, try to be up high to catch the sun setting over the Renaissance buildings and the hills of Tuscany. You'll be glad you did.

The Rooftop Bar at La Rinascente

The department store opposite Piazza della Repubblica (La Rinascente) has a rooftop bar. The wine list is good, as is the appetizer menu. Neither will make any *best-of* lists, but who cares? You are here for the view. And everyone I have ever brought here has absolutely loved it. I love bringing people up here for the transition from afternoon to sunset to evening. I often bring my groups here after shopping for shoes across the street at Antica Cuoieria. There can be a wait to get up here as the bar is quite small, so I recommend getting here well before sunset. I bring my travelers an hour or so before sunset just in case the wait is long. By the time we get ushered upstairs there is usually a long line waiting behind us.

When you get up the stairs to the bar, turn right and try to get the corner table. It has the best view of the Duomo, and that is the view you have come for. You'll see some satellite dishes across the rooftops, but you'll have a wonderful view of the cathedral dome in all its sunset glory, and then when it lights up as night falls. Piazza della Repubblica is below the bar on the opposite side. After dark it's fun to look down on the carousel all lit up and listen to the street musicians.

The dress code is smart casual, so as long as you're not in shorts and a tank top with sneakers and a fanny pack, whatever you were wearing to explore the city should be fine.

Address: Piazza della Repubblica, 4

What's Nearby: You're opposite Piazza della Repubblica, midway between the Duomo and Piazza della Signoria.

La Terrazza del Minerva at the Hotel Grande Minerva

From April until October, the rooftop bar at the Hotel Grande Minerva opens for drinks with a 360 degree view and some good snacks. This is a great spot to enjoy a glass of Prosecco while looking out over the city. The bar is a little expensive but is worth it for the view.

In the off-season the bar is closed but you can still come up for the view.

Address: Piazza Santa Maria Novella, 16

What's Nearby: Basilica Santa Maria Novella and the Officina Profumo Farmaceutica are both right here. San Lorenzo is a couple of blocks to the north.

La Terrazza at the Hotel Continentale

This one has a sophisticated, luxe, lounge-type feel. It is located atop the medieval Consorti Tower at the Hotel Continental. You can see the cathedral from up here, but I prefer the view over the river. La Terrazza is close to Ponte Vecchio, and the sunset views over the Arno are stunning.

The décor is modern and I particularly like the outdoor lounge sofa running the length of the wall, facing the river. It's stylish and chic and a lovely place to enjoy some early evening bubbles.

Be aware: La Terrazza is quite expensive and reservations for non-hotel guests come with a €200 minimum spend.

Address: Viccolo dell'Oro, 6R

What's Nearby: Ponte Vecchio, Piazza della Signoria and the Uffizi Gallery, Orsanmichele and the Porcellino Market are all close.

Loggia Rooftop Bar at Hotel Palazzo Guadagni

I love this one. The views from the loggia on the top floor of the Palazzo Guadagni are gorgeous, not only of the city but also over the Florentine hills. The ambience here is delicious and not at all pretentious. The loggia are beautiful, the décor tasteful – it's lovely. You'll feel far away from the tourist crowds as you enjoy a glass of Tuscan wine with the sounds of Santo Spirito floating up to you. This spot is historical and completely charming.

Address: Piazza Santo Spirito, 9

What's Nearby: With Piazza Santo Spirito in the middle, you are only a few minutes from the Brancacci Chapel in Santa Maria del Carmine to the west and Palazzo Pitti to the east. Ponte Vecchio is five minutes away.

The Angel Bar at the Hotel Calimala

This rooftop bar with its 360 degree panorama is one of Florence's best kept secrets. You can eat or drink up here all day long, but I love late afternoon/early evening. The terrace is on multiple levels, with wrought iron tables and chairs, foliage and thatched canopies. The views are ridiculous, especially looking into Palazzo Vecchio and down to the Duomo. Their fabulous signature cocktails and wines are not particularly expensive, the atmosphere is great and the dress code is smart casual. This is a great little spot to start your evening – or to end it. Don't be surprised if you pop up here for an aperitivo and don't want to leave.

Address: Via Calimala, 2

What's Nearby: You're midway between Piazza della Repubblica and Piazza della Signoria, and a couple of blocks from the Duomo. The Badia Fiorentina and the Bargello are each maybe a minute away.

B-Roof at Hotel Baglioni

I walked past this hotel a million times not knowing the interior was gorgeous or that it had a fabulous rooftop bar just waiting for me. The restaurant is open year round, but the B-Roof garden bar only opens during summer and let me tell you, it is amazing. The cocktails are well made, the wines are wonderful, and Good Lord – the views!

This has the most sensational after-dark view of the Duomo all lit up with the dome of the Medici Chapel in front of it.

You need a reservation to visit both the restaurant and the bar.

Address: Piazza dell'Unita Italiana, 6

What's Nearby: Hotel Baglioni is beside Santa Maria Novella, across from the train station, and a one minute walk to San Lorenzo and the Medici Chapel.

Divina Terrazza at Hotel Grand Cavor

Another bar with a completely spectacular view, this time looking directly into the Duomo. There are also beautiful views of Palazzo Vecchio, but it's so hard to turn away from the Duomo, especially from the position this bar affords you. The bar decor is contemporary and completely uninteresting, but frankly you could be sitting up here on wooden boxes and still be happy as a clam. The drinks are good and the snacks are fine, nothing particularly memorable, but who cares? The view is mind blowing. I really don't think there is one better in all of Florence.

Address: Via del Proconsolo, 3

What's Nearby: This is midway between the Duomo and the Piazza della Signoria.

Sesto Bar at Westin Excelsior

Another bar and restaurant with a great view. Perched on top of the 5-star Westin Excelsior, the bar serves old-school cocktails and good wine from 7pm until 9pm each night. It makes every *best-of* list, and has a diehard loyal clientele.

Address: Piazza Ognissanti, 3

What' Nearby: You're close to Ognissanti, Santa Maria Novella, and if you are in the market for some really sensational bespoke men's shoes, Saskia is only a couple of blocks away.

Food & Restaurants

20.

What to Eat in Florence

If you've read my other books, *Glam Italia! How To Travel Italy* and *Glam Italia! 101 Fabulous Things To Do in Rome* you'll already know that Italian food is regional. Each region of Italy has its own cuisine, most of it so specific that each area even has its own pasta shapes. The shape and cut of a piece of pasta, be it a Tuscan variation on spaghetti, *orecchiette* in Puglia or *trofie* in Liguria, is all about the sauce it's served with, and how that sauce will be picked up by the pasta. As well as the pasta itself having variables, simple sauces like a tomato-based ragu are quite different in different regions of Italy.

Not only is Italian cuisine regional, it's also seasonal. In most cases you'll only see ingredients on a menu during their particular season. Mass tourism has a way of messing this up, but if you are reading one of my books then chances are you are not looking for a mass tourism experience! You are looking for something authentic.

Before you travel to Italy, I recommend reading the **How to Choose a Restaurant in Italy** section of my book, *Glam Italia! How To Travel Italy*. If you stick to my hard and fast rules for choosing where to eat, you will never go wrong!

Cucina Povera

When I talk about food in Florence I'm generally talking about a cuisine that sweeps over a large area of Tuscany, rooted in *Cucina Povera* (poor food or peasant food). This cuisine is all about making do with what you've got, transforming simple, humble ingredients into hearty, satisfying meals. It is a way of eating that was born of economy, but continued by choice.

Typically only a handful of ingredients comprise any dish, but these are ingredients of this land. They have been grown in fertile Tuscan soil, ripened in the Tuscan sunshine, and have quenched their thirst in pure, clean Tuscan water. Unlike in America, where many ingredients have been tampered with, and where seed is owned and modified by Monsanto, GMOs are banned in Italy. This means the food here is real and flavorful. It doesn't need endless additives to coax out flavor – bite into something as simple as a local tomato and the flavor explodes in your mouth. Tuscan food doesn't have to travel far, it comes from the nutrient-rich, rolling hills nearby, the Tuscan stretch of coastline, and the flatlands in between. Each ingredient is so full of flavor, that Tuscan bread (designed to scoop up sauces or be layered with fresh local ingredients in a sandwich) has no salt. One theory for this is that salt will only compete with the flavors, which have been paired with precision to create perfection.

Some recommendations on this list are specific to parts of Tuscany outside Florence (such as panforte), but are found in abundance in Florence and have become part of the local cuisine. They are so good I would hate for you to miss them!

This is not America (or any other place in the world)

Before we move forward there is a really important point I want to make. I consider it the number one rule of dining out in Italy. But first – there are two types of restaurants in the high tourist cities and towns:

- **Tourist restaurants** with photos of the food on plastic menus, translations into 15 languages and bottles of ketchup on the table. Tourist restaurants are about high turnover of quick-to-prepare, unchallenging food. Quality and authenticity are low priority, prices are high, and no self-respecting Italian would be caught dead there unless he was flirting with the waitress.

- **Local restaurants** where local residents eat. The menu is in Italian, (sometimes with a couple of translations) the food is authentic and of high quality. It's cooked slowly, and intended to be enjoyed bite by delicious bite. The clientele is Italian and the price points are far more reasonable.

If you eat at tourist restaurants the food will cost more, but it will come out quickly. You'll recognize more items on the menu, and they won't necessarily be seasonal. The chances that your pasta sauce simmered away for hours in the kitchen are exceedingly slim – it probably came from an industrial size can. It's unlikely that the pasta was handmade this morning – it's probably out of a box. If you choose to eat here, knock yourself out, no rules apply.

BUT

if you choose to eat in a trattoria populated by locals (and I can't imagine why you wouldn't), you must be on board with the Number One Rule Of Dining Out In Italy…

The Number One Rule of Dining Out in Italy is...
DON'T CHANGE THE MENU.

It's not unusual in America for a restaurant patron to be making a mental list of changes to request while snapping open their napkin: fat-free ranch on the side, no onions, swap the asparagus with green beans, separate the pasta from the sauce, oh, and can I have fries with that? While I realise this is considered quite a normal thing to do in the US, in Italy it can be seen as incredibly rude and uninformed.

In local Italian restaurants, the dishes are created to ensure a perfect pairing of ingredients. Often the recipes go back generations. So, if you don't like onions, don't order a dish with onions in it. Asparagus is included in the dish because that's what is perfect. While you're in Italy, go with the flow, order the food as it appears on the menu, and delve into the experience of eating the local cuisine. Don't change the menu.

Vegetarians

I'm often asked about vegetarian options in Italy, and I'm pleased to tell you that Italy may be the easiest place on Earth to eat out as a vegetarian. Florence has many specifically vegetarian restaurants, but there are also endless vegetarian options on menus everywhere.

Vegetarians on my Glam Italia tours never have a problem anywhere we go. I myself haven't eaten red meat in more than 30 years. In my normal life, I eat seafood and occasionally chicken or turkey, neither of which seem to feature much on Tuscan menus. (When I am in Italy, I do make an exception for pork in its myriad forms, because it's too good to miss.)

Gluten-free

At first glance you may think that carb-heavy Italy is the worst place for anyone gluten-intolerant. Not so fast, my friend – Italy is fantastic for the gluten-free!

I've had clients with Crohn's and more recently Celiac's disease on my Glam Italia tours. Eating out has been a breeze! They're often astonished when almost every eatery offers gluten-free options. If you simply google 'gluten-free near me' a big list pops up. The need for gluten-free options has had zero adverse impact on our dining out options.

What To Eat

Here are a few foods specific to this region. I always suggest asking your waiter which foods are from the immediate area. So while you're here, ask them to recommend something specifically Florentine.

Depending on the season and how long you are in Tuscany, keep an eye out for the following items and try a few!

Bread

Don't be surprised when you bite into that first piece of Tuscan bread and find there's no salt! This dates back to the Middle Ages when a heavy salt tax was levied, so the stubborn Florentines decided to just make bread without it. Most table bread will be quite dense and chewy. Step inside a Tuscan supermarket and you will be blown away at the variety of breads available. I have never tried one I didn't like.

A couple of my favorites are the local **focaccia**, and **schiacciata all'olio** (*schiacciata* means 'squashed'). There are many varieties of this type of bread but the three main types are:

- **High and soft.** This is a bread that you can stuff with sandwich fillings. It's not normally salted so is great with cured meats (which are typically salty).
- **Traditional.** This looks like traditional focaccia, is salted, tastes of local olive oil, and often has rosemary on top. The base is crunchy and the body is soft. This is bread perfection.
- **Thin and crisp.** This is like a cracker and comes in a big rectangle. I often buy spicy pepper flavors and serve it with cheeses and antipasti.

Appetizers

With so many appetizers specific to Tuscany, one of the best ways to get a good sampling is to order **antipasto misto** or **affetati misti**. This is a platter with a variety of different nibbles. You usually get a variety of *salumi* (cold meats such as prosciutto and salami), cheeses, cheese drizzled with local honey, spicy grilled vegetables and a selection of crostini.

In the crostini department look for **crostini di fegatini**. (Actually, it may be wiser to bite into one without looking because they look pretty gross.) The *fegatini* part is the Tuscan version of pâté, normally made from chicken liver but sometimes pork liver. Slightly more liquid than the French counterpart, what it loses visually is more than made up for in taste. The first time I ordered Crostini di Fegatini I was a little horrified when it arrived. I sat there for a few minutes contemplating converting to veganism, before starvation won and I tried a (*tiny*) bite. It was fantastic. Now it's a favorite of mine.

Crostini vs Bruschetta

So what's the difference between crostini (one crostino) and bruschetta (two bruschette)? You may see both on a menu.

Crostini are made by slicing thin rounds from a small, round, baguette-shaped bread. The bread has a fine texture so when brushed with oil and toasted it has more crunch to it. Due to their size, these 'little bites' are paired with more densely flavored toppings. If served as an appetizer there may be three or four different types on the plate.

Bruschetta is a wider slice of more rustic or sourdough bread, rubbed with garlic and drizzled with olive oil, then traditionally roasted over coals. These larger slices are eaten in multiple bites, so you are likely to have only one or two on a plate. Although there are endless varieties of toppings, you will likely see some version of a diced tomato and basil. Another popular Tuscan bruschetta has puréed fava beans.

BRUSCHETTA IN SAN GIMIGNANO

If you make it to San Gimignano there is a wonderful bruschetteria behind my usual apartment, called **Pane e Pomodoro** (Vicolo dell' Oro, 2B.) This is a little side alley where San Matteo meets the Piazza del Duomo.

Beatrice slices her bruschetta the full length of a loaf of bread, so they're huge. She has loads of different toppings but my favorite is sliced pear with melted pecorino, drizzled with local honey. Simply heavenly.

Salad

While still in the bread category, there is a wonderful Tuscan bread and tomato salad called **panzanella**. Every eatery and home seems to make their own version of it using the same core ingredients: bread, tomatoes, basil and olive oil. It's especially good with a densely flavored olive oil. This salad is a Tuscan summer staple.

Soup

A few years ago Florence had a mid-summer hail storm. That night, chilled and wrapped in scarves, my friend and I stumbled into a fabulous back street trattoria (one I've never been able to find my way back to) filled with happily noisy Florentines, and ordered steaming bowls of pappa al pomodoro (you'll find the rest of this story in **Chapter 21: Where to Eat in Florence**).

Soup is one of my favorite foods in Florence and throughout Tuscany. Tuscany is known for hearty, thick soups, which in my opinion is one of the joys of traveling there in the cooler months! Most recently, I've been in Tuscany in the summer which feels too hot for soup. But when I'm here from fall through to late spring, Tuscan soup is my favorite thing to eat. I recommend these ones in particular...

PAPPA AL POMODORO

This is my favorite Tuscan soup and although you can get it everywhere I especially love the way it's made in Florence. Using two-day-old Tuscan bread, fresh ripe tomatoes, garlic, basil and bold local olive oil, this is the greatest thing ever on a cold day, but beware – it really fills you up.

You would think that with all the time I spend in Italy I would be able to eat the multiple courses the Italians eat but I just can't. One bowl of Pappa al Pomodoro and I'm done, with no room even for dessert. You may fare better than I do in the endless food-fest that is the average Tuscan meal, and if so I applaud you, but in case you are like me, go easy on the ordering!

RIBOLLITA

Considered to be the most Tuscan of soups, just like Pappa al Pomodoro, Ribollita is a hearty comfort food. It starts with a minestrone – a stock-based soup loaded with vegetables and beans. The minestrone will feature seasonal vegetables from the garden, such as onions, celery, carrots, zucchini, even potatoes, as well as wild herbs from nearby fields.

Historically, the leftover soup would be served again on the second day, this time with yesterday's toasted stale bread. It might be served cold in the summer, but in the winter it would be re-boiled (*ribollendo*) or re-heated in a pan with olive oil and the stale bread (hence the name *Ribollita*).

Today Ribollita is made with seasonal vegetables, perhaps with kale added in the winter and cabbage in the summer.

CACCIUCCO

I always order whatever seafood is on a menu, and I love this soup. Every restaurant has its own recipe, but essentially it uses a fish stock base to which shellfish and chopped up chunks of white fish are added. Some places use sage, the way they make it in Livorno, others will add chili, which is closer to the recipe from Viareggio. However they are making it, I've never had a bowl I didn't enjoy!

ZUPPA DI FAGIOLI

This is a super hearty Tuscan white bean soup. If you have a constitution that can handle beans, this soup could be a winner for you.

There has not been a single instance when I have read 'zuppa di fagioli' on a menu and not thought about Michael Rips' hysterically funny book, *Pasquale's Nose*. If you've read it you will understand my aversion to any bowl densely packed with beans. (In a nutshell, while taking a stroll after eating a bowl of particularly powerful beans the night before, Rips found himself encountering an intestinal *phenomenon* worthy of a trip to the hospital. He braced himself against a wall for support, then careened across the piazza looking for help. A local stepped forward and threw him face first over the hood of a parked Fiat, hoisting his legs skyward in some form of gastric Heimlich maneuver that created a sonic boom heard throughout the piazza. The church ladies came out to see what was going on, and then apparently completely understood that the newcomer hadn't yet developed the constitution needed to handle local beans.) And so I don't order it. But you should give it a whirl, and if you find yourself doubled over with gas, just dive belly-first over a parked Fiat 500 and have a friend do the leg thing…

Pasta

Tuscan pasta dishes frequently involve gamey ragus (wild boar, hare, venison), and as such their pastas are designed to be coated well with these sauces.

PICI

Pici (pronounced *pee – chee*) is a thick spaghetti, stretched by hand. As far as pastas go, pici is dense and filling and is normally paired with a simple sauce, such as *all'aglione* (tomato and garlic), *con le bricole* (cheese, garlic and breadcrumbs) or *all'etrusca* (hard boiled eggs).

I always think of pici as being from Pienza, but it's actually Sienese. Regardless, this is an incredibly good but very filling pasta.

GIGLI

Gigli is specifically a Florentine pasta. Fluted in shape, it is named for the city's flower, the lily. You may know this one as *campanelle*, it looks like a cone with ruffles. Although you will see it paired with game sauces, you will also find gigli served with creamy sauces and vegetable sauces.

I'll order it if it's on the menu when I'm in town, just because it is the pasta of Florence.

TORTELLI MUGELLANI

These are little pasta parcels filled with potato or a potato/cheese/meat variable. Originating in the hills to the north of Florence around the Mugello area, this pasta can be made with wheat or chestnut flour.

PAPPARDELLE

This has to be the number one pasta in Tuscany, and is my favorite. Pappardelle are long, wide ribbons of egg pasta. Frequently homemade that morning, so invariably fresh, this pasta, in my totally biased opinion, is the best of them all!

Pappardelle is the perfect density, not too heavy and not too light, so you can eat a bowl of it and not require a nap afterwards. You'll see it paired with creamy sauces or maybe fresh porcini, but it is the perfect partner for Tuscany's game ragus. Try it with a venison ragu or hare (**pappardelle con la lepre**), both are popular, typical Tuscan dishes. My only personal foray into four-legged creatures is with *cinghiale* (wild boar). You will see **pappardelle al cinghiale** on the menu everywhere you go in Tuscany, and you really cannot get more Tuscan than this dish!

Meat

CINGHIALE

Pronounced *chin-gyah-leh*, this is wild boar, the taxidermied head of which is mounted on the wall of every delicatessen, salami shop and butcher in Tuscany, as well as in half the restaurants you walk past. Cinghiale should be at the top of your must-try list. Although technically considered game, local wild boar doesn't taste overly gamey. It just tastes like a more intense version of pork.

You can get cinghiale everything, from salami to sausage to… heaven knows what else, but I think the best way to try it is with pappardelle. *Pappardelle al cinghiale* finds its way onto most Tuscan menus and is always fantastic. No two restaurants prepare it the same way, but I've never had a merely average plate, it's always sensational.

One year on an extended stay in Tuscany, my then-12-year-old son ordered *pappardelle al cinghiale* every single day. We didn't eat at the same place twice and we were galivanting all over Tuscany, so his non-scientific study met lots of variables, but it had a standard outcome: although everywhere prepared it differently, it was universally delicious.

BISTECCA FIORENTINA

Walking past restaurants on the streets of Florence you see giant thick steaks in the windows, waiting to be ordered and grilled. These are the steaks used in another of the most famous dishes in Florence and all of Tuscany, the *bistecca Fiorentina* (Florentine steak). I don't eat red meat so have no personal experience with this one, but steak-lovers go crazy for Bistecca Fiorentina.

The steaks come from Chianina cows. Indigenous to the Valdichiana area, these huge white cows are one of the oldest breeds in the world, records of them date back 2200 years. Known for the incredible quality of their meat, Chianina are also the tallest and heaviest breed of cow in the world. If you are a steak-eater, plan on arriving hungry or maybe splitting it with someone. I can't imagine how one person could eat something this huge!

Traditionally the Bistecca Fiorentina is a porterhouse steak, about three inches thick, weighing 2–3.5 pounds. It is always prepared using only five ingredients: rosemary, sage, olive oil, kosher salt and pepper. Most restaurants cook it on an open flame, but it can be cooked in a skillet. The Florentine steak is typically served rare, but you can probably order it medium or well done too.

TRIPPA & LAMPREDOTTO

Once again, you won't see me eating either of these, but I would be remiss not to tell you about *trippa* (tripe) and one of Florence's most famous sandwiches, *Lampredotto*.

Trippa: Florence is famous for tripe. Condé Nast *Traveler* describes the tomato sauce-based **trippa alla Fiorentina** as one of the world's great dishes. They are one of the foremost travel authorities in the world, so I'm going to take their word for it.

Lampredotto is a warm tripe sandwich on a crusty roll. You can buy it at Sant' Ambrogio market, and all over town from food trucks and carts – think of it as an anytime street food. When you spot a lampredotto truck or cart, you'll see flocks of locals eating nearby, sitting on benches, leaning on counters, even sitting on the curb. Everyone leans forward into each bite – this sandwich is juicy and no self-respecting Florentine wants it dripping down their front.

There are multiple types of tripe, but lampredotto specifically comes from the cow's fourth stomach. Seasoned with herbs and slow cooked in vegetable broth, the tripe is sliced and layered onto a crusty roll, and topped with *salsa verde* (a green sauce made of mixed herbs, capers, anchovies, garlic and olive oil with a little vinegar). I'm told the tripe is tender, not rubbery. You can also ask for the roll to be *bagnato* (dipped into the cooking broth).

If you do eat red meat, you must try a lampredotto in Florence. Some people argue you can't have a more Florentine experience.

Cheese

Tuscany is heaven for cheese eaters, absolute *heaven*. One of my favorite things to do when roaming Tuscany is to buy fresh cheeses at local village markets. They slice wedges from giant wheels of cheese, are happy to let you sample, and wrap your purchases in waxy paper to carry home.

My Glam Italia tour travelers and I have enjoyed many Tuscan nights with bottles of local wine, schiacciata bread, olives, prosciutto and an assortment of local cheeses. (I come home from Italy needing to go to Betty Ford's for cheese!)

Although there are more than 30 types of cheese from this region and endless variables within each, I want to tell you about two in particular.

PECORINO

Everywhere in Tuscany you'll be spoiled with a huge variety of pecorino – this is a sheep's milk cheese made using ancient techniques passed down through the centuries. For a long time this cheese was known as *cacio marzolino*, because pecorino production traditionally began in March and continued through the spring.

Tuscany's pecorino history reaches back to the Etruscans (850–350 BC). The highest concentration of sheep farming is in the provinces of Siena and Grosseto, and is almost exclusively dedicated to the production of milk. There are variations in the methods used to make pecorino, and depending on where you are trying it, there are huge differences in the taste. (So if you try it once and don't like it – keep trying!)

Pecorino Toscano DOP has a soft or semi-firm consistency and is made from full fat ewe's milk. Produced all over Tuscany, it is one of three cheeses from the region to have the European DOP quality appellation.

Another DOP pecorino to keep an eye out for is **Pecorino della Balze Volterrane DOP**. Made with raw sheep's milk and rennet from the cardoon flower, it comes from one of my favorite Tuscan towns near Florence, Volterra.

What makes the various pecorinos so wildly different is the sheep roam the pastures of Tuscany, eating wild herbs and grasses. Just as areas produce grape varieties that differ based on the soil and the climate, the same happens with the grasses the sheep dine on. Pienza for example is a clay area that grows its own wild aromatic herbs, which make the sheep's milk particularly fragrant and incredibly tasty. Pienza is considered the capital of pecorino cheese.

Different production techniques also impact the flavor of the cheese. There is a cheese from Pienza called **pecorino di Pienza stagionato in barriques**, which is aged for at least 90 days in oak barrels, giving the cheese an oaky element. In another area near Siena you can find **pecorino stagionato con foglie di noci** which has been aged in terracotta jars with walnut leaves. Near Pisa there is a pecorino that gets dipped into olive oil flavored with rosemary, mint, sage and basil within a few days of ripening, which gives it its own incredible flavor. I love pecorino with truffles, and at local markets I will buy pecorino spiced with chili peppers.

There are many different pecorinos from all over Tuscany to try! While in Florence/ Tuscany do your best to try as many as you can. It may be served with a dollop of jam, with figs, drizzled with honey, offset by nuts, or on its own. There are endless ways local pecorino can be served. If dining out it will be perfectly paired, so rather than ask for a specific accompaniment let yourself be guided by the way the eatery is serving it.

RICOTTA

Ricotta is another of the many cheeses you need to try in Tuscany. Ricotta shows up in many different places in Italian food, including in pasta dishes, and often replaces the cream-fillings we use in the US. Pastries filled with cream in America might be filled with ricotta in Italy. Before you back away and say *uh-uh – not trying it*, do yourself a favor and take a (big) bite. This is nothing like the ricotta you know from home.

If you're not familiar with Italian ricotta, it is a soft, white cheese made from whey, the watery liquid you're left with after cheese is made. Technically ricotta is not a cheese but a *latticino* or dairy byproduct. In Italy you can find ricotta made from cow's milk, sheep's milk, goat milk, even buffalo milk down in Campania and Puglia, where buffalo mozzarella is made.

Ricotta has a lengthy history too. During the Roman Republic Cato the Elder (234–249 BC, pre Julius Caesar) regulated the production of ricotta with laws governing sheep farming and agriculture. Even more than 2000 years ago, they used the whey instead of discarding it. The first ricottas were most likely an accidental byproduct of the manufacture of pecorino.

Ricotta means *re-cooked*. The whey is allowed to ferment for a couple of days to become more acidic, then is cooked to near-boiling, after which the residual proteins solidify and become curds which are then filtered through a cloth. The final product has a consistency similar to cottage cheese but is sweeter. It is also low fat.

Made without additives, the best ricotta you will ever taste comes straight from the farm. You'll find it both in local village markets and in cheese shops. Many local restaurants buy theirs direct from the farm too, which is yet another reason not to eat at a tourist joint.

One of my best friends in Tuscany, Silvana, serves a large ricotta she orders from a farmer near her *agriturismo* (farm stay – a popular style of accommodation in Italy). It looks like it has come out of a jello mold. She slices it like a cake and sprinkles nuts over it before drizzling it with honey from her farm. It is honestly one of the best things ever. I hope you get the chance to try a sheep's milk ricotta with nuts and honey. Although served all over Italy, to me it is a very Tuscan experience.

Here are four common forms of ricotta:

- **ricotta di mucca** is made from cow's milk
- **ricotta di pecora** is made from sheep's milk
- **ricotta di capra** is made from goat's milk
- **ricotta di bufala** is made from buffalo milk.

Most commonly you will find sheep or cow's milk ricotta. They are quite different too. Cow's milk makes a milder ricotta which you find in many pasta dishes from the north such as ravioli, tortelloni and stuffed crepes, cakes and pastries. Areas where sheep farming is bigger (Tuscany, Lazio, Abruzzo, Sardinia, Campania and Puglia) have more sheep's milk ricottas. Within each region the taste varies depending on where the sheep graze. Typically sheep's milk ricotta is richer than cow's milk ricotta.

When buying cheeses or when ordering them in a restaurant in Tuscany, ask specifically for local cheese. Actually, this is my gold standard when ordering anything, from wine to food. I always ask for the food and wine from the immediate surrounding area. It gives the waiter or salesperson an opening to tell me the story behind it, it supports local businesses and gives you another touch point to the history and culture of the town or village you are visiting.

Crespelle alla Fiorentina: This is a very traditional Florentine dish but you don't see it so much anymore. If you see it on a menu do give it a try. *Crespelle* are essentially Italian crèpes. *Alla Fiorentina* has them stuffed with ricotta and spinach, and either covered in béchamel sauce or a tomato-based sauce and loads of fresh parmesan, and then baked in the oven. It has been a while since I have had it, but it is incredibly good!

Sweet Stuff

There are two items on my sweet list that you absolutely must try while in Florence and/or Tuscany.

PANFORTE

Panforte is my kryptonite. You'll see it everywhere that sells coffee. *Panforte* translates to *strong bread*, and is a flat cake made with spices, honey, dried fruit, chopped nuts, with just enough flour to hold everything together.

Papers from 1205 recorded that the servants and inhabitants of Montecelso had to bring the nuns 'breads with pepper and honey' as a form of tax. Over time it became a Christmas delicacy, and in the archives in Genoa it was recorded centuries ago as being one of the most famous sweets in Italy. Originally from Siena, panforte is sometimes called *Panforte di Siena*, but now you see it everywhere in the Siena–Florence areas, year round.

There are chocolate versions but my favorites are the golden *Mandorlata panforte* (almond) and the also golden *Margherita panforte* which tastes like ginger cookies and chai tea.

A narrow slice of panforte with a cappuccino is a glorious way to start the day. And don't worry about the calories – this is Tuscany! You will be walking more than enough (and outside of Florence it is all up and down hills) to burn off not only your panforte but also a gelato later on in the day!

CANTUCCI

The perfect way to end dinner in Florence is with cantucci and a glass of vin santo. Cantucci are little crunchy halfmoon-shaped almond biscotti that you dip into your vin santo. You could of course have them with coffee, especially if you are planning on staying up all night, but I think the best way to enjoy them is with vin santo or a hearty red wine. Now, I am neither a sweet wine person nor a drinker of heavy reds, but the wine served with cantucci is a very small glass. Vin santo is a sweet dessert wine that is delicious soaked into a cantuccio.

Cantucci can be eaten at any time of day, but because I usually have them at night, in my mind they have become the best way to end a long Italian dinner before taking a stroll through the nighttime streets of Florence.

Foodies can take foodie walking tours of Florence. You can download my list of recommended private guides a

www.glamitaliabooks.com/florenceguides

21.

Where to Eat in Florence

If you have read the chapter on **How To Choose A Restaurant In Italy** in my book, *Glam Italia! How To Travel Italy*, you will already have the restaurant thing sorted.

So long as you avoid tourist joints (like the plague!), Florence will afford you endless fantastic dining options and experiences. Over the years I have ambled into so many totally wonderful eateries, some with names and/or locations I can't remember, but I have seldom if ever been disappointed. Sadly, my penchant for wandering aimlessly and discovering fabulous little places off the beaten path hasn't always aligned with my years of travel journaling – there are so many fabulous places I never found again!

Being Lucky

As I mentioned earlier, one time while staying in the Santa Croce area my friend Denise and I got caught in a hail storm. We were soaked and starving, the city was darkening quickly as we ran through the streets holding jackets over our heads, looking for a local trattoria with *pappa al pomodoro* on the menu.

We ended up in a wonderful restaurant, filled to bursting with cool young things on their way home from work, well-to-do older couples, and everything in between. The bubbling noise of them all talking and laughing and doing life Florence-style on a random Tuesday night immediately told us that A) this was the place to be and B) that we wanted, if only for a few hours, to be a part of this life. The hostess magicked up towels to dry us off then put us at a little table in the middle of all the action. The waiter brought us steaming bowls of the best papa al pomodoro I have ever had, and a bottomless jug of local red wine. We sat there as happy as a couple of clams, eating, drinking and barely even talking because we were both so absorbed in people-watching. The people, the banter, the fun, the outfits and the hairdos – to be honest, even if the food had been awful we would have loved it. But the food was *soooooo* good, and we ended up ordering more than just soup.

The entire experience was totally fantastic. And totally, totally normal Florence. When we eventually left, the rain had stopped and after a handful of course corrections we found our way back home, burning off every damn calorie we had just consumed by climbing the 1000 (or maybe it was only 60) very steep stairs up to our apartment. I'm blaming it on the wine, but wouldn't you know it, I didn't write down the name of the restaurant on a napkin, didn't pay attention to which streets we walked along when we left, and I have never been able to find it again!

Where I'm going with this story is that so long as you avoid the tourist eateries, you are in all likelihood going to have fantastic dining experiences in Florence, especially if you veer off the main streets. I don't bother making notes from articles about the best restaurants in Florence anymore, because there are outstanding restaurants and eateries *everywhere*. This is what they do here! They create amazing food for a very discerning clientele who only like amazing food. So long as you eat at places that are full of Italians you can not go wrong.

Being Unlucky But Lucky

I've only had one less than fantastic restaurant experience in all the years I've been coming to Florence. It was a cold evening in December, I had been exploring on foot all day, fog blanketed the city, and once again all I wanted to do was get a hearty bowl of Tuscan soup and an even heartier glass of red wine. I wandered into a hustling, bustling, busy restaurant and, not wanting to take optimal table space that a family of eaters could otherwise occupy, told the host I was only planning on having a bowl of soup. He looked at me like I had lost my mind, then handed me off to an uppity waiter who proceeded to take me downstairs and tuck me into the dingiest corner. The only other table down there was a big table with a large family having a high volume birthday party. The waiter was so irritated that I was having only soup that he actually slammed the bowl on the table, splashing some out, and getting the attention of the birthday family.

I couldn't have cared less. I just wanted to eat and go home. However, the birthday family didn't like it one bit. They started asking me questions about visiting Florence, where I had been and what plans I had, the dad kept filling my wine glass and handing me plates of food. Before I knew it they had moved me over to their table and I became part of their party. Thanks to the neverending wine refills I was not only one of the heartiest singers of the birthday song but also one of the most enthusiastic clappers in the entire bunch! I had the time of my life.

So, the less than fantastic restaurant experience was only the bit with the snippy waiter and host. The evening itself was wonderful. And that's the thing about eating in Florence, even the tiniest hole-in-the-wall joint is in all likelihood going to be tremendous. The trattoria you randomly wander into is going to be fabulous. As long as you avoid the tourist restaurants and only go into places filled with Italians, you don't need anyone to tell you where to eat. Unless it's a local, and they are probably going to send you to their cousin's restaurant anyway (which will be magnificent).

Just remember, Italians eat later than we do. Don't expect anywhere to be full at 7:30pm. Also remember, pizza isn't served until evening as it takes all day for the wood fire to heat up to 800 degrees. Pizza for lunch isn't necessarily going to be your most authentic experience, so unless you are in Tuscany for only one day I would save your pizza eating for evening (because Tuscan pizza is sensational and you don't want to miss it).

Because so many readers of my book *Glam Italia! 101 Fabulous Things To Do In Rome* send me photos of themselves in the restaurants I talked about in the book, and have told me how much they loved both the meal and the experience, I couldn't publish this book without naming a handful of my favorite eateries in Florence. (So be sure to tag me on Instagram @CorinnaTravels when you go to them!)

These are the places that I *have* to revisit for a meal every time I'm in town.

Caffè Pitti

For many years I ate here on my first night in Florence, every trip. (And I still come here every trip, but now it's not always on the night I arrive.) It started when my friend Michelle and I did our first trip to Italy together (which I talk about in the *Glam Italia! How To Travel Italy* book). I hadn't been to Florence in ages, but Michelle came frequently, and said we had to have dinner at her favorite place. Her routine was to always eat there on her first night in Florence. Sounded like a plan to me!

We walked 30 minutes across town to get there (which is hilarious because it's maybe a 10 minute walk from where we were staying, we just didn't know our way around so well back then). We walked through the night, crossed the Ponte Vecchio, and headed up to Piazza Pitti. Although it was cold outside and the waiters tried to encourage us to sit inside, we parked ourselves outside in the sidewalk seating, wrapped up in coats and scarves like a couple of fabulous abominable snowmen. Michelle always sat out here, never inside, so in spite of the cold, here we were. (Funnily enough, I've always sat outside here since, regardless of how hot or cold the weather is. If nothing else, I'm a creature of habit.)

Caffè Pitti is opposite the Pitti Palace. The view is commanding, and the food is *fabulous*. Once when Michelle and I were here, there was an asparagus pasta dish on the menu that was so totally out of this world we actually came back the following night and had it again. (The waiters thought that was hilarious.) I've *never* had a meal here that was less than wonderful. In addition to their traditional Tuscan fare, they also have a special menu and a truffle menu. The owner, Massimo Gori, owns a *tartufaia* (truffle farm), which not only cuts out the middle man but seriously makes this a farm to table operation! As for Massimo, let me tell you, he is gorgeous. That first night when we sat outside in the cold (while the sensible people ate inside in the warmth) at the end of our meal Massimo braved the chilly air and brought out a bottle of limoncello and three glasses, plopped himself down at the table and regaled us with hilarious stories and many rounds of my favorite after-dinner drink. There is something glorious about finding yourself on an evening in Florence with a bellyful of pasta, surrounded by more staggering history than your brain can comprehend, drinking limoncello with a dashingly handsome Italian.

So of course we keep coming back!

I have brought many of my Glam Italia tour groups here over the years and I also come with friends and family. It is consistently excellent. The waiters are fun. And of course if Massimo comes out at the end of the night (with or without limoncello). It's just perfect.

Address: Piazza Pitti, 9 | http://www.caffepitti.it/

What's Nearby: Caffè Pitti is opposite the Pitti Palace. You are a two minute walk from Ponte Vecchio, and a five minute walk from Santo Spirito.

Francesco Vini

Francesco Vini is another restaurant that I discovered with Michelle on our first trip to Florence together and is another one that I visit every single time I'm in town. I *love* this place!

I bring all my tour groups here (I travel with a maximum of six people, so it's not like I'm dragging in a busload of 42), and I always bring my family and friends when any of them are in town. In fact, since I first discovered it, I have never come to Florence and *not* eaten here. If I am only in Florence for the day I come here for lunch. At this point it has been over a decade of dedicated eating at Francesco Vini and I have always been thoroughly thrilled with the entire experience. In my opinion they have the best pappardelle al cinghiale anywhere. I've ordered the dish all over Tuscany and have never had better.

Over the years I got to know the entire Francesco Vini family except for one son, (who, funnily enough, lives in my hometown in New Zealand – what are the odds of that?? Francesco and his wife Anna Lisa spend more time visiting my hometown than I do!)

Francesco Vini has an outstanding wine list and everyone who works here is super knowledgeable about all of the wines. The menu is fantastic and *everything* that comes out of the kitchen is wonderful. Their pasta is outstanding, regardless of which sauce you choose. When you take that first bite, chew slowly, *slowly* and analyze everything happening inside your mouth, not just the taste but the texture, the absolute perfection. I challenge you to find better anywhere. They have a pizza oven too, but pizza isn't served before 7:30pm.

On hot days in the summer, I love lunching here in the shaded area in the back. I usually order one of their fabulous salads. If you are unsure of what to order and don't feel like having cinghiale, just close your eyes and point to anything on the menu – you won't be disappointed! I hope you will love Francesco Vini as much as I do.

Address: Borgo dei Greci, 7R | https://en.francescovini.com/

What's Nearby: Francesco Vini is on Borgo dei Greci, a short street that runs between Piazza di Santa Croce and the Palazzo Vecchio. The Bargello is a three minute walk, as are Palazzo Vecchio and Badia Fiorentina.

La Grotta Guelfa

One of my recent travelers described the food here as 'outrageously good'. I would have to agree. He and his wife shared a *bistecca alla Fiorentina* (giant Chianina steak) that was about the size of a human torso. They said it was the best steak they had ever eaten anywhere, which is saying something as they have lived around the world as well as all over the US. (It was fun watching them close their eyes and swoon over every bite.) I don't remember what I had that particular night, but I do remember we were drinking €15 bottles of Chianti Riserva that were insanely good. (I don't think I've ever described a $15 bottle of restaurant wine in the US as being insanely good.) La Grotta Guelfa of course has plenty of expensive wines available too, but I get a kick out of finding fantastic wines that are inexpensive.

Another time I was here I had a lemon pasta dish that defied belief – it was one of the best meals I have had anywhere in the world. When I was in Florence again a few weeks later, I raced back to order it again but it was no longer on the menu. The chef said he would happily make it for me, but I have a policy of never messing with the menu in Italy. If something isn't there chances are it isn't in season, or in this case perhaps the lemons weren't as good as they were a few weeks prior. Instead I asked him what he would recommend, and he sent me out a ravioli dish from the specials menu that was To Die For. Trust your chef.

This is another restaurant where I've spent many, many long, lovely Florentine evenings, sitting outside with great company, the sound of musicians playing nearby, excellent food and great wine. There are two outdoor spaces, one is in the loggia, which dates back to somewhere around the early 1400s, and the other is a permanent tented terrace on the sidewalk. Both are marvelous. Sometimes you have to wait to get a table, but it's worth it. I will happily wait any length of time for a table outside here. You can make a reservation, but I never think that far ahead, I tend just to show up.

Address: Via Pellicceria, 5R, Piazzetta Di Parte Guelfa | https://grottaguelfa.it/

What's Nearby: La Grotta Guelfa is almost directly behind the Porcellina market. You are less than a five minute walk from Ponte Vecchio, Piazza della Signoria and Piazza della Repubblica.

Al Antico Vinaio

This place makes the best sandwich in the world and will ruin you for all other sandwiches from this point forward. Since opening in 1991, Al Antico Vinaio has built a cult-like following in Florence. On any given night expect a line of hungry Florentines stretching down the street, waiting to get their hands on the greatest sandwich of all time. Scattered along the via dei Neri you will find happy Italians leaning against the walls with their sandwiches, or sitting on the curb nursing their giant panino and a hearty glass of red wine. It doesn't matter what time of year or which day of the week you show up, this place is always hopping. (It's open during the day too, but I always come at night.)

I discovered Al Antico Vinaio several years ago when I was renting an apartment a couple of blocks away. Walking home one night I spotted a long line of Italians winding along the sidewalk and heard the hub bub of chatter and laughter that indicated that whatever was going on involved happy people. Being that I am always looking for fun, and thinking this must be a party of some sort, I decided to crash it and maybe make some new friends. You can imagine my surprise at finding out this was a line for a *sandwich*!

It's not as though there is a shortage of sandwich options in Florence. Frankly, panini are a dime a dozen here – you can find a decent sandwich on any street, so I knew there had to be more than met the eye with this place. I started chatting with the people in line around me, who quickly let me know that this wasn't just any old panino, it was *the best sandwich in the world*. Watching people exiting the store carrying these huge sandwiches, half of them with a big glass of wine in their other hand, I realized I'd need a game plan before reaching the counter. Luckily for me my sandwich brethren took great interest in explaining the system to me – this is not like Subway or any other American sandwich chain; you don't order mustard and mayo or specify your ingredients. There is a list of sandwiches to choose from, and you don't deviate. *Don't mess with perfection.* My new friends started identifying the different sandwiches as people walked out with them in hand, telling me which from the menu each one was. I appeared to be the only non-Italian around, so they told me to stick with them and they would help me order. In the end it was pretty simple actually – I ordered *La Favolosa* ('the Fabulous', with pecorino cream, artichoke cream and spicy aubergines).

The sandwiches at Al Antico Vinaio start with a giant square loaf of *schiacciata* which gets cut into four equal pieces (schiacciata is like focaccia). Not only is the bread a generous size but the fillings also are supersized. The meat alone is at least an inch (2.5 cm) of freshly sliced Tuscan sandwich meat (prosciutto/salami/capocollo/porchetta). Instead of mayo they use artichoke or truffle spreads, or creamy local cheeses. Some sandwiches have a slice of spicy eggplant. You may not recognize all of the ingredients but don't worry – you're going to fall in love with your sandwich. Not only is this the best sandwich you will ever have (and quite possibly the biggest), it only costs €6! All of the sandwiches here are only €6 each (except for the Limited Edition menu, which are €8) and there's not a processed ingredient in sight! It's all fresh, local, real, Tuscan food. If you want to double down and get a glass of wine to go with your panino, that will set you back only €10 for a glass of good local Tuscan wine. Seriously.

Since that first night I have been here about a million times and typically there are people from all over the world waiting to order, along with a consistently huge local tribe. Before long a second Al Antico Vinaio opened across the street, and now there are three of them all on the same little street. And all three are always packed!

I bring all my Florence-based Glam Italia tour groups here. Everyone always says they couldn't possibly eat a sandwich that big and assures me they will take half of it back to the palace to finish the next day. So far not one of them ever has! These sandwiches are so good, everyone always eats the whole thing.

Sit on the curb with your glass of wine and watch the locals, or take your sandwich around the corner to the river and eat with a view.

Al Antico Vinaio needs to be on your must-do list for Florence, but don't just take my word for it – in 2014 it was the *most reviewed restaurant in the world*! Home of the world's best sandwiches

Address: Via dei Neri, 65, 74, 76R | https://www.allanticovinaio.com/

What's Nearby: This is just around the corner from the Uffizi and Palazzo Vecchio, and maybe a five minute stroll from Ponte Vecchio.

Lungarno 23

If you're in the mood for a burger there is no better place than Lungarno 23. The restaurant has a full menu which, even without the burgers, is still tremendous, and the wine list is outstanding. But let's talk burgers. Lungarno 23 serves handmade Chianina beef burgers. Their Chianina beef is sourced from small farms and is PGI certified (Protected Geographical Indication). They offer a variety of burger options from a simple bacon and cheese burger to burgers with olive tapenade. The most popular is the Cinta Burger which is prepared with premium Cinta Senese bacon. Apart from the huge Chianina beef patty (which I'm told is the ultimate burger, the best burger on the planet), every ingredient is sourced to be the very best. You also may find that these are the very best French fries you have had, anywhere, ever.

The view from the restaurant is lovely. While chewing away in burger heaven, you can look at the Ponte Vecchio, Uffizi Gallery, the tower of Palazzo Vecchio and even the top of the Duomo.

Lungarno 23 pride themselves on excellent service, so don't be intimidated if you are the only non-local here. The staff are multi-lingual, really friendly and will make you feel at home.

Address: Lungarno Torrigianni, 23 | https://www.lungarno23.it/

What's Nearby: Lungarno 23 is in the Oltrarno neighborhood just beyond the Ponte alle Grazie. Opposite the Uffizi, close to Ponte Vecchio, the Bardini Museum, Giardino Bardini, and Piazzale Michelangelo.

Gelato

I have two strict rules when it comes to buying gelato in Italy (not just for myself but also for my tour groups too).

1. Only buy artisanal gelato.
2. Try a flavor you wouldn't find at home.

Gelato could have its own entire chapter! But let's start with the artisanal-only rule. There are two types of gelato. The first is made onsite using local ingredients, all of which are in season. The other type is chain store gelato, made in factories and shipped in, full of preservatives and food coloring. The factory type sometimes arrives powdered and gets whipped up into gelato in the store. You don't travel across the world to Florence to eat McDonald's, so don't come all the way here and eat the McDonald's of gelato. You're in Florence – eat the real stuff! There's no comparison.

Here's the difference between artisanal and factory gelato:

- **Artisanal gelato:** This product is made in the store, or sometimes an owner will have a few stores and make the gelato in one centralized location. It is made daily in small batches, with fresh ingredients. Artisanal gelato is made to be consumed immediately so it doesn't need to be frozen. It has no preservatives, colorants, or chemicals. The sweet/cream balance is perfection, and it is not loaded with sugar. Think of artisanal gelato as being a handcrafted product, produced by artisans. If you support these businesses they can keep going forever.
- **Factory gelato:** This product is made in giant batches in factories, using heavily processed and artificial ingredients,

artificial colors, and chemicals. It is made to be frozen and stored for months, and it is sugared up to the max.

Artisanal gelato and factory gelato cost the same, so there is zero reason to buy the crappy stuff.

Any highly touristed city will have an abundance of tourist eateries, designed to fill the bellies of the undiscerning. The same applies to gelato shops. You'll see tourist gelato shops everywhere, serving up factory product to people who don't know or don't care. But you, my friend, have made it this far through my book, so clearly you care what you're getting.

Factory gelato joints are quite easy to spot and to avoid. They are located on busy streets or near big tourist sites. The gelato case will be full of brightly colored, whipped up mounds of gelato.

How To Spot The Difference – Artisanal or Factory?

HIGH VS LOW

Factory gelato is whipped and sits high above its container in the glass case. A popular flavor may leave a container half full, but don't be misled. Look across the case and you will see the flavors that aren't selling as quickly, piled up high. They are almost never in covered containers and can even sit in direct sunlight without melting. The only way to make gelato hold its shape like this is with chemicals and preservatives.

Artisanal gelato is made from fresh ingredients that you couldn't whip to any height no matter how hard you tried. Therefore the gelato sits lower and flatter in its container in the glass case. Often they even keep a lid on it to maintain its quality.

THE VIBRANT COLOR PALETTE

Factory gelato has loads of added colorants so its colors will be bright. Looking across the glassed case, vivid colors will pop at you.

Artisanal gelato doesn't have any added coloring, so the colors will be flatter and more muted. Strawberry won't be a bright, hot pink, instead it will add a pinkish hue to a cream tone. Mint will be whitish, not bright green. Chocolate gelato normally has an intense dark brown color, but this comes from the natural ingredients. Pistachio will be greyish green. (I always go by the color of the pistachio. If it is a bright color you know you're not looking at the real deal.)

THE FLAVOR PROFILES

Factory gelato shops tend to only carry mainstream flavors, flavors you can find in any supermarket freezer section or at Baskin Robbins or any stateside ice cream chain.

Artisanal gelato tastes different. It is much, much more flavorful than the chemical stuff, so try flavors you don't typically find at home. Artisan shops will have some common flavors but will also feature some interesting, sometimes complex, and totally inspired flavor profiles, like raspberry and rosemary, white peach and sage, white chocolate and basil, ricotta, almond and fig, fennel and almond. Now before you get all weird and want to run for the comfort of chocolate chip at the factory gelato joint, know that A) *stracciatella* is vanilla + chocolate, with chocolate shavings instead of chips, B) there will always be simple flavors that you are familiar with, and C) they'll let you taste a few before ordering.

I recommend trying anything you would consider unusual in ice cream flavors. If it has rosemary, basil, sage, bergamot, lavender, rose or anything you are not used to seeing as a flavor partner at home, at least taste it. Step out of the box for just a moment and experience something different. You have a lifetime of chocolate chip ahead of you. So live a little.

Is it Gelato or Ice Cream?

My favorite gelato shop in Volterra has a big sign outside saying 'This Is NOT Ice Cream!' Some Italians get quite feisty on the subject, probably because one takes craftsmanship and the other takes a factory and some chemicals.

The ingredients do have some cross over, both contain milk and cream although the ratio is different – gelato has more whole milk and less cream. Ice cream has egg yolk. Gelato has no eggs. Ice cream is typically 10% fat and gelato is generally around 5–7% fat. The texture of each is quite different, as is the process of making them. Gelato uses a slow churn, only allowing 25–30% air, which gives it a creamier, denser texture. Ice cream is whipped faster, allowing up to 100% air. A one liter tub of ingredients can make a two liter tub of ice cream.

Where to Get Gelato in Florence

You will find plenty of gelato shops scattered all over that have the word *Artisanal* or *Artiginale* on their signage, or you can google *artisanal gelato in Florence* and your smartphone will guide you to the nearest one. There will be one within a block or two – remember Florence is a really small city, so nothing is far away.

I do have a handful of favorite gelaterias, so if you'd like a recommendation, try one of these:

PERCHÈ NO!

This means *Why Not!* in Italian. Perchè No is one of the oldest gelaterias in Florence. Revered by locals since opening in 1939, this family owned business makes gelato fresh each morning, offering classic flavors and some fun, interesting ones. The last time I was here I had gelato with rose in it, and it was incredible.

Address: Via dei Tavolini, 19R

What's Nearby: You're across from Orsanmichele, two minutes from Piazza della Signoria, Piazza della Repubblica and the Porcellino market. It is right in the heart of everything, and very easy to find.

VIVOLI

Vivoli opened in 1929, making it the oldest gelato shop in Florence. It started as a café then at some point added gelato. Vivoli has an old world feel to it, all wood and tile and handmade everything. This is another family owned business, and one of the things I love about it is, with the exception of the hazelnuts and pistachios, all the ingredients are grown by the family – farm to table!

They don't have cones, only cups, their servings are quite large, and their gelato is extra creamy.

Addresss: Via Isole delle Stinche, 7R

What's Nearby: Vivoli is one block from Piazza Santa Croce, roughly halfway to the Bargello, close to the Accademia and Piazza della Signoria.

GELATERIA LA CARRAIA

This one has two shops, one by Santa Croce on via dei Benci and the original on the Oltrarno side of Ponte alla Carraia. Don't be surprised to see a long line of Florentines and in-the-know travelers outside, patiently waiting to get some of this incredible gelato! Gelataria La Carraia is owned by a husband and wife and opened in 1990. It is well loved for its classic gelato flavors and its house specialties. Die a little over the ricotta and pear, or the white chocolate with pistachio sauce. They offer the standard €2.50 serving or you can get a mini cone for €1 if you want to try something without the full commitment.

Address: Piazza Sauro Nazario, 25R (Oltrarno) /via dei Benci 24R (Santa Croce)

What's Nearby: Ponte alla Carraia is one bridge west of Ponte Santa Trinita', two bridges away from Ponte Vecchio. It is on the Oltrarno side, a five minute walk from Piazza Santo Spirito, close to the vintage shop Recollection By Albrici.

CARAPINA

This is next level, gourmet gelato, and a little more expensive than most but totally worth it. They have two shops, the closest one is between the Uffizi and the Ponte Vecchio. The gelato is made fresh each morning and again during the day if needed. They are strictly seasonal, so don't be disappointed if your favorite flavor is not on the menu. To keep it fresh they keep the lids on the gelato pans, so you only see the gelato when they lift the lid to stir the flavor you are ordering.

In the summer of 2017 they also had a chic food truck on the Lungarno del Tempio, but at the time of writing this I don't know if it was a one-time thing or if it will continue (I haven't looked for it since).

Address: Via Lambertesca, 18 /Piazza Oberdan, 2R

What's Nearby: The Piazza Oberdan location is further out so look for the via Lambertesca location. This is only a minute from Ponte Vecchio and the Uffizi, two or three minutes from the Porcellino market and Piazza della Signoria.

GELATERIA DEI NERI

Gelateria dei Neri has a *huge* selection of flavors, from the classics to some really different and quirky ones and everything in between. I don't normally care for chocolate gelato but I did try a chocolate and chili flavor here that was insanely good, so at least try a sample if it's on the menu.

Address: Via dei Neri, 9

What's Nearby: This is close to the Uffizi and Palazzo Vecchio. Only a block from Piazza Santa Croce, it's also close to the Ponte alle Grazie.

It's Worth the Effort

In Florence you are spoiled for choice with gelato shops. There are modern shops, old fashioned shops, vegan shops, really there's something for everyone. If you're in the mood for gelato just ask a local where the nearest artisanal gelato shop is and they will direct you to somewhere good. Just promise me you won't go to a chain store – hold out for the good stuff!

A Walk with Michelangelo

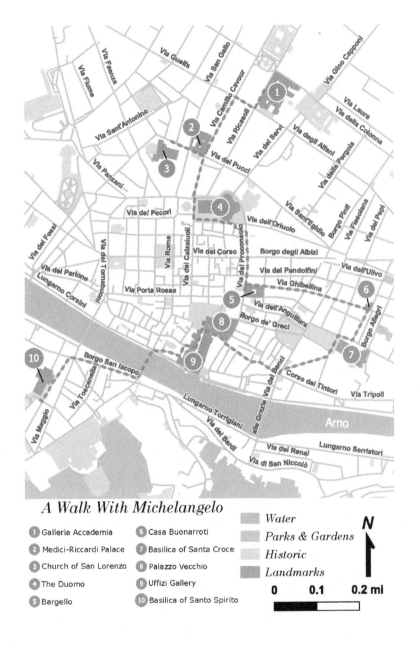

A Walk With Michelangelo

1. Galleria Accademia
2. Medici-Riccardi Palace
3. Church of San Lorenzo
4. The Duomo
5. Bargello
6. Casa Buonarroti
7. Basilica of Santa Croce
8. Palazzo Vecchio
9. Uffizi Gallery
10. Basilica of Santo Spirito

Water
Parks & Gardens
Historic
Landmarks

N

0   0.1   0.2 mi

22.

A Walk with Michelangelo

I get a huge kick out of doing walks that follow the lives of artists, writers and historical figures as well as Dan Brown's books and movies. On numerous occasions I've been asked to take fans on Dan Brown walks in Florence and in Rome, and each time I am so happy that I'm not the only geek that loves doing this! Taking walks like these not only lets you experience a different side of the city but also gets you out of the main tourist circuit. It is great for your sanity when Florence gets packed with tour buses and cruise groups.

One way to experience Michelangelo in Florence is to take a walk through the city with him, tracing his life here as well as the progression of his life's work. Few artists have had as much impact on the history of art as Michelangelo. Although he lived most of his life in Rome he considered himself a Florentine. Many of his masterpieces are in Florence, and exploring the city looking for them helps not only to understand the home of the Renaissance, but also adds to your understanding of the master himself. He was born March 6, 1475, in the village of Caprese. Before he was a month old, his family moved back to Florence. His mother was too sick to nurse him so he had a wet nurse. He later joked that he absorbed more from her than just milk – she came from a family of stone carvers. Michelangelo's mother died when he was six years old.

Explore Michelangelo's Florence

Because everything in Florence is relatively close, the guide below is in chronological order, which I find more logical. However, you may want to follow his work geographically instead, as indicated on the map provided.

We are going to start our walk at the Medici Palace.

The Medici-Riccardi Palace

Lorenzo the Magnificent discovered Michelangelo when the 13 year old was apprenticed to Domenico Ghirlandaio, the greatest painter of the time. Recognizing the child's incredible talent, Lorenzo moved him into the Medici palace and gave him access to the sculpture garden in San Marco. Living in the palace from 1490–1492, Michelangelo was exposed to Lorenzo's incredible art collection. He took part in family dinners and social events, putting him in the company of contemporary artists, philosophers and the Florentine elite. Although we can't know for certain, it is reported that Lorenzo treated Michelangelo like a son. At this time Lorenzo was also raising his orphaned nephew, Giulio. Giulio would go on to become the second Medici pope, Pope Clement VII. Michelangelo and Giulio become lifelong friends (and sometimes enemies). As pope, Giulio commissioned Michelangelo to work at San Lorenzo, the Laurentian Library and, shortly before Giulio's death, *The Last Judgement*.

On the ground floor at the corner of the Medici Palace you can see Michelangelo's *Kneeling Windows*. He created them in 1517, and they were named because the supports below the window sill look like kneeling legs. Years later the Medici used this style again at Palazzo Pitti.

Be sure to go inside the palace.

Address: Via Cavour, 1

Santo Spirito

The next stop chronologically is Basilica di Santo Spirito, across the river in the Oltrarno. One of the prettiest of Florence's Renaissance churches, it also an important piece in the young artist's life.

After Lorenzo's death in 1492, 17-year-old Michelangelo found shelter here with the monks. The Prior allowed him to dissect dead corpses in the church hospital at night to learn the inner workings of the human body. This was a crucial step in his artistic development. When you look at the musculature in his sculptures, the cording of veins, the bodies he created, you can see that Michelangelo had learned how the insides of humans worked. In exchange for this permission in 1493 Michelangelo carved an exquisite wooden crucifix for the church. The crucifix shows Christ, with a frail, possibly teenage body, no doubt inspired by the corpses of young men and boys Michelangelo had seen at the hospital. There is something very emotional and sad about this piece, suspended from the ceiling, perhaps an allusion to human weakness, but hauntingly beautiful.

Address: Piazza Santo Spirito, 30

What's Nearby: While here in the Oltrarno, stop for a coffee and a slice of panforte before moving on to our next stop.

The Bargello Museum

In 1494 with the Medici family now in exile, Michelangelo moved to Rome. Much of his most famous work happened in Rome, including his frescoes in the Vatican, his sculpture of the *Pieta'* and much of his architectural work. While in Rome he created his sculpture of *Bacchus*, which is now in the Bargello Museum in Florence.

The Bargello is a fabulous museum, but I want to direct your attention to the sixteenth century Tuscan works on the ground floor, where you find Michelangelo's *Bacchus and Brutus*. Also here, you can see one of his most important works, a marble bas relief called the *Tondo Pitti*. He created this piece for a private client, Bartolommeo Pitti while working on the *David*. The tondo shows a meditative Mary with an open book on her lap, looking into the distance sadly, perhaps contemplating the fate of the sweet son leaning into her. She takes up most of the space in the tableau and although folded into herself, the forward movement of her knee makes you think she wants to burst forward and escape. I find many Madonna and Child artworks to be quite static, but this one conveys great emotion. There is something in her expression we don't normally see, and she is incredibly beautiful. I love it.

Another piece to look at while at the Bargello is the *David/Apollo*. This was created 27 years later in 1530 for Baccio Valori, Governor of Florence and Medici ally. Because this piece is unfinished it is unknown whether it was to be Apollo or David.

Address: Via del Pronconsolo, 4

Accademia

In 1501 Michelangelo began work on one of his most famous pieces, the *David*. Interestingly the block of marble from which *David* emerged had been neglected for 25 years. Two other artists had their turn with it before Michelangelo, only 26 at the time, persuaded the *Arte de Lana* (Wool Guild) to let him finish the *David*. His *David* became a symbol of Florence and of the Florentine Republic and is without question, an absolute masterpiece. (For more about *David*, see **Chapter 8: Piazza della Signoria**.)

There are several other Michelangelo sculptures in the Accademia. His *non-finito* (unfinished) pieces are haunting, they look like they'll be struggling to escape their marble block confines for eternity. Be sure to see the famous *Prigioni*, a series of prisoners writhing and coiling, trying to get out. They were originally meant for the tomb of Pope Julius II. You can almost *feel* their struggle as you look on. As beautiful as *David* is, I find the prisoners even more compelling.

Address: Via Ricasoli, 58

What's Nearby: If you swap the order of the Accademia and the Bargello, you can walk over to Al Antico Vinaio on via dei Neri and get the sandwich of a lifetime and a big glass of red wine for lunch. Once you've had a nice lunch break we'll head to the Uffizi, just around the corner.

The Uffizi

There is so much to see at the Uffizi. I can happily arrive at opening time and leave when it closes, spending all day with the art (especially in the off season). But we are walking with Michelangelo today, so you need to go to room 41, the new Michelangelo and Raphael room. Here you will find another of his masterpieces, the *Tondo Doni.*

It was commissioned 1505–1506 by Florentine merchant Agnolo Doni to celebrate his prestigious marriage to Maddalena Strozzi and the birth of his first child.

Still in its original frame this oil and tempura on panel shows the Holy family in the foreground and Saint John in the middle right. This is an incredibly important piece on many levels, one being that it is the only finished panel painting of Michelangelo's to survive. Giorgio Vasari pinpointed this specific painting as being the beginning of the 'modern style' of Florentine art. The painting is beautiful and almost looks like a sculpture in its structure. Notice the pyramid-like form the bodies take, from the wide base at the bottom to the peak point at the top of Joseph's head. Then see how Mary's left elbow and right knee almost come out of the painting toward you. I love that she is in motion, twisting around to Jesus, while supported inside Joseph's leg. Added to the majesty of this work of art is the beauty of the colors Michelangelo used. This piece is mesmerizing.

Address: Piazzale degli Uffizi, 6

Palazzo Vecchio

Our next stop is next door to the Uffizi in the Salone dei Cinquecento/Salon of 500 in the Palazzo Vecchio.

The *Genius of Victory* is a nine-foot-tall statue created in 1532–1534 for the tomb of Pope Julius II. After Michelangelo's death, Vasari persuaded the sculptor's nephew to gift the statue to Duke Cosimo I de' Medici, and it became a symbol of Florence conquering Siena.

This statue is of two male figures. A victorious young man wearing a crown of oak leaves, twists up and around while his left knee pushes down into the back and head of an old, conquered warrior. From the expression on the old man's face and the hunching of his body you can sense him wanting to throw off the younger man, but the power and strength of the younger man have him beaten. The sculpture is unfinished at the bottom, which makes the old man look more beaten down while elevating the young man to an even higher level of perfection. The oak leaves are the symbol of the house of Della Rovere (which means 'of the oak tree'), the family of two popes, Sixtus IV and Julius II. Julius II commissioned Michelangelo to paint the Sistine Chapel ceiling. Known as the 'Warrior Pope', he wanted the papacy to be the dominant political and military force in Italy, making this allegorical image of the victorious squashing down the defeated, ideal for his tomb. In 1505 Julius commissioned Michelangelo to create his tomb but a combination of it being a bad luck omen to create your own tomb while still alive, and lack of funds delayed the project.

The model for the young man is thought to be Tommaso dei Cavalieri, a handsome 23-year-old nobleman who Michelangelo fell in love with in 1532 (when he was 57). Michelangelo decribed Tommaso as being 'light of our century, paragon of all the world', and he was the inspiration for several other works. The artist was so enamored of him he wrote 30 of his 300 poems about/to Tommaso. The younger man married and had two children but the two remained lifelong friends, Tommaso was even present at Michelangelo's death.

Address: Piazza della Signoria

L'Importuno de Michelangelo

On the exterior wall of the Palazzo Vecchio, behind Hercules' bum, if you look carefully you can see the face of a man etched into one of the huge stones. (I go into this in more depth in **Chapter 13: Unusual & Interesting Things** chapter). This is the *Importuno de Michelangelo*, or Michelangelo's Graffiti.

Legend says Michelangelo etched this image with his back to the wall. There are three possibilities for who the face belongs to, which you can read about in Chapter 8, but while here in the piazza outside the Palazzo, be sure to look for it!

Basilica San Lorenzo

Zig-zagging back across the historic center, our next stop is Basilica San Lorenzo. San Lorenzo was the Medici family church and the site of the family mausoleum, the Medici Chapels.

Between 1515 and 1534 the Medici produced two popes, Leo X (the party pope) and Clement VII. Pope Leo was Lorenzo the Magnificent's son and Pope Clement was his orphaned nephew, Giulio de Giuliano, son of his brother Giuliano. Michelangelo lived with them as their brother for three years during his teens. They commissioned him to build the *Sagrestia Nuova* in the Medici Chapels, as well as the Laurentian Library. Lorenzo the Magnificent and Giuliano are buried in the Sagrestia Nuova, so the two popes had Michelangelo create the mausoleum for their respective fathers. Even though he left Florence for Rome before they were finished, both works are attributed to Michelangelo and are a fantastic example of the diversity of his skills. He was both architect and artist on the projects and his use of space in the Sagrestia Nuova was considered revolutionary.

Michelangelo's relationship with the Medici was complex, and at one point he hid from Clement VII in a secret room next to the Sagrestia Nuova for three months, fearing for his life. This secret room is hopefully opening to the public in 2020. Only seven meters long and two meters wide, Michelangelo covered the walls with sketches while in hiding there. (Read more **in Chapter 13: Unusual & Interesting Things**.)

Between 1520 and 1534 Michelangelo built the New Sacristy (*Sagrestia Nuova*). He worked on sculptures, completing Lorenzo and Giuliano, the allegorical *Night and Day* and *Dawn and Dusk* and the *Madonna and Child*. The New Sacristy is an unfinished work, and no doubt would have been covered in paintings as well.

The sculpture of *Night* is considered to be one of his greatest works, but frankly I can't get past her wonky boobs.

The Sagrestia Nuova is a claustrophobic place. Perhaps due to being unfinished it can feel a little menacing, almost purgatory-like and, in my opinion anyway, feels turbulent like the artist's relationship with the family. The space is square and confined, but vaults upward. I am intrigued by the concreted window spaces around the lower level. It is as if there is no escape for the souls buried there. You can imagine them frantically bouncing from blind window to blind window in confusion, with only the good and strong being able to lift themselves upwards to the windowed mezzanine level where the light floods in, and onward to the perfect circles of heaven above.

Then there is the beauty in the sculptures he created at the bottom. The statue of Giuliano de' Medici is an exercise in beauty and elegance. He is exquisite. Rather than contemplative, he is active, as if about to push himself up and stride forward toward you. He is positioned with the sculptures of *Night and Day*. Where Giuilano is active, the statue of Lorenzo is contemplative, his face in the shadows, calmly thinking, maybe strategizing. He is fantastic. Below Lorenzo are *Dawn and Dusk*. He looking old and worn, she young and lovely.

The experience of standing in this space is quite something. While the sculptures are mesmerizing, the energy of the space vacillates between heavy and frantic, and is decidedly odd. I've heard it described as power, strength and dominance, but in my mind those souls are still bouncing around the windows with no escape...

Address: Piazza di San Lorenzo, 9

What's Nearby: I always need a mental break after the Medici Chapels, so now is the perfect time to drop in to a coffee spot in San Lorenzo and knock back a couple of espressos. I love La Menagere at via dei Ginori, 8R. Turn left at the Medici-Riccardi palace and you'll find it down the block on your right.

Opera del Duomo

From San Lorenzo, walk to the back of the Duomo to the cathedral's museum, the Opera del Duomo, and one of Michelangelo's final works, *The Deposition*. Known by several names including the *Bandini Pietà* and the *Florentine Pietà*, Michelangelo worked on the marble sculpture between 1547 and 1555. Jesus' body now removed from the cross is held up by Nicodemus as it falls into Mary's arms, supported by Mary Magdalene. You can almost feel the weight of Christ's body as it drops into Mary.

Vasari said Michelangelo made the Florentine Pieta' for his own tomb in Santa Maggiore in Rome, beginning work on it at the age of

72. It wasn't a commission, but rather a project he worked on to 'amuse his mind and keep his body healthy'. He worked on it at night by the light of a single candle.

After eight years of work Michelangelo tried to destroy it, removing one of Christ's legs, damaging an arm and removing other components. We'll never know why, perhaps it was due to a flaw in the marble or a fit of frustration. Regardless he sold it and it became the property of Francesco Bandini who hired an apprentice to restore it to its current state.

Look under Nicodemus' hood to see a self-portrait of Michelangelo.

Address: Piazza del Duomo, 9

Basilica Santa Croce

Michelangelo died in Rome on February 18, 1564, at the ripe old age of 88. He had lived in Rome for three decades but still considered himself a Florentine. His exile to Rome was self-imposed, based on his loathing of the first Duke of Florence, Alessandro de' Medici, who he considered a tyrant. Rather than live under Alessandro, the artist preferred living under the rule of the popes.

Michelangelo was first laid to rest in the church of SS. Apostoli in Rome, but Duke Cosimo I de' Medici decided that since he couldn't work with Michelangelo in life he could at least honor him in death with both a state funeral and a tomb. Michelangelo's nephew Leonardo was tasked with stealing the body, which he did by hiding it in a bale of hay and sneaking it out of Rome. Cosimo I hired Giorgio Vasari to work on the tomb, which sits inside the front right doorway of Basilica Santa Croce, from where Michelangelo could see the Duomo, 800 meters away.

Next to the bust of Michelangelo, three intertwined laurel wreaths represent the artistic fields of painting, sculpture and architecture, all of which were profoundly impacted by Michelangelo's work. These three laurels also make up the logo of the Academy of Art and Design, created by Cosimo I in 1563. The logo turn was inspired by the three circles Michelangelo used to mark the pieces of marble he would use for the tomb of Pope Julius II. Below him, three muses representing Painting, Sculpture and Architecture mourn the loss of their master, each holding the tools of the trade she represents. Look at the figure of Sculpture resting one foot on top of a slab of marble, chisel and hammer in hand. This pose dates back to antiquity and symbolizes power and control over something. Think of a soccer player posing with his foot on the ball, Jesus ascending to heaven with his foot on the tomb, David resting his foot on the head of Goliath. To me this is a beautiful tribute, designating Michelangelo the master of sculpture.

Michelangelo keeps good company at Basilica Santa Croce. Should he wander around in the night he could pass the time chatting with Galileo, Machiavelli and Rossini amongst others. The permanent residents here are so accomplished that the basilica is known as the Temple of the Italian Glories. I love the idea of Michelangelo perusing Giotto's frescoes after we've all gone to bed, or walking the cloisters when he needs fresh air during Florence's hot summer nights.

Address: Piazza Santa Croce

Casa Buonarotti

The Buonarotti house (*Casa Buonarotti*) in Santa Croce isn't actually the childhood home of Michelangelo. The palace was built by his much loved nephew Leonardo, and then passed down through the family.

You could either start your Michelangelo walk here or make it your final stop. On one hand it came to being after his death, but on the other hand it holds two important bas reliefs from his youth: *The Battle of the Centaurs* and the *Madonna della Scala*.

The *Madonna della Scala* (1490) was completed while he lived with the Medici, and *The Battle of the Centaurs* (1492) was his last work for Lorenzo de Medici, who died shortly after its completion.

If I am walking with Michelangelo in Florence, I usually finish at Basilica Santa Croce or at Casa Buonarotti, then wander down Borgo dei Greci to my favorite restaurant in Florence, Francesco Vini.

Address: Via Ghibellina, 70

A Walk with Dante

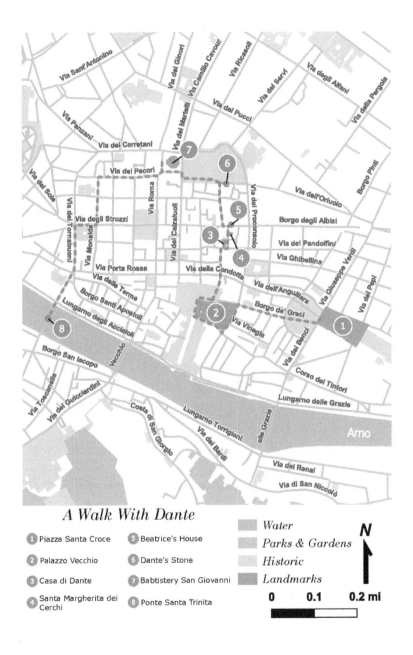

A Walk With Dante

1. Piazza Santa Croce
2. Palazzo Vecchio
3. Casa di Dante
4. Santa Margherita dei Cerchi
5. Beatrice's House
6. Dante's Stone
7. Babtistery San Giovanni
8. Ponte Santa Trinita

Water
Parks & Gardens
Historic
Landmarks

N

0   0.1   0.2 mi

23.

A Walk with Dante and *Inferno*

If you're a fan of Dante, or of Dan Brown's *Inferno*, a stroll through Dante's Florence can be fun. Most of this walk is also in the movie *Inferno*. You will recognize places that Robert Langdon (Tom Hanks) and Dr. Sienna Brooks (Felicity Jones) run through as they chase down the answers to the puzzle Langdon must decipher in order to save the world.

You can actually take an *Inferno* walking tour with a licensed guide. (Download a list of private guides at www.glamitaliabooks.com/Florenceguides. I haven't done it yet, but I *love* doing things like this so it's definitely on my list. The great thing about doing a walk with an officially licensed guide is that they know 1000 times more than just the tour they are taking you on. Talking about Florence is their favorite thing in the world so they're happy to tell you as much as you want to learn. They also have the *best* recommendations for places to eat and drink.

First let's learn about Dante and take a walk with him. At the end of the Dante walk, I have listed for you the places you would visit to make your own *Inferno* walk.

Dante Alighieri (1265–1321)

Dante Alighieri is Italy's most famous and most beloved poet. He is also the protagonist in one of the most enduring love stories of all time.

Best known for his 32,000 word poem *The Divine Comedy*, an allegorical journey from Hell through Purgatory and up to Heaven, warning a corrupt society to correct itself and find the path of righteousness. Written in the first person, the poem follows Dante's journey through its three parts, Inferno (Hell) and Purgatorio (Purgatory), through which he is accompanied by the Roman poet Virgil, and then Paradiso (Heaven) where he is guided by the love of his life, Beatrice. Dante wanted the Italian language to be seen as a serious literary language, so he wrote *The Divine Comedy* in Italian rather than in Latin. *The Divine Comedy* is considered one of the greatest literary masterpieces of all time.

Born in Florence in 1265 to a family involved in the very complex Florentine political scene, the city became a feature in his *Inferno* years later. Although he died while exiled from Florence, Dante and the Renaissance city are forever intertwined. Florence loves Dante and pays homage to him not only in the expected ways (with statues and museums), but also in a series of 40 commemorative plaques quoting lines from *The Divine Comedy*, affixed to walls throughout the city (see **Chapter 13: Unusual & Interesting Things**).

A TALE OF UNREQUITED LOVE

Dante's story is a love story, albeit a tale of unrequited love. He first met Beatrice Portinari when he was nine years old, and it was, at least for him, love at first sight. His father had taken him to a May Day party at her house, a meeting he detailed in his poem La *Vita Nuova*. It is possible the two also spent time together as children during the summers as the Portinari and Alighieri families had neighboring summer villas outside of Fiesole.

Their next known meeting was nine years later at the stone bridge where the Ponte Trinita' now stands. Beatrice was walking along the Lungarno, wearing a white dress, and accompanied by two older women. She turned and greeted Dante, who was so overwhelmed he ran away without saying a word. So overjoyed by the meeting, he went to his room to think about her, fell asleep, and dreamed what would become the subject for his first sonnet in *La Vita Nuova*. After this there were only two more known meetings, one in Beatrice's family church, Santa Margherita de Cerchi, and one at a wedding feast.

There was no hope for Dante's love for Beatrice, as both had marriages prearranged. Dante married Gemma Donati in 1285, with whom he had four children. Beatrice was married to Simone di Bardi in 1287. Beatrice died unexpectedly, only three years into her marriage, and five years later Dante published *La Vita Nuova*, detailing his tragic love for her.

Once exiled Dante never returned to Florence, even in death. His body remains in Ravenna, although he has a tomb in Santa Croce. The city of Florence tried repeatedly to get his body back, but the monks of Ravenna keep his bones hidden.

Interestingly, were Dante to arrive back in Florence tomorrow he would still be able to find his way around. Much of the city is unchanged and would be familiar to him, although he would no doubt be amazed at the cathedral!

Dante in Florence

You shall leave everything you love most, this is the
arrow the bow of exile shoots first.

- Paradiso XVII

Because everything in Florence is relatively close, the guide below is in chronological order, which I find more logical. However, you may want to follow his work geographically instead, as indicated on the map provided.

Casa di Dante – The Dante Museum

I think this is the perfect place to start a walk through Dante's life in Florence. Although not Dante's actual home, this museum was built to honor him in what is thought to be the location of the Alighieri home. In the late 1800s, when Florence was the capital of Italy, the government wanted to commemorate Dante's life, but the funds to purchase the land and buildings and begin the restoration weren't available until 1911. Researchers pinpointed the exact location of the Alighieri house from city archives where documents from the early 1300s indicated a dispute over a fig tree on the border of the Alighieri property and that of a neighboring priest.

The museum covers three floors, marking three important stages of Dante's career. It not only tells the story of Dante, but also celebrates important aspects of Florence during this time.

The first floor introduces you to thirteenth century Florence and takes you through Dante's early life, from baptism at 'beautiful San Giovanni' (the Baptistery), through his youth, public life and political life. There are reproductions of thirteenth century weapons too.

The second floor is dedicated to his exile in 1301 and his life in Ravenna until his death in 1321.

The third floor looks at iconography of Dante over the centuries, with reproductions of artworks by Giotto, Fra Angelico, Ghirlandaio, Signorelli, Raphael and Michelangelo.

The little piazza in front of the Casa Dante has a bust of him on the wall, and is a nice spot for a photo.

Address: Via Santa Margherita, 1

Santa Margherita dei Cerchi

What it lacks in grandeur, art, and size, this church makes up for in story. First documented in 1032, Santa Margherita dei Cerchi is amongst the oldest churches in Florence. Also amongst the smallest! Best known as the Church of Dante, located in one of Florence's oldest neighborhoods and just twenty meters from his home, you would walk right past if you didn't know to look for it. From early childhood, Dante attended mass here with his family, as did his future wife Gemma Donati and his great love, Beatrice Portinari. He and Gemma may have even have been married here.

Initially run by the Cerchi family, in later years the Donati and Adimari families were patrons. Several other wealthy families came to mass here including the Portinaris from around the corner in the via del Corso. (That's lots of high powered action for a one roomed church down a side alley!) Many of the Donati and Portinari families are buried here.

A tomb is attributed to Beatrice, although she was probably interred across town at the Bardi family church. In Italian culture, Beatrice is a symbol of pure, everlasting love, so her 'tomb' is constantly covered with flowers, notes and letters from visitors asking her to help them with their love lives.

Another interesting person buried here is Beatrice's nanny, Monna Tessa. She inspired Beatrice's father to build the Hospital of Santa Maria Nuova.

People don't come here for the art. Most of the paintings are a bit kitchy and just refer to the life of Dante. But it is an important stop when exploring Dante's Florence.

Address: Via Santa Margherita

Beatrice's House

Beatrice's father Folco Portinari owned several houses. In 1456 the houses were purchased by Jacopo Salviati and transformed into a single, glorious palazzo at via del Corso, 6. (Salviati was Lorenzo the Magnificent's son in law, married to Lucrezia de' Medici.) Beatrice's actual childhood home was absorbed into the building, so although the palazzo is referred to as her childhood home, she didn't know it as it stands now.

Walking from Casa Dante past Santa Margherita dei Cerchi and over to Beatrice's house you can imagine how nervous Dante would have been walking this same route, hoping for a glimpse of his true love. It also seems crazy that living so close together they saw each other so few times!

The palazzo itself has a fascinating history and it is worthwhile googling to learn about the Medici's activities here (including a baby thrown out a window (and caught by his dad), the King of Denmark and much more).

The Palazzo Portinari Salvati was sold in 2016 to the Taiwanese LDC group and is now home to 44 luxury apartments.

Address: Via del Corso, 6

Dante's Death Mask

Fans of *Inferno* will already be familiar with Dante's Death Mask. Theoretically the mask was carved directly from the face of Dante, to capture his final expression at the time of his death. But it is now thought to have been carved by Pietro and Tullio Lombardo 150 years *after* he died. Regardless, it changed hands several times and now resides here, in the Palazzo Vecchio. The mask is a symbol of Dante's political contribution to Florence and his contribution to Italian literature and culture.

If doing a Dante walk, stopping here to see the mask is a must.

Address: Palazzo Vecchio

Badia Fiorentina

Walking from Piazza della Signoria along via del Proconsolo toward the Duomo you'll pass the Badia Fiorentina, a monastery whose bell not only regulated medieval life during Dante's time but is also mentioned in Paradiso XV 97–98. . Look for one of the 40 plaques in Florence commemorating Dante, here at the entrance to Badia Fiorentina

In 1373 Boccaccio used the Badia to give public lectures on Dante's works.

In the movie *Inferno* this is where the billionaire Bertrand Zobrist jumps/falls to his death.

Opposite the Badia is the Bargello Museum, the oldest seat of government in Florence. This is where Dante's banishment was proclaimed, the place from which his exile was born.

Dante's Stone at the Duomo

Construction of Santa Maria del Fiore (the Duomo) began in 1296, roughly five years before Dante's exile from Florence in 1301. It is said he would sit on a rock at the building site watching the work happening, deep in thought, no doubt absorbed in his poetry. The original stone is long gone, but a plaque marks the spot where Italy's greatest poet would sit.

On the south side of the cathedral, look for two little side streets, via dello Studio and Piazza della Pallatore. Midway between the two, between street numbers 54 and 55 you will see a pink marble plaque framed in grey, set down low. It says,

SASSO DI DANTE

Legend tells that one day a man passing by the poet sitting on his rock called out, 'Dante, what do you like to eat?' to which Dante replied, 'Eggs!' A year later the man passed him again, still sitting on his rock and asked him, 'How do you like them?' and Dante answered, 'With salt!'

Address: Piazza Duomo

The Baptistery

Dante's Bel San Giovanni is one of the oldest buildings in Florence. For centuries all Florentines were baptized here in the large octagonal font, Dante included. It is said the original font was damaged by Dante as he rescued a drowning baby.

While sitting on his rock watching the construction of the foundations of Santa Maria del Fiore, he would have looked directly across the piazza at the Baptistery.

Address: Piazza Duomo

Ponte Santa Trinita'

We can't be certain Dante's encounter with Beatrice took place here, but it was immortalized in 1883 when British painter Henry Holiday painted *Beatrice and Dante*. The painting lends itself to the romance of their story. The colors are magical, the clothing is as it was at the time, and there is something gorgeous about Dante looking up and seeing Beatrice coming towards him with the iconic Ponte Vecchio as a backdrop, and being so moved by the experience that he was compelled to write *La Vita Nuova*.

During Dante's lifetime a stone bridge stood here. It washed away in a flood in 1333, and the construction of the Ponte Santa Trinita', which stands there today, was completed in 1569.

Basilica Santa Croce

From Ponte Trinita' walk up the river to Ponte alle Grazie, turn left onto via dei Benci and head to the spectacular Basilica Santa Croce, where Dante *isn't*.

Dante died and was buried in Ravenna in 1321. Two hundred years after his death, Florence wanted the remains of the exiled Dante back. Florence made several requests to Ravenna to return him, but Ravenna stood firm, ignoring them all. In 1519 the first Medici pope, Leo X, issued a papal order to return Dante to Florence. The Franciscan monks in charge of Dante's body pulled a fast one on Leo X and Florence, sending them an empty coffin! The monks removed Dante's body (or what was left of it), and hid him in their monastery. Meanwhile Florence had built a tomb for Dante inside Basilica Santa Croce which sits empty to this day.

Outside the Basilica, in Piazza Santa Croce, a statue of Dante was erected in 1865 to commemorate the poet's 600th birthday. He looks a little fierce but at least on some level he is here.

As you wander the heart of the *centro storico* in Florence keep an eye out for the plaques celebrating Dante's work. There are 40 in total, affixed to walls, each quoting a line from *The Divine Comedy*.

Your Own *Inferno* Walk

If you want to take your own walking tour of Dan Brown's *Inferno* there are some other places to add to your list:

The film starts with Zobrist being chased across Ponte Vecchio, through the streets of Florence to Badia Fiorentina. It also goes to the Porta Romana, which I left off this list as it is a bit out of the way.

To make the walk geographically easier, start at the **Pitti Palace**, which serves as a backdrop in the film, and head into the **Boboli Gardens**. This is where Langdon and Sienna run through the trees chased by a drone, escaping into the Vasari Corridor through a secret door. From the gardens, cross the **Ponte Vecchio.**

In *Inferno* they take the **Vasari Corridor** (closed to the public until 2021) to Palazzo Vecchio. Follow the corridor above you through Piazza degli Uffizi to **Palazzo Vecchio.** At the end of the Uffizi building look up and see the bridge section of the corridor leading into the old palace.

If possible at the **Palazzo Vecchio,** take the *Secret Passages* tour or the *Inferno* tour. These take you into the **Salon of 500** where Langdon and Sienna decipher the frescoes and where the assassin Vayentha falls through the ceiling. Both tours will take you up into **the rafters above the Salon of 500,** which is cool enough on its own, but also is where Vayentha chases Langdon and Sienna before falling through the painting to her death. As far as I know, you can only get up here with one of the tours.

While at Palazzo Vecchio, visit **Dante's Death Mask.** You can see this on your own or with either tour. When Langdon and Jones find the death mask is missing they follow the clues to the **Baptistery**.

From Palazzo Vecchio walk along via Proconsolo to the Duomo. Once on via Proconsolo, **Badia Fiorentina** is immediately on your left. Zobrist fell to his death from the tower here.

Continue straight along via Proconsolo until you reach the Duomo. The **Baptistery San Giovanni** is the freestanding octagonal building at the opposite the cathedral.

From this point filming in Florence stops, but you can follow the story further by walking to Santa Maria Novella train station and taking the Italo train to Venice.

24.

Tips For Travelers

I cover some of these elsewhere in this book, but this summary of tips will be helpful if you're coming to Florence for the first time.

Don't Drive in Florence

Don't rent a car for your stay in Florence. Parking is extremely limited, there is almost no traffic allowed in the city center and the ZTL's are hard to avoid. A ZTL is a camera-monitored limited traffic zone that will earn you a steep fine every time you enter it. Only residents with special passes, taxis and delivery trucks can drive inside these zones in the historic center, and only during certain hours. It's too easy to cross in and out of a ZTL multiple times in one day without realizing. If you're in a rental car, it gets even more expensive. For each infraction, the authorities will send the rental car company a notice. The rental company will charge your credit card €35–60 for the inconvenience *every time* they have to pass your information to the authorities. Then the authorities also fine you directly for each infraction.

Instead, pick your rental car up at the airport after visiting Florence. There are rental car offices inside the city but you won't necessarily get a car. (One time we went to collect our rental car only to find a note on the door telling us they were closed and to go to the airport location.) Another great thing about picking up your car at the airport is that you get straight onto the motorway with only a little maneuvering, and you don't risk inadvertently getting yourself into a ZTL as you make your way out of the city.

GETTING ONTO THE MOTORWAY

In my experience, GPS can never direct you from the rental car lot to the motorway correctly. You will be in traffic for two minutes, making a sideways horseshoe shape, doubling back so the airport is on your right, immediately before the onramp. The GPS will put you in the wrong lane and send you around in circles, which is stressful. Once you're out of the rental car area, get into the left lane below the bridge as you start the horseshoe, then once you've doubled back move over to the right lane to exit onto the motorway as you pass the airport.

Have a rental car employee show you the route on the map.

Walk Everywhere

Central Florence is really small. From the Duomo to almost anywhere in this book you have a maximum 20 minute walk. Unless it is pouring with rain or you are carrying a lot of luggage, don't bother with taxis. The GPS on your phone works really well for walking directions, so you won't get lost.

Florence is a city to be experienced on foot. You discover so much by just walking around. I avoid places overloaded with tourists – drop back a block and you'll find streets with plenty of room to walk, full of fascinating things to discover.

Go for an Early Morning Walk

If you're staying overnight, go walking before the tour buses arrive. I love heading out around 7:30am and walking all over the city center. You have the big attractions all to yourself, or you'll share them with very few others. It's a wonderful time to see the Duomo, wander around Piazza della Signoria and see every statue with no one getting in the way. Walk through Piazza Uffizi while it's empty (again, the statues will be standing there just for you and you alone) then wander over to Ponte Vecchio. Beyond a few locals heading to work the bridge will be empty, the shops' ancient shutter doors closed and locked. They are a fantastic sight to see!

I've stumbled upon some of the best finds in Florence on these early morning walks when the city belongs to just me.

Walk at Night

Florence is a very safe city, where you can feel secure wandering alone at night. Nights in Florence are magical. The buildings look so beautiful, all summer long there are musicians in the streets, and the smells from the restaurants are intoxicating. All of your senses come alive here – Florence by night is a sensory banquet.

At night always look up. When people turn on their living room lights you see frescoed ceilings and incredible artwork that remains hidden during the day. Apartments and homes here are inside historical buildings, many of which have frescoes dating back centuries. My friends complain that as kids they couldn't put posters on their bedroom walls because of the frescoes – can you even imagine growing up with that kind of art in your home?

Seek Out the Medici

The Medici are everywhere in Florence. Look for their crest on buildings, look for art they commissioned and track them all over town. My Glam Italia tour travelers who've watched the Medici series on Netflix get a huge thrill out of every building and every work of art that they recognize as being part of Medici lore.

Go On Walking Tours

I outlined two walking tours for you in this book, but you can also design your own, or book a tour with a licensed local guide. Even after decades of visiting Florence, I always learn so much from local guides and will take a walking tour at any opportunity. A guide will point out tiny details, will give you insight and background color, and will tell you stories you can't find in guide books. Try to book a small group tour while you're here. There are tours for everything – not only sightseeing but also foodie tours, aperitivo tours, art tours, church tours, you name it.

Only Use Officially Licensed Guides

I talk about this in all my books because it's really important. Becoming a licensed tour guide in Italy is not easy. They must hold degrees in history/archaeology, art history/Roman history or something similar. Training is intensive and they must be fluent in at least two languages.

There are limited openings for licensed guides and many years there are no openings at all. There might be 200 applicants trying out for just a handful of guide jobs. In order to become a licensed tour guide, applicants sit written exams, do oral exams in front of a panel of judges, and take judges on a trial walking tour, the destination of which they only find out at the time of the exam.

In short, these experts are brilliant at what they do and have more than earned the right to do it. Licensed guides must wear their license (normally around their neck) while working. There is no 'special license for Russians' or any other exceptions.

You can download the list of official licensed guides that I work with at **www.glamitaliaboks.com/Florenceguides.**

Only Hire NCC Drivers

Whether moving from city to city or taking a day trip into Tuscany, only ever hire officially licensed NCC drivers. If your hotel or Airbnb is booking your driver, specify that it must be an NCC driver, otherwise they may hook you up with unemployed cousin Bob who needs some cash, opening you up to a world of potential problems and dangers.

NCC is the official license for professional drivers all over Italy. Amongst other things, the NCC appellation means your driver is properly and fully insured, and is subject to random drug and alcohol testing with zero tolerance. He has passed all the required road testing, is medically certified and his vehicle is regularly inspected to meet all safety standards.

NCC drivers will have a metal shield on their rear license plate and an NCC logo on their front windshield.

Beware of Pickpockets and Scammers

Expect pickpockets anywhere there are large crowds. Men should keep wallets in their front pockets and keep a hand on their wallet when in crowds. Women should wear cross-body bags, fastened closed, with their hand on the bag. If your bag has a front fastener or opening, wear it with the opening against your body.

Don't put your handbag on the floor or hang them from chairs in restaurants.

Separate your cards and cash. Have one card and the cash you need for that day in your wallet and keep the rest in a money belt or in your apartment/hotel safe so that if you do get pickpocketed you don't lose everything.

- Beware of woven bracelets. The scammer tries to either give you a bracelet or tie one to your wrist, then shakes you down for money. They can get aggressive and try and intimidate you into paying them. There are police everywhere, so grab one if you find yourself in this situation.

- Don't give money to beggars, no matter how helpless they look. Most are scammers – I've been seeing the same ones for years. They may kneel in the gutter in rags looking destitute, but when you are out of sight they pull out the latest iPhone and text their mates that you're coming.

- Don't let strangers approach you. Tourists are easy to spot a mile away. No Italian is going to confuse you with a local, and they definitely won't approach you for directions or with questions. Other tourists are unlikely to ask you either.

Not all con artists dress like gypsies – some dress as priests and nuns, tourists and moms, students and average folks.

- If someone approaches you with questions or asking for directions, assume they are up to something and keep your distance. There are police officers everywhere, so anyone who is genuinely lost can ask one of them.

Don't Use the Money-changing Booths

Your very worst exchange rate is at the money-changing places. Don't bring cash to change into euros, instead use your ATM card at bank ATMs. Check the fees with your bank before leaving home. Some banks charge as high as 5% of each withdrawal as well as a $3 ATM fee. If your regular bank has high fees, open an account with another bank to store and access your travel money before you travel.

Order Small Currency

I recommend that my tour travelers only carry currency in €20 notes and smaller. Most vendors won't risk potential counterfeits, and not all can make change for larger bills.

Use the Trains

Florence is a major train hub. You can get almost anywhere in Italy from here. The high speed trains get you to Rome in 90 minutes or to Venice in two hours. Much of Tuscany is accessible via local rail, Lucca, Arezzo, Pisa, Pistoia and many other fantastic towns are a quick and inexpensive trip away by train. This easy access makes Florence a great base for an Italy vacation.

Book Ahead Online

If you're planning on visiting the Accademia or Uffizi be sure to book tickets online well in advance.

High speed rail tickets are also much less expensive if booked ahead of time, but local rail can be purchased at the station.

Getting To and From the Airport

Florence Peretola/Amerigo Vespucci airport is 4 km from the city center/Santa Maria Novella train station.

The best ways to get to and from the airport are:

TAXI

A taxi takes 15 minutes to get from the airport to the city center. The cost is a base rate fee of €22 with an additional €1 per suitcase. If you have heavy luggage or are exhausted from a long flight, this is the easiest way to get door to door. Florence has many cobblestoned streets, so dragging luggage can be difficult and can also ruin the wheels on your suitcase.

T1 TRAM

Since February 2019, Florence has a tram service from the airport into the city. The tram takes 15 minutes to Santa Maria Novella station and costs €1.50.

When exiting the airport terminal, turn left and follow the signs to the T1 Tram. There are ticket machines at the tram stop. You may need to purchase an additional ticket for oversized luggage. Once on the tram, **YOU MUST VALIDATE YOUR TICKET** in the yellow machine by the door. Your ticket is open for use if not validated (so you could use it again and not pay for this ride), so if guards or police come on the tram to check tickets you will be fined if yours isn't validated, no excuses.

IF YOU FLY INTO PISA

Pisa is the other airport in Tuscany and often has better deals for flights than Florence. If you fly into Pisa, from Pisa Airport (Galileo Galilei) take the Pisa Mover Shuttle from outside the arrivals area to the Pisa Centrale train station, and take the train from there to Florence (Firenze SMN).

There are also bus charter companies offering coach service from Pisa airport directly into Florence Santa Maria Novella train station.

City Tourist Tax

As with everywhere in Italy there is a city tourist tax when you are staying overnight. Depending on where you stay it ranges from €3–€7 per person, per night. Hotels may build this into your charge but Airbnb /vacation rentals usually get paid separately, in cash.

Ask ahead of time how much the tax will be per person and have that amount in cash when you arrive (it makes everything easier).

Be aware that hotels and vacation rentals have to photocopy or photograph the picture page of your passport when you arrive. This is the law.

The Firenze Pass Museum Card

For €85 this card gets you discounts into 75+ museums, galleries and tourist sites within a 72 hour time frame. Some swear by it, but I don't use it myself. Check their website firenzecard.it and see if it will benefit your plans. The museums and galleries in Florence are not particularly expensive and I have never spent €85 going to museums in a 72 hour period. Every museum in this book is on the Firenze Card list but you'd need to visit eight of them in three days in order to break even.

No Big Bags

Don't bring a big bag or backpack to museums and galleries. Most will not allow them inside, but check their websites to be sure. Also don't bring bottled water/drinks, as most sites won't allow them either.

Wi-Fi

There is public Wi-Fi available around the city and in bars, coffee shops etc, but be careful using it. I (*emphatically*) advise against using public Wi-Fi as it can allow hackers easy access to your banking/email/social media etc.

Check your phone carrier's international plan before leaving home. Some offer free international data, others have affordable plans.

You can rent a Wi-Fi hotspot in Italy. I've used Expresso Wifi in the past (now called Onemyfi) and was very happy with the service. For US$10 per day I had unlimited Wi-Fi. The unit had eight hours battery life so I needed an external battery pack/mophie to keep it working all day. I now own a portable hotspot. They can be purchased at TIM or Vodafone stores in Italy for around €60, with SIM cards costing an additional €15. This is much more economical than renting a device or using my cell carrier's international plan. If you will be spending more than 10 days in Italy and plan on uploading photos and videos to social media, using GPS, and apps such as WhatsApp to stay connected with people back home, you may want to consider this option.

TIM and Vodafone have stores at the airports and major train stations, as well as scattered around the city. You'll need to have your passport with you when you purchase one.

25.

What To Do Next

Now that you've made it all the way through this book I would like to ask you a favor. Please leave a review on Amazon. Reviews are crucial to the life of this book and, more importantly, to travelers trying to find quality, informative, interesting books to help plan their trip to Florence.

Want More?

BLOG

Follow my blog CorinnaBsWorld.com for more information on Italy and general international travel tips.

If you want help finding an officially licensed guide in Florence you can download my personal list at **www.glamitaliabooks.com/Florenceguides.**

NEWSLETTER

Sign up for my newsletter. On the blog there is a link to subscribe to my Private Members Newsletter. Twice each month I send a newsletter with specific information for travelers to Italy, including secret little towns to visit, lists of festivals happening, and foods you need to try. The newsletter is full of great information that isn't on the blog or in the books.

SOCIALS

Follow me on social media! You'll find me in the following places:

Instagram: @CorinnaTravels

Facebook: Corinna Cooke Author

Pinterest: @Corinnamakeup

MY OTHER BOOKS

My books are available worldwide exclusively on Amazon.com. All books are available in the travel friendly eBook version (Kindle/Kindle App) and in paperback. *Glam Italia! 101 Fabulous Things To Do In Florence* is the third book in my *Glam Italia!* series.

Glam Italia! How To Travel Italy (Secrets To Glamorous Travel On A Not So Glamorous Budget)

Glam Italia! 101 Fabulous Things To Do In Rome (Beyond the Colosseum, the Vatican, the Trevi Fountain and the Spanish Steps)

Glam Italia! How To Travel Italy (Secrets To Glamorous Travel On A Not So Glamorous Budget)

My first book *Glam Italia! How To Travel Italy (Secrets To Glamorous Travel On A Not So Glamorous Budget)* helps you plan your trip to Italy. It covers everything from getting the best flight deals, to avoiding jet lag, to how to decide where to stay and for how long.

Once we have your trip planned, the second half of this book guides you through all the help you may need on the ground: how to use the trains, essential information about renting cars, how to order coffee, which foods and wines to order in each region of Italy, what to do if things go wrong, what to do if you get sick – and much, much more. It's like having me there to help you!

Glam Italia! 101 Fabulous Things To Do In Rome (Beyond the Colosseum, the Vatican, the Trevi Fountain and the Spanish Steps)

My second book *Glam Italia! 101 Fabulous Things To Do In Rome (Beyond the Colosseum, the Vatican, the Trevi Fountain and the Spanish Steps)* shows you incredible things to do in Rome to avoid the tourist crowds. Similarly to my book about Florence, you'll be amazed just how many spectacular things are hiding in plain sight, just down the street from the big attractions. This book will make you fall in love with the Eternal City the way I have, and will leave you desperate to come back for more.

ANDIAMO!

So my friend, I hope you enjoyed this book and that it gave you plenty of ideas for your Florence itinerary, places to visit, things to see, eat, drink and do while you are in town. Be sure to tag me in your social media posts so I can enjoy your travels.

I've had so much fun meeting readers of my books in airports, train stations and all over Italy. Chances are if you see a bright red ponytail bopping its way across the piazza it's me, so please come over and say hi!

Finally, I wish you the very best for your travels. Have a totally fantastic time, do things you wouldn't normally do, and make this the trip of a lifetime!

See you in the piazza,

Corinna

Acknowledgments

Thank you to my editor Anna Jemima Golden, for your patience and your brilliance. I love bouncing ideas off you, your clever replies and your magic with words. We are three books into this journey together now, who knows how many we will have done by the end? I'm so lucky to have you in my corner!

Thank you to Jimmy, for years and years of friendship, for introducing me to so many of Florence's secrets and for always finding me when I get lost! To lovely Gaia, for making my dear friend the happiest man in the world and to Faisal and the entire crew at Jimmy's Leather Collection, for all the fun and friendship over the years.

Giorgio and Maria Chiara Montini, thank you for your friendship and kindness, your patience when my flights get delayed, and for giving me a dream home in Florence. I can't wait to see you again soon.

Luca Benfaremo, thank you for all the planning, preparation and fun! I love riding shotgun with you and hearing all your fascinating stories as we traverse your beautiful Tuscany. My travelers love your caring and your kindness and the way you make everyone feel like a VIP. I am so lucky to work with you and to call you friend.

Marta Halama, my brilliantly talented artist and friend. Thank you for taking on my projects and for being so creative and clever! I adore working with you.

To the lovely Jennifer, thank you for a lifetime of encouragement, for always believing in me and supporting all my crazy plans and ideas. You infused my life with wanderlust, taught me to see myself as a world citizen and gave me a love of languages and cultures that has enriched my life more than you can imagine. You showed me that as women we can be everything we want to be, you taught me to stand up for myself and to design the life I wanted. I am so lucky you are my mother. I love you so very much.

Finally to Tommy, I am so proud of the man you have become. You are my greatest joy. Never lose sight of your dreams, travel the world as much as you can, keep making music and know I love you more than life itself.

XO

About the Author

Corinna Cooke is an international makeup artist, blogger and bestselling author.

A lifetime fascination with archaeology, art and history, paired with a love of languages resulted in years of non-stop travels to Italy.

Her blog posts about exploring the country and discovering off the beaten path places to visit led to an accidental boutique, private tour-guiding business. For two months every year she takes small groups of women on glamour-filled, a' la carte tours of Italy.

Originally from New Zealand, Corinna has lived around the world, and now calls sunny Arizona home.